To Kenneth from Jean on
his 85th Birthday, March 13, 2001

CREATION, CATASTROPHE, AND CALVARY

*Why a Global Flood Is Vital
to the Doctrine of Atonement*

JOHN TEMPLETON BALDWIN, EDITOR

REVIEW AND HERALD® PUBLISHING ASSOCIATION
HAGERSTOWN, MD 21740

This book was
Edited by Gerald Wheeler
Copyedited by William Cleveland and Jocelyn Fay
Designed by Willie Duke
Electronic makeup by Shirley M. Bolivar
Typeset: 11.5/14 Bembo

PRINTED IN U.S.A.

04 03 02 01 00   5 4 3 2 1

R&H Cataloging Service
Baldwin, John Templeton, ed.
    Creation, catastrophe, and calvary.

    1. Creation.   2. Creationism.   3. Atonement.   4. Death.
5. Bible and geology.   6. Deluge.   I. Title.

                        213

ISBN 0-8280-1323-3

CONTENTS

Foreword / 5
Harold G. Coffin
Introduction / 7
John T. Baldwin
Meet the Authors / 14
John T. Baldwin

CHAPTER 1

Revelation 14:7: An Angel's Worldview / 19
John T. Baldwin

CHAPTER 2

The "Days" of Creation in Genesis 1:
Literal "Days" of Figurative "Periods/Epochs" of Time? / 40
Gerhard F. Hasel

CHAPTER 3

Genesis 2: A Second Creation Account? / 69
Randall W. Younker

CHAPTER 4

Biblical Evidence for the Universality of the Genesis Flood / 79
Richard M. Davidson

CHAPTER 5

The Grand Canyon and the Genesis Flood / 93
Ariel Roth

CHAPTER 6

The Geologic Column and Calvary: The Rainbow Connection—
Implications for an Evangelical Understanding
of the Atonement / 108
John T. Baldwin

CHAPTER 7

Evolution: A Theory in Crisis / 124

Norman R. Gulley

CHAPTER 8

The Role of Creation in Seventh-day Adventist Theology /159

Ed Zinke

CHAPTER 9

Science and Theology: Focusing the Complementary Lights of Jesus, Scripture, and Nature / 172

Martin F. Hanna

Index /209

Visit us at *www.rhpa.org* for more information on other Review and Herald products.

FOREWORD

Harold G. Coffin

The secular worldview of the origin of matter and the gradual development of the great variety of living organisms during hundreds of millions of years has so dominated the civilized world that the biblical narrative of creation and then global catastrophe only a few thousand years ago has been difficult to maintain even in churches that consider Genesis to be literal history. Impressed with what appear to be compulsive scientific evidence, and growing weary of swimming against the current, scholars have attempted to reconcile science and religion through reinterpretation of Scripture. Such efforts have succeeded so well that few religious entities, even fundamentalist churches, hold to a recent creation week and subsequent destruction by a worldwide flood. (Creation, catastrophe, and time measured in thousands of years are three inseparable aspects of the biblical doctrine of creation.) Even the Seventh-day Adventist Church has not been immune from such influences.

Many of those who promote theistic evolution[1] or progressive creation[2] either have not followed their line of reasoning far enough to see or do not wish to present the theological consequences of their position. Many conservative Christians do not realize that long ages for life on earth, or slow evolutionary development, or uniformitarian earth history (even modified catastrophism within geologic time), can destroy the weekly cycle, greatly weaken the significance of the seventh-day Sabbath, and raise questions regarding the integrity of God's Word. They do not understand that if fossils represent life-forms that God created long before Adam, death would not be the result of Adam's sin, but would be part of God's original plan for the creation that He called "very good" (Gen. 1:31). Also, they fail to realize that the core of the gospel, the substitutionary death of Christ to cancel the death penalty for our sins, comes into question.

Did Moses give us a true history of the earth? Were all the New Testament authors and Jesus, who all accepted Genesis as authentic history, mistaken? Do Lyell and Darwin now take the place of Moses as the source for a correct interpretation of earth history?

This presentation by seven different authors is a much-needed volume. It is the first major attempt to make a definitive statement of the theological outcome of rejecting a literal reading of Genesis. The writers clearly present the results of compromising with biblical history. The book will become a useful and important reference in many personal and institutional libraries.

---

[1] Theistic evolution teaches that God created the original spark of life and then used evolutionary processes to bring living organisms to their present complexity and diversity.

[2] Progressive creation suggests that each day of creation, in which God instantaneously created living organisms, was either a long period of time or was separated from the next day by a long period of time.

INTRODUCTION

John Templeton Baldwin
Seventh-day Adventist Theological Seminary
Andrews University

In a celebrated line about the mixing of sun and rain, William Wordsworth writes, "My heart leaps up when I behold a rainbow in the sky."[1] The visual power of that awesome heavenly arch only deepens as we grasp its theological and geological significance in this book written from the perspective of faith seeking understanding. The articles are written by Christian scholars who do not claim to have all the answers, but who are enjoying the whitewater ride through the spray-filled canyons of the creation and flood texts and nature itself, and as a result are finding new harmonies between Scripture and science.[2]

The authors do not suggest that the empirical data discussed in the essays rise to the level of demonstration or of direct proof. Rather, Philip Clayton helpfully suggests that given the Christian's belief in God as creator, "[t]o the eyes of faith, it is impossible not to find signs of God's purpose and design within the world."[3] In this light the writers understand the role of evidence as being suggestive of and/or consistent with what we might expect in view of biblical claims, and thus as reinforcing our faith in its inspired history. This understanding means that the efforts of the authors represent work in progress.

On the other hand, the authors hold that biblical and contemporary scientific evidence combine to indicate convincingly that the total galactic universe is at the minimum billions of years old.[4] In addition, the writers laud Darwin's discovery of the concept of natural selection and its effectiveness in the clearly obvious process of microevolution as it accumulates small variations in populations. However, on theological, philosophical, and biological grounds the authors question whether we can properly extrapolate microevolution as capable of producing the large and complex changes evident between biological forms considered, for example, at the taxonomic ordinal level. Thus, given a biblically based commitment to the imminent return of the resurrected Lord (and for other important reasons presented in this book), many, if not most, mainline Adventist members, pastors, biblical scholars, and systematic theologians are reluctant, for instance, to subject the protological (origins—Gen. 1-11), and eschatological portions of Scripture to space/time category translation when discussing what the text means for us today.[5] In line with this conviction the present writers embrace the biblical teaching more or less as classically understood by Reformers such as Luther that God rapidly and recently created our world's basic life forms.[6] In part this explains why the authors adopt a largely univocal (having one meaning) historical interpretation of the mighty acts and words of God articulated in the biblical narrative.

Being fully aware of the distinctiveness of taking seriously—in a post-enlightenment critical and post-modern context—the orientation indicated above, we ask readers with a contrasting worldview to resist the understandable impulse to lay the volume down. We believe that the reader's journey through the essays will be rewarded with something of enduring value. The Word of God and nature continue to be full of pleasant surprises.

As we near the beginning of the third millennium A.D., more and more people are asking questions about human and cosmic destiny in light of evolutionary and geological theory.[7] In response to developments, this volume joins efforts such as the new intelligent-design movement by presenting fresh, readable, yet responsible, research concerning the philosophy of origins, creation, intelligent design theory, and flood geology.[8] The book introduces several unpublished pieces presented by Adventist scholars at the time of the annual joint sessions of the Evangelical Theological Society and the Adventist Theological Society in 1994, and other essays devoted to the interface of science and religion. It addresses current issues that in one way or another are linked to the event symbolized by the rainbow.

Here is a sampling of some of the questions raised: What about the length of the days of the creation week? Can we take the Genesis creation account literally in light of the postmodern quarrel with "first principles" and with the metaphor of truth as foundation,[9] and in view of the findings of geology that so many interpret as suggesting that we cannot construe a literal creation week and a global flood as historical events? Does the creation story of Genesis 2 conflict with Genesis 1 (an idea that some have used to explain the apparent differences between the two chapters)? What about God's global flood?[10] Is such a phenomenon really in the mind of the biblical author and demanded by the text? What difference does it make theologically whether one believes that the flood was a planet-wide or a local event? Does the extent and effect of the flood have an impact upon, for example, the forgiveness of sins? Are traces of an aquatic catastrophe discernable in the geologic column on scales of magnitude consistent with what we would expect in a global flood?

In short, this book examines the reasons a group of gospel-loving Christians known as Seventh-day Adventists, who are also committed to doing good, responsible science, continue to accept in this postmodern period the biblical teachings of a seven-day creation week and a global flood. The book serves as a response to the understandable claim voiced in some scholarly circles suggesting that it is a sacrifice of the intellect to equate the biblical account of a seven-day creation week and a global flood with historical reality. In the discussion both the geological difficulties and the potential negative theological implications of positions being assessed need to be recognized.[11] Here Del Ratzsch presents a helpful and timely reminder to the authors and readers of this book:

"On all sides we need to unhitch our egos and do some hard, maybe even painful, work. And maybe the various sides should talk. Not debate—talk. It is just possible, neither side being omniscient, that both sides could gain something from serious contact with competent practitioners on the other."[12]

Chapter 1 discusses biblical and theological evidence indicating how the first angel of Revelation 14 presents a literal seven-day creation worldview as a critical issue during the last days before Christ's return. Authored by the late Old Testament biblical scholar Gerhard Hasel, chapter 2 returns to the much-discussed and controversial issue of the Genesis understanding of the length of the days of creation. Does the biblical text intend the reader to understand the days of creation literally or figuratively? Leading thinkers such as Charles Hodge felt that we should interpret the days of the creation week as long indefinite periods of time because it would offer a way to harmonize Scripture with the findings of science. Hasel's essay may constitute the most scholarly consideration and critical evaluation available of key arguments representing all major positions concerning this important issue.

In chapter 3 Randall Younker considers the relationship between the first two chapters of Genesis. Traditionally, scholars have presumed both creation accounts to be complementary. But more recently many biblical scholars have viewed the two creation narratives as stemming from differing traditions, in which Genesis 2, understood as the older version, presents a creation narrative standing in contradiction to Genesis 1. Continuing biblical research has led to some surprising findings. Building on the groundbreaking work by Cassuto, Younker advances a comparative word study argument showing the complementarity of the two chapters.

Richard Davidson, in chapter 4, focuses specifically on the Genesis understanding of the extent of the flood described in Genesis 6-9. Does the text consider the deluge to be a truly historical event or rather a figurative construct? If we understand the flood historically, does the text intend that we interpret the flood as a global event or a local affair? In a recent dissertation entitled "The Diminishing Flood"[13] Rodney Stiling traces a four-phase shift in thinking by nineteenth-century American geologists and theologians regarding the extent of the flood as a result of what they consider to be compelling geological evidence against a worldwide deluge. First they considered the flood as a deep-water universal event responsible for shaping the many-layered geologic column itself. Next they reduced the flood to one that disturbed only the uppermost surface of the globe. In the third phase they regarded the Genesis flood as only a local event. Finally they concluded that there had been no real flood in history at all.

Davidson lets the biblical text speak eloquently for itself concerning the extent of the flood by means of unpacking, among other ideas, the profound theological significance of the Hebrew term "flood" *(mabbul)* as a planet-wide undoing of creation. That the biblical text portrays the flood as the global undoing of creation is a point of critical importance that seems to have nearly vanished in recent evangelical scholarship. This concept needs to return to the center of the discussion of the biblical account of the flood.

Ariel Roth addresses the question, in chapter 5, of whether geologists can convincingly trace, in the broken surface of the earth, data consistent with what we might expect in God's global flood.[14] In view of Davis A. Young's recent book, *The Biblical Flood: A Case Study of the Church's Response to Extrabiblical Evidence,* which claims that "there is no geological evidence to confirm the idea of a universal deluge,"[15] it is important to reopen the question of whether we can discern physical evidence of a planet-wide flood in the present geologic column. Roth samples current, accountable, scientific field research projects that are discovering geological evidence calling for some form of causality consistent with a global catastrophic aquatic event of the type narrated in Genesis 6-9. Such evidence suggests that embracing a global flood model does not require sacrificing the intellect.

In the essay "The Geologic Column and Calvary: The Rainbow Connection" (chapter 6), I raise the question What, if anything, does the way in which the geological column was formed have to do with Calvary, that is, with the forgiveness of sins? In other words, do key theological conclusions flow from the way in which one interprets the making of the geologic column in respect to the biblical flood? For example, did major fossil-bearing portions of the geologic column build slowly over a span of 570 million years, entombing animals long before Adam's sin? Or did these portions of the column form rapidly through physical forces associated with and subsequent to a flood of global proportions? What impact, if any, do the answers to such questions about the extent and effect of the biblical flood have upon our salvation?

This chapter suggests that we need to discuss the geological as well as the theological difficulties associated with flood geology. In this fashion we can make healthy headway as we place all issues onto the table for discussion. Above all, the chapter outlines how we account for the formation of the geologic column significantly affects the integrity of the substitutionary atonement, thus showing the connection between the geologic column, Calvary, and the rainbow.

Next Norman Gulley's essay constituting chapter 7, "Evolution: A Theory in Crisis," addresses the fundamental question of origins. Gulley does not dispute what many sometimes call "microevolution." However, whether one can properly extrapolate the actions of microevolution to account adequately for the full range of biological forms descending gradually by means of an interlocking chain of very small modifications is another matter entirely. Gulley's article questions the biological adequacy of the idea of "macroevolution." He describes and evaluates the mounting biological evidence that shows with utter compelling power the inadequacy of Darwinian theory concerning the origin *de novo* of biological forms. His conclusion suggests the need for some kind of causality other than that offered by Darwin. Information from another source of truth, namely revelation, supplies such a cause in the form of a personal, caring Creator-God. Gulley's discussion indicates the complementary nature of science and Scripture.

The final two essays deal with broad theological issues. In "The Role of Creation in Seventh-day Adventist Theology," Ed Zinke assesses the impact that progressive creation or theistic evolution may have upon the theology of the Seventh-day Adventist denomination. Many evangelical theologians have for some time endorsed some form of progressive creation. What is less widely known is that major thought leaders of the North American evangelical community are now embracing some form of theistic evolution. Zinke shows how adopting the postmodern evolutionary worldview of theistic evolution shapes our understanding of the nature of the Bible, humanity, God, Christ's work of redemption, and His second coming.

Finally, Martin Hanna tackles the issue of whether we can harmonize the worlds of science and religion. Should they be? If so, in what way? He relates three "lights" of authority—Christ, Scripture, and nature. After identifying tensions among the approaches of Barth, Tillich, Gilkey, and Torrance concerning the relation between natural science and theology, Hanna discusses what he calls the "inclusive model" appropriate for evangelical theology.

This book brings biblical issues, recent geological assessments, and major theological implications to the table for discussion in the ongoing dialogue regarding the basic issue of origins, design, creation, and flood geology. All too often such discussions tend to omit areas of possible sensitivity and seem to focus on "assured results." The contributors hope that readers will carefully probe all the issues and evaluate them with openness. The timely counsel offered by John Macquarrie needs to be heeded by all participants in the discussion of science and religion: "Our first step must be . . . to learn a new respect for one another, and to ensure that no group is marginalized."[16] It will facilitate the important goal of "mutual understanding and progress."[17]

In sum, this volume enables the reader not only to develop a deeper understanding of the creation and the flood, but makes these crucial biblical truths come meaningfully alive in our personal daily life.

---

[1] William Wordsworth, "My Heart Leaps Up When I Behold," in J. E. Tobin, ed., *English Literature* (New York: American Book Co., 1949), p. 676.

[2] For aspects of this portrayal I am informed instrumentally in part by language employed by Thomas G. Long, Princeton professor of preaching and worship, in his article "The Use of Scripture in Contemporary Preaching," *Interpretation* 44, No. 2 (April 1990): 352.

[3] Philip D. Clayton, *God and Contemporary Science* (Grand Rapids: W. B. Eerdmans, 1997), p. 114. While Philip Clayton himself stands outside the special creation tradition, his position regarding the relation of empirical evidence and biblical claims nicely characterizes one operating principle of this book. Clayton's position helpfully brings balance and humility to the table.
A sensitive historical mapping of the relation of science and religion appears in the book by John Brooke and Geoffrey Cantor, *Reconstructing Nature: The Engagement of Science and Religion* (Edinburgh: T & T Clark, 1998). In these revised Glasgow Gifford lectures, John Brook echoes Clayton's orientation to the relation of evidence and faith. Natural theology can confirm or encourage faith, when belief is already present.

[4] In addition, on biblical and scientific grounds Adventists welcome the various lines of contemporary anthropological and theological research underscoring the holistic understanding of the human person. This research questions the concept of human personhood as involving a separable eternal soul. For some recent perspectives regarding this recent exploration of human nature see: Nancey Murphy, *Whatever Happened to the Soul? Scientific and Theological Portraits of Human Nature* (Minneapolis: Fortress Press, 1998).

[5] For a masterful assessment of the implications of category translation see: Langdon Gilkey, "Cosmology, Ontology, and the Travail of Biblical Language," *The Journal of Religion* 41, No. 3 (July 1961): 194-205; and Langdon Gilkey, *Religion and the Scientific Future* (New York: Harper and Row, 1970; reprint ed., Macon, Ga.: Mercer University Press/ROSE, 1979), especially chapter 1, "The Influence of Science on Recent Theology," pp. 3-34.
Category translation, for example, treats the biblical activities and figure of Satan as no longer that of a real historical agent, but rather as metaphors, symbols, or allegories for evil. The biblically indicated space and time categories of satanic persecutions (Job 1 and 2), or his temptations of Christ (Matt. 4), for instance, are translated into the category of metaphor.
While cultural and existential translation represent central tools in Adventist scholarship, cate-

gory translation remains problematic in Adventist academic circles. In part the present volume represents an attempt to address the issue.

[6] For Luther's interpretation of the days of creation week as literal days as contrasted with the position of Augustine, see Martin Luther, *Lectures on Genesis,* ed., J. Pelikan, *Luther's Works* (St. Louis: Concordia Pub. House, 1958), vol. 1, p. 6.

[7] Cf. Dermot A. Lane, *Keeping Hope Alive: Stirrings in Christian Theology* (New York: Paulist Press, 1996).

[8] Five landmark publications have fueled this new discussion: Michael Denton, *Evolution: A Theory in Crisis* (1985); Phillip E. Johnson, *Darwin on Trial* (1991); Alvin Plantinga, "When Faith and Reason Clash: Evolution and the Bible," *Christian Scholar's Review* 21 (1991): 80-109; Michael Behe, *Darwin's Black Box: The Biochemical Challenge to Evolution* (1996); and a group of publications from scholars calling themselves "design theorists." Individuals such as Michael Behe, William Dempski, Paul Nelson, and Johnson are examples of leading figures in the new interest in design theory. In fact, Johnson summons "paleontologists to interpret their evidence without Darwinist prejudice" ("Response to Hasker," *Christian Scholar's Review* 22 [1993]: 303, n. 7). In evaluating this remarkable invitation, William Hasker magnanimously allows that Johnson's research proposal "could produce a genuinely viable special creationist alternative" ("Reply to Johnson," *Christian Scholar's Review* 22 [1993]: 308). Then Hasker articulates a window-opening opportunity: "I hope he [Johnson] will find scientists who are willing and able to undertake the research he has in mind" *(ibid.).*

The first major meeting of the intelligent-design movement occurred in November 1996 at Biola University in La Mirada, near Los Angeles. See the January 6, 1997, issue of *Christianity Today* for two articles covering this event: David Neff's editorial "The Pope, the Press, and Evolution," pp. 18, 19; and Scott Swanson, "Debunking Darwin? 'Intelligent-Design' Movement Gathers Strength," pp. 64, 65.

[9] See Stanley J. Grenz, *A Primer on Postmodernism* (Grand Rapids: Eerdmans, 1996), p. 158.

[10] If we are to call the biblical flood by its technically more accurate name, i.e., "God's global flood," rather than "Noah's flood," we might evaluate the event with greater care. Although associated with the flood, Noah did not send it; God did.

[11] In the final chapter of his revised doctoral thesis, University of California, San Diego, entitled, *Chronic Vigour, Darwin, Anglicans, Catholics, and the Development of a Doctrine of Providential Evolution* (Lanham: University Press of America, 1996), Gregory Elder concludes that one major religious response to Darwin was an intentional avoidance of discussing potential theological difficulties that might arise from the transmutation theory. The present essay seeks to be one step in redressing such avoidance.

[12] Del Ratzsch, *The Battle of Beginnings: Why Neither Side Is Winning the Creation-Evolution Debate* (Downers Grove, Ill.: InterVarsity, 1996), p. 198.

[13] Rodney Lee Stiling, "The Diminishing Deluge: Noah's Flood in Nineteenth-Century American Thought" (Ph.D. diss., University of Wisconsin at Madison, 1991).

[14] Cf. the language used by Ellen G. White in this context in manuscript 62, 1886.

[15] Davis A. Young, *The Biblical Flood: A Case Study of the Church's Response to Extrabiblical Evidence* (Grand Rapids: Eerdmans, 1995), p. ix.

[16] John Macquarrie, "Foreword," in Alister E. McGrath, *The Renewal of Anglicanism* (Harrisburg, Pa.: Morehouse, 1993), p. 2.

[17] J. P. Moreland, ed., *The Creation Hypothesis: Scientific Evidence for an Intelligent Designer* (Downers Grove, Ill.: InterVarsity, 1994), p. 37.

MEET THE AUTHORS

John T. Baldwin

Although the contributors are academic professionals, they are real human beings with family, children, pets, hobbies, and interests in enjoyable enterprises as varied as sports, book collecting, and music. For instance, Randall Younker, director of the Institute of Archaeology, is also the quarterback for a football team during the summer intramural season at Andrews University. John Baldwin, professor of theology, directs the seminary chorus at the same institution. Above all, each author is deeply committed to Jesus Christ, family, seminary teaching, and the gospel ministry.

The late Gerhard Hasel, after completing a Ph.D. program in biblical studies at Vanderbilt University in Nashville, Tennessee, served for 27 years on the faculty of the Seventh-day Adventist Theological Seminary, Berrien Springs, Michigan, from 1967 to his tragic death in the summer of 1994. He was dean of the seminary from 1981 to 1988, director of the Ph.D. and Th.D. programs from 1976 to his demise, and the first John Nevins Andrews professor of Old Testament and biblical theology. Hasel wrote more than 10 books and 158 scholarly and popular articles, the last of which appears as the second chapter here.

Randall W. Younker is associate professor of Old Testament and biblical archaeology at the Seventh-day Adventist Seminary, Andrews University. In addition to a B.A. in religion and an M.A. in biology from Pacific Union College, Younker has earned an M.A. and a Ph.D. in Near Eastern archaeology from the University of Arizona. His current seminary duties also include directing the Institute of Archaeology and the Ph.D./Th.D. program.

Younker has participated in numerous archaeological projects in Israel and Jordan, including the Tel Dor Project in Israel and the Tell el 'Umeiri survey in Jordan. He has codirected excavations at Tell Gezer (Israel), Tell Jawa (Jordan), and el-Dreijat (Jordan), the latter two as part of the Madaba Plains Project. Currently, he is directing excavations at Tell Jalul, the largest site in central Transjordan, for the Madaba Plains Project.

In addition to archaeological field work, Younker has also served as a trustee on the board of the W. F. Albright Institute of Archaeological Research in Jerusalem and is currently a trustee for the American Schools of

Oriental Research. He has coedited two books and published more than 40 scholarly articles and reviews. Also, he serves on the editorial boards of several scholarly journals, including *Andrews University Seminary Studies, Journal of the Adventist Theological Society,* and *Origins.*

Richard M. Davidson is J. N. Andrews professor of Old Testament interpretation and chair of the Old Testament Department at the Seventh-day Adventist Theological Seminary, where he has taught since 1979. His wife, Jo Ann Mazat Davidson, teaches in the seminary in the Department of Theology and Christian Philosophy. Born in California, Davidson earned his Master of Divinity degree summa cum laude from the Seventh-day Adventist Theological Seminary and his doctorate in biblical studies from Andrews University in 1981. Entitled "Typological Structures in the Old and New Testaments," his dissertation is now published under the title *Typology in Scripture.*

Before coming to Andrews, Davidson served as pastor in Arizona for several years and received ordination to the ministry in 1974. In addition to holding membership in the Society of Biblical Literature, the Evangelical Theological Society, the Chicago Society of Biblical Research, and the Adventist Theological Society, Davidson has written a number of articles for reference journals and Adventist denominational papers, including the article "The Flood," in *Evangelical Dictionary of Biblical Theology* (1996). Recent books include *A Love Song for the Sabbath* (Review and Herald, 1988) and *In the Footsteps of Joshua* (Review and Herald, 1995).

Born in Geneva, Switzerland, Ariel A. Roth holds a Ph.D. in zoology from the University of Michigan. He has taken additional training in geology, mathematics, and radiation biology at various campuses of the University of California. In addition to holding a number of college and university academic appointments and memberships in several learned societies, Roth directed the Geoscience Research Institute of Loma Linda University for 14 years and has served as editor of the journal *Origins* for 23 years.

Roth's research focuses on living and fossil coral reefs in both the Pacific and Caribbean oceans, where he has investigated the effects of light and pigment on the rate of coral reef growth. The Atomic Energy Commission (DOE), the National Institutes of Health, the National Science Foundation, and the National Oceanic and Atmospheric Administration have funded his research.

Active in the evolution-creation discussions in the United States, Roth has served as a consultant or witness to the states of California, Oregon, and Arkansas. He has conducted numerous paleontological and geological field trips in Australia, New Zealand, Europe, and North America in areas significant to creation-evolution issues. His publications number more than 125 articles in both scientific and popular journals, and Roth has lectured around the world.

John T. Baldwin, currently professor of theology in the Seventh-day Adventist Theological Seminary, holds a Ph.D. in theology from the University of Chicago (1990). Having written a dissertation entitled "The Argument to Design in British Religious Thought: An Investigation of the Status and Cogency of Post-Humean Forms of Teleological Argumentation With Reference Principally to Hume and Paley," Baldwin continues to follow his research interest regarding the philosophical relationship of science and religion. He won a John Templeton Foundation prize in the 1994 Call for Papers on Humility Theology for his article entitle "God and the World: William Paley's Argument From Perfection Tradition—A Continuing Influence," published in the *Harvard Theological Review* (85, No. 1 [1992]: 109-120).

Baldwin serves on the editorial board of the journal *Origins* and on the editorial advisory board of the journal *Origins and Design,* while holding memberships in the American Academy of Religion, the American Scientific Association, the Adventist Society of Religious Studies, the Adventist Theological Society, and the Society of Biblical Literature.

Norman R. Gulley is professor of systematic theology at Southern Adventist University. He graduated with a Ph.D. in systematic theology from the University of Edinburgh, Scotland, where he studied under Professor Thomas F. Torrance and wrote a dissertation on the eschatology of Karl Barth. Gulley served as chair of the Theology Department at Japan Missionary College, chair of the Graduate Theology Department at the Adventist University of the Philippines, and director/academic dean of the Graduate Seventh-day Adventist Theological Seminary (Far East) in Manila. He is a member of the Evangelical Theological Society, the British Theological Society, the Society of Biblical Literature, and the American Academy of Religion, and has been an officer in the Adventist Theological Society since its inception.

His publication record is extensive, including more than 100 articles and seven books. Gulley has written three major articles for the *Anchor Bible Dictionary* and contributed the chapter "Reader-Response Theories in Postmodern Hermeneutics: A Challenge to Evangelical Theology" in the book *The Challenge of Postmodernism: An Evangelical Engagement* (Victor Books, 1995). His *Christ Is Coming* (Review and Herald, 1998) is a major textbook on eschatology. Currently he is writing a three-volume systematic theology.

Ed Zinke, a theologian with a specialty in the history of method in theology, is a graduate of the Seventh-day Adventist Theological Seminary. He served as a pastor in the Arkansas-Louisiana Conference and as research scholar for 14 years in the Biblical Research Institute of the General Conference of Seventh-day Adventists. Ed has been president of the Adventist Theological Society and later its treasurer. He and his wife, Ann, own and operate a company that supplies the retail trade with packaged quality nuts and dried fruit. They generously contribute financially to the Ph.D. programs of the Seventh-day Adventist Theological Seminary.

Martin Frederick Hanna, currently a Ph.D. candidate at the Seventh-day Adventist Theological Seminary, originates from the Bahamas. Upon completion of his doctorate, Hanna looks forward to returning to previous teaching responsibilities at West Indies College.

Ordained to the ministry in 1986, Hanna served as teacher and pastor in the Bahamas for seven years; dean of men and lecturer in theology at West Indies College in Jamaica (1987-1991); president of the Midwest Chapter of the Adventist Theological Society (1994-1996); and research assistant at the seminary (1991-present).

Hanna's research focuses on systematic theology in general and upon the role of science in theology in particular. His publications include: *The Seventh-day Adventist Theological Bibliography (1851-1994)* (Seminary, 1995); reviews and articles in the *Andrews University Seminary Studies,* the *Journal of the Adventist Theological Society,* and *Celebration: An Adult Leadership Resource Journal.*

CHAPTER 1

REVELATION 14:7: AN ANGEL'S WORLDVIEW

John T. Baldwin

Seventh-day Adventist Theological Seminary

Andrews University

Introduction

Current New Testament research has discovered a vastly significant allusion to Exodus 20:11 resulting from a profound cosmological statement by the first angel of Revelation 14.

Eight far-reaching implications of the allusion serve as the foundational principles undergirding the various essays in this volume and provide the basis for the possibility of unparalleled contemporary Christian theological, scientific, and spiritual unity.

In a recent exegetical study, New Testament scholar Jon Paulien examines what he shows to be the high point of the last half of the book of Revelation, namely, the summons in Revelation 14:7 of the inhabitants of the earth to worship the true God.[1] The passage contains a direct verbal parallel between Revelation 14:7 ("made heaven and earth, and sea") and Exodus 20:11 ("made heaven and earth, the sea"). According to Paulien, this verbal parallel, along with thematic and structural parallels, shows that the latter portion of the first angel's message constitutes a clear, direct allusion to the fourth commandment of Exodus 20:11 within the broader context of a worldwide call to worship the true God.[2] Thus, the allusion and its implications acquire distinctive importance because they form the integral parts of the high point of the second half of the book of Revelation.[3] In the following discussion we will analyze and evaluate eight possible theological, scientific, and spiritual implications that flow from this exegetical insight. But first we must consider the nature of the allusion.

Revelation 14:7: Endorsing Exodus 20:11

Four distinct verbal parallels between Revelation 14:7 and Exodus 20:11 help to demonstrate that the New Testament passage is a definite allusion to the fourth commandment of the decalogue. The first verbal parallel is between the verb "made" in Revelation 14:7 and the "made" of Exodus 20:11. The next three verbal parallels involve three specific nouns ("heaven, earth, and sea") that appear in both passages in the same identical order. Along with thematic and structural parallels, these striking verbal parallels establish that Revelation 14:7 constitutes a definite allusion, not merely an echo, to the cosmogonic (origin of the earth) portion of the fourth commandment (Ex. 20:11).[4]

Two initial considerations help to suggest that the allusion of verse 7 to Exodus 20:11 also endorses all the elements of Exodus 20:11. First, verse 7 makes the allusion in the context of listing specific divine acts that identify the One whom human beings should worship. By doing so it clearly affirms these divine creative acts as the approved criteria for knowing who the true God is. Second, when the Revelation passage alludes to the same acts of creation mentioned in Exodus 20:11, it thereby endorses them and the entire text as indicated below. This wide endorsement leads to the eight implications that we will now examine.

A First-Century Biblically Endorsed Six-Day Creation Worldview[5]

The first and most basic implication is that a six-day creation cosmogony, or worldview, is inherent in the first angel's message. By alluding to the Sabbath commandment, containing the phrase "For in six days the Lord made," verse 7 upholds the entire proclamation of the seventh-day Sabbath. Thus Revelation 14:7 by implication endorses all the cosmogonic elements of Exodus 20:11, thereby affirming the concept of "For in six days the Lord made."

The exegetical research of New Testament scholar C. H. Dodd underscores the conclusion that the allusion to Exodus 20:11 approves of not only the specific creative acts of the Old Testament passage, but also the wider context of the commandment as a whole and thus the concept of creation in six days. In *According to the Scriptures* Dodd indicates that New Testament writers such as Paul and John used the Old Testament in a way that is based upon a widely accepted Old Testament textual "substructure."[6] Dodd points out that the biblical writers were not "bringing together isolated 'proof-texts,'"[7] but were using key portions of passages as pointers to "whole contexts."[8] Thus, for example, when Paul with deep thankfulness asks, "Death, where is thy sting?" he is not "employing a casual literary reminiscence [proof-text level], but referring [alluding] to a passage already recognized as a classical description of God's deliverance of His people out of utter destruction"[9] as found in Hosea 13:14. The New Testament writers intended for such allusions to send their first-century hearers back to the original Old

Testament context for reinforcement and illumination of "certain fundamental and permanent elements in the biblical revelation."[10]

Applied to Revelation 14:7, Dodd's research and language indicate that the first angel's allusion to Exodus 20:11 is not a casual literary reminiscence, but seeks to direct the reader to a whole textual context, in this case the fourth commandment and the concept of creation in six days. As we shall see, such a conclusion has implications for an angel-endorsed worldview of creation in six days.

The fact that Revelation 14:7 implicitly endorses the concept of a creation in six days gives the exegete, theologian, scientist, or lay reader hermeneutical authorization to take the temporal "in six days" concept of Exodus 20:11 and insert it into Revelation 14:7 and thus to interpret the latter passage as "worship Him who, *in six days,* made the heavens, and the earth and sea." Figure 1 illustrates this endorsement.

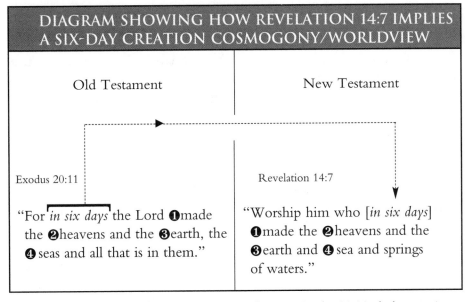

DIAGRAM SHOWING HOW REVELATION 14:7 IMPLIES A SIX-DAY CREATION COSMOGONY/WORLDVIEW

Old Testament	New Testament
Exodus 20:11	Revelation 14:7
"For *in six days* the Lord ❶made the ❷heavens and the ❸earth, the ❹seas and all that is in them."	"Worship him who [*in six days*] ❶made the ❷heavens and the ❸earth and ❹sea and springs of waters."

Figure 1: *This diagram shows that through an allusion to Exodus 20:11, the latter portion of the first angel's message implies a six-day creation cosmogony or worldview. See discussion above. The numbered words indicate the four verbal parallels existing between the two passages.*

The above exegetical analyses indicate that Revelation 14:7 is a divinely intended first-century confirmation of the six-day creation worldview. In other words, if it were possible today for the reader of Revelation 14 to ask the first angel how long God took to make the heavens, earth, sea, and springs of water, the celestial messenger would probably reply, "I just directly alluded to an Old Testament passage that explicitly answers your question—it took six days."[11] Because in this discussion of Revelation 14:7 no categories foreign to the cultural setting of the text are imported into or overlaid upon the passage by a reader who might be considered in some sense as a so-called "co-author," the conclusions drawn from Revelation 14:7 in this section are not those resulting from the application of conventional reader response theory.[12] Rather, the conclusions represent straightforward exegetical implications or insights.

If the messenger in Revelation 14:7 offers an endorsement of a six-day creation cosmogony does that mean that modern readers should continue to accept as historically true the biblically implied worldview? The next section discusses whether the first angel's message in general contains additional indicators that suggest we should accept the biblical worldview as historically accurate for today.

A Twenty-first-Century Biblically Endorsed Six-Day Creation Worldview

Does the biblically endorsed worldview implied in Revelation 14 have any theological and scientific relevance for us today? This concern introduces the specifically systematic theological and interdisciplinary aspects of the question. The following three contextual factors point to the end-time location and contemporary relevance of the worldview of Revelation 14:7, which is the second implication of the allusion.

The Apocalyptic End-time Sweep of Revelation 12-14

As we view Revelation 12 in light of the historicist principles of interpretation noted below, we witness a dragon persecuting a woman (the church) for 12 centuries after the ascension of Christ. After the same dragon empowers two beasts in chapter 13 to enforce a global system of false worship, three angels in chapter 14 deliver God's final warning to humanity against participating in such worship. They passionately summon everyone to worship the only true God. This indicates the end-time relevance of the first message of Revelation 14.

The Contextual Location of Verse 7 Within Revelation 14

Revelation 14 links the messages of the three angels with the second coming of Jesus and places them immediately before a striking description of the Second Advent. Such a contextual location suggests that they constitute a divinely crafted end-time series of messages that must go to all of humanity before Christ returns.

End-time Relevance of the Phrase "The Hour of His Judgment Is Come"

The type of apocalyptic interpretative principles we bring to the text will determine whether we consider the six-day creation concept as still relevant or not. For example, we will obtain different answers depending on whether we use preterist, futurist, historical-critical, or historicist presuppositions and hermeneutical principles. It would seem, for example, that the preterist and the classical historical-critical methods would relegate the six-day creation in verse 7 to little more than an ancient cosmogony with little or no current scientific significance.

However, we arrive at an altogether different answer when we approach the text from a particular historicist perspective.[13] According to this interpretation, the phrase "the hour of his judgment is come" (Rev. 14:7) signals the precise temporal commencement of the first message of Revelation 14 in the mid-nineteenth century.[14] Viewed in this light, Revelation 14's three messages represent God's final appeal to humanity as wholly reliable historically and scientifically because they are God's "present truth" for the end of secular history.

These historicist assumptions and interpretations, along with the two contextual pointers we analyzed above, suggest that the six contiguous creative[15] days implied in verse 7 are to be taken as historically and scientifically true even in a neo-Darwinian or postmodern age. As a result of such assumptions, we discover in these texts that the resurrected Lord Himself not only helps to unite both Testaments by embedding a six-day cosmogony in the first angel's message of Revelation 14, but also endorses such a worldview for the last days.

An Objection Evaluated

Before we explore some additional implications, we should first consider a question that might arise about the conclusion thus far. Does the absence of the words "in six days" in Revelation 14:7 suggest that God is in some way implying that we should, in fact, no longer regard a six-day creation as historically true? Otherwise, would God not have explicitly said "in six days" in the first angel's message?

Four considerations combine to indicate that such a conclusion is clearly unwarranted biblically. First, it would make Jesus contradict Himself. In 1 Corinthians 10:4 Paul states that it was Christ who accompanied the Israelites in their deliverance from Egyptian slavery. Theologically, this suggests that it was the pre-Incarnation, second person of the Godhead, the Logos, who spoke the fourth commandment from Mount Sinai, declaring that "in six days the Lord made heaven, the earth, and the sea." If we try to make Revelation 14:7 hint that the six-day creation event is no longer historically true simply because it lacks the words "in six days," we have Jesus contradicting what He presented from Sinai.

Second, the fact that Revelation 14:7 indeed approvingly alludes to Exodus 20:11 means that the allusion endorses the seventh-day Sabbath, and thus by implication the reason that Scripture states that God chose the seventh day as the Sabbath in the first place—namely, because He completed the creation in six working days. Such considerations indicate how the allusion of Revelation 14:7, far from denying the truth of the six-day creation, is in fact an important and divinely inspired confirmation of the continuing significance of the six-day creation worldview. Thus verse 7 substantiates the "in six days" concept even though it does not directly quote the words.

Third, one of the main benefits of a biblical allusion is that it enables God or His spokespeople to use an economy of words. With a few select terms God can bring to mind a biblical passage without actually having to cite it. This means that the absence of part of a passage in an allusion to another text does not necessarily signal God's disapproval of the missing words. On the contrary, a cryptic allusion can be His shorthand method of endorsing an entire passage, and thus, in the case of Revelation 14:7, confirming the concept stated in the phrase "in six days" even though the explicit words do not appear in Revelation 14:7.

Fourth, to claim that the absence of the explicit "in six days" in verse 7 means that God somehow suggests that in the last days the concept of creation in six creative days[16] is no longer historically true would force a later portion of Scripture to directly contradict an earlier one. But the Word of God clearly rejects such an idea. For example, in 1 Corinthians 14:32 Paul states that the "spirits of prophets are subject to prophets," meaning that later revelation will not go against earlier presentations of truth. In addition, Isaiah 8:20 states: "To the law and to the testimony! If they do not speak according to this word, it is because there is no light in them" (NKJV). The passage indicates that we must judge the implications of Revelation 14:7 by previous Scripture. In the case of the allusion to Exodus 20:11 it would involve nothing less than the Ten Commandments of Exodus 20. Thus the absence of "in six days" in Revelation 14:7 cannot mean that the worldview of creation in six days is no longer true. Rather, the truth is just the opposite—namely, that today, despite the fact that we live in a postmodern, evolutionary era, the six-day creation worldview remains the truth in the mind of the One who created life on our planet in precisely this fashion.

Divine revelation is progressive in the sense that successive portrayals provide wider and deeper understandings of what God has already disclosed in the past. Fresh insights do not contradict what God has already given. The notion of "present truth" does not mean that we replace past truth with "present truth". On the contrary, the idea of "present truth" implies, for instance, the current existence of concepts whose time has arrived according to the prophetic time clock, but such concepts do not invalidate former revelations.

We turn now to a discussion of some additional implications of the conclusion that Revelation 14:7 confirms a worldview of creation in six days.

Macroevolutionary Theory Addressed

The third implication is that Revelation 14:7 speaks directly to the Darwinian macroevolutionary worldview in a most timely and cogent fashion. Toward the end of July 1844, Darwin completed a 189-page handwritten manuscript summarizing his species theory. It expanded the version he had prepared two years earlier. Scholars refer to it as "Darwin's 1844 Sketch."[17] Like his later *Origin of Species,* the essay proposed the development of biological species through an evolutionary process involving millions of years. However, according to the apocalyptic historicist interpretation, God raised up during the summer of 1844 in North America an initial proclamation of the first angel's message of Revelation 14 as a present truth that would go to the entire world. Thus when Darwin in his 1844 manuscript sketch suggests that major biological forms developed over millions of years, God in the same year sends a special message to the world that He created the basic life-forms in six days, not millions of years.[18] His timing is brilliant. Only by means of a historical six- day concept of creation can we adequately address Darwin's idea of macroevolution and its cousin concepts of progressive creation and theistic evolution.

A Global Flood

The fourth implication may be somewhat surprising. A six-day creation worldview, if historically true, actually requires a corresponding historical global flood. A creation week of six contiguous creative days necessarily places all the newly created animals onto essentially the same surface or geological strata together at the same time. It means that when death entered the world after Adam's sin, animals would be buried in the same geological strata with human beings. All kinds of organisms from simple to complex would be jumbled together on the surface of our planet. They would not be sorted and buried deeply in distinct and different groups at different levels as we actually find when we examine the strata today. The fossil record demonstrates a definite sequence in fossil types as we ascend the geological column. But nature has no natural sorting process currently operating that would cause selective burial of animals all living at the same time together on essentially the same surface. Thus, in light only of the biblical creation and fall narratives, clearly the fossil-sorted geologic column should not exist.

However, the stark truth is that it does exist. Its thousands of feet of layers of rock reveal definite order and pattern to the fossils. According to contemporary geologic theory, the column formed relatively slowly by many local catastrophic spurts over 540 million years. Each sediment deposit or lava flow buried the constantly evolving organisms. How can the believing Christian account for the existence of the present geological column? For many Christians the current geological state of affairs requires the application of the biblical narrative of God's flood. Thus, the geological implications of a six-day creation demand a catastrophic aquatic geological event of global proportions able to create the kind of fossil record that we find today. It alone could sort and bury organic forms into many thousands of feet of sediment after the sin of Adam. Genesis 6-9 describes an event of such magnitude. A global flood can bury at the colossal scale we find in the rocks. Clearly, a local flood theory cannot account for a planetary geologic column. Although a discussion of a planet-wide flood lies outside the scope of this chapter, fresh field evidence continues to be discovered that is consistent with such a concept.[19]

Our analysis indicates how the last part of the first angel's message encourages the Christian to interpret Genesis 6-9 as describing a global flood as a scientifically valid event. Viewed in this light, Revelation 14:7 can provide the basis for a new and unparalleled theological and scientific Christian unity. Most mainline Christian denominations no longer believe that the biblical flood was a historical, global event. They suggest various kinds of explanations to account for today's natural world. However, the biblical worldview can bring conceptual unity to this diversity.

A Possible Significance of the Surprise Phrase "Fountains of Water"

Before we turn to a fifth implication of the worldview of Revelation 14:7, let us consider a striking phrase that appears in the first angel's message. Alluding to Exodus 20:11, the first angel unexpectedly refers to "the fountains of water" rather than to the familiar Exodus 20 "and all that is in them" (Ex. 20:11). In other words, after having followed the lead of Exodus 20:11 virtually word for word in specifying what God created, the messenger in Revelation surprisingly deviates from the parallel listing by specifying a single class of items existing among the "all that is in them." Is the vision signaling something of importance here? If so, what might it be?

Assuming divine intentionality behind the phrase "fountains of water," why does Jesus have the messenger break the parallel listing of things mentioned in Exodus 10:11? Why does the angel mention "fountains of water" and not some other class of created thing, such as trees, birds, fish, or mountains? Perhaps the reference to "fountains of water" in the context of a divine announcement of the arrival of a unique time of divine judgment seeks to direct the reader's attention to a previous period of divine judgment.[20]

First, the general biblical usage of the concept "fountains of water" includes all springs or fountains and hence the famous "fountains of the great deep" referred to in Genesis 7:11. The book of Proverbs informs us that divine wisdom created the fountains of the deep (Prov. 8:24, 28). Above all, the fountains of the deep, according to the book of Genesis, broke up at the time of the biblical flood that God sent as a divine judgment against intractable human sin. Thus the expression "fountains of water" in Revelation 14:7 may intentionally point to the event when God washed the earth of its corruption.[21]

Second, the Greek word for "fountain" in Revelation 14:7 is a form of *pēgē,* the same Greek word used in the LXX (the second-century B.C. Greek translation of the Old Testament) for the Hebrew term for "fountain" *(ma'yān)*[22] employed in fountains of the deep in Genesis 7:11 and Proverbs 8:24. This usage of "fountains" in the original biblical languages permits the reader to grasp a possible connection between "fountains of water" (Rev. 14:7) and the "fountains of the great deep" (Gen. 7:11), and hence to when the "fountains of the deep" burst at the time of God's divine aquatic judgment against human sin. Thus the reference to "fountains of water" in Revelation 14:7 may be an inspired hint of the divine judgment of flood the Lord sent to sweep away human iniquity.

Perhaps God intends that the possible allusion to the flood by the words "fountains of water" should underscore the truth that He is indeed a God of judgment, as well as a God of everlasting faithfulness and graciousness (both evidenced in the narrative of the Genesis flood). If so, the personal and spiritual implications of the flood connotation triggered by the phrase "fountains of water" might be to encourage the reader to take seriously the momentous arrival of a new end-time process of individual divine judgment now announced by the first messenger of Revelation 14.

If we can properly interpret the concept "fountains of water" as pointing to God's previous act of judgment in the Genesis flood, the phrase constitutes still another divine endorsement of the historical reality of the biblical flood.

Finally, given the judgment context of Revelation 14 as an end-time message in preparation for the *eschaton,* and in view of the fact, as shown by Davidson's essay in this volume, that the flood constitutes a divinely initiated aquatic global undoing of creation in judgment upon human sin, is it possible that by alluding to the Genesis flood in the phrase "springs of water" John might also be implicitly warning of the immanence of a second global undoing of creation—this time, as indicated in Revelation 19:20-21:1, not by means of water, but by fire?[23]

Testifying to God's Goodness

Fifth, one of the most significant spiritual and theological contributions made by the last part of the first angel's message may be its support of God's goodness in view of what we can only characterize as a pernicious, even demonic God, if the Creator in fact uses the evolutionary process as His method of choice. Why? As Holmes Rolston III rightly indicates, the process of evolution is extraordinarily wasteful and cruel, filled with "predation, parasitism, selfishness, randomness, blindness, disaster, indifference, waste, struggle, suffering, death."[24] In this setting Richard Rice reminds us that "God is responsible only for the possibility of evil," not its actuality.[25]

In this context Philip Clayton recently pinpoints the problem for God's character when God is interpreted as directly creating through evolution. "A God who allows countless billions of organisms to suffer and die, and entire species to be wiped out, either does not share the sort of values we do, or works in the world in a much more limited and indirect way than theologians have usually imagined."[26] His perceptive comments show that if Christians accept the disease-ridden, wasteful, and suffering- and death-filled macroevolutionary process as God's way to produce directly new life-forms, then nature clearly depicts God with a demonic face.[27] In other words, the geologic column, if interpreted as the product of millions of years of organic evolution guided by God, actually portrays the way Satan would develop life-forms, not God. In light of these negative theological implications that seldom get mentioned, Thane Hutcherson Ury asks perceptively, "Is this the God before whom David would rejoicefully dance?"[28] Revelation 14 helps to resolve this weighty challenge to divine beneficence.

The good news is that the momentous historical events of a rapid creation and a global flood required by Revelation 14:7 directly safeguard God's goodness by removing from Him any responsibility for producing life-forms through an evolutionary process. A literal creation necessitates a global flood (Gen. 6-9) to produce the geologic column after the entrance of sin. Assuming the historical reality of the two events, the Christian may correctly conclude that God, in fact, did not use macroevolutionary processes to create life-forms, and that the divinely initiated global flood formed the massive fossil-bearing layers of rock that so astound us today. Thus we cannot charge God with creating life-forms in a demonic manner.

It is important that we point out that the biblical narrative does not portray the flood as a capricious act on God's part. It depicts the totality of divine grace. God's spirit strives to bring everyone to repentance (Gen. 6:3). In addition, God suffers deep anguish over the breakdown of human relationships (verse 6). Through the preaching of Noah for 120 years God warns humanity of coming destruction and provides a way of escape (verse 6). A high point of the narrative is the statement that "God remembered Noah" (Gen. 8:1). Even during the storm itself God provides abundant divine grace, showing that His loving character continues in full strength even during the darkest movements of earthly tragedy.

As we have seen, to interpret the geologic column as the record of God's direct way of creation diminishes and even demonizes Him. It presents a pernicious deity wholly unlike the compassionate biblical God who weeps over the recalcitrant people He comes to save (Luke 19:10, 41). We would find it hard to imagine Him caring when one sparrow falls (Matt. 10:29). By contrast, the last part of the first angel's message responds to the theodicy issue.[29] Through its implications of a six-day creation and a global flood, Revelation 14:7 provides the geological basis for the encouraging truth that God's character is everlastingly benevolent and fair, thus identifying Him as truly worthy of our love, trust, worship, and praise. The geological, spiritual, and theological implications of the Revelation passage are indeed far-reaching, showing again how important a six-day creation and global flood are to our understanding of the kind of God we worship and serve. We turn now to perhaps the most practical implication of Revelation 14:7.

Hermeneutics

As Langdon Gilkey correctly observes, "cosmology [worldview] does make a difference in hermeneutics."[30] A sixth implication of the cosmology of verse 7 is its capacity to illustrate how God desires that we interpret the Bible. The passage encourages a return to a distinctive biblical hermeneutic.

Interpret the Bible Literally When Called for by the Text

Revelation 14:7, with its allusion to a creation in six historical days (Ex. 20:11), encourages us to regard Genesis 1-11 in a straightforward historical sense and thus to make substantive hermeneutical decisions. Verse 7 reminds us that we need to interpret the Bible literally and historically when called for by the text. Moreover, the fact that this hermeneutical principle appears in a

New Testament text alluding to an Old Testament passage shows us how the New Testament interprets Genesis 1. It makes the hermeneutical concept doubly significant.

In addition, because it was Jesus who appeared in the visions (Rev. 1:1, 10, 12, 17, 18), it means that in Revelation 14:7 none other than the resurrected Lord Himself interprets Genesis 1 literally, thus illustrating Christ's preferred post-Resurrection method of Bible hermeneutics. He offers it as a model for us today. We too would do well to understand the Bible literally when common sense tells us that is what a passage intends, just as Jesus does here. Because the book of Revelation speaks to the last days and uses this type of hermeneutic, it strongly suggests that it is the one divinely intended for the end-time.

Addressing the Distinction Between "What the Text Meant/What the Text Means"

By implying that a six-day creation and a global flood represent actual historical events, Revelation 14:7 effectively addresses the widely applied hermeneutical principle distinguishing between "what the text meant and what the text means."[31] According to this concept, many post-Enlightenment and postmodern exegetes believe there is a massive worldview and cultural break between what the biblical writers held to be true and what evolutionary science believes to be historically factual. They consider the cosmological divide as so great that one must pass many of the claims of Scripture through a hermeneutical filter that separates what the biblical writer held as true from how we must interpret a passage today, i.e., category translation needs to occur.

By contrast, the allusion in Revelation 14:7 implies that what the text meant in the first century is essentially what it teaches for us today. In this sense our passage from Revelation dissolves the distinction between what this text meant and what it means today. Such a conclusion in no way lessens the need to consider cultural aspects when interpreting the Bible. But it does remind us that what the Bible meant in principle then is what it means in principle for the last days.

The six-day creation concept has a number of significant aspects for us today. For example, the concept of the length of creation is equally as important as the "when." How long did God take to create? A second question involves whether God intentionally created our world's basic life forms in one week or over a period of millions of years.[32] The worldview embedded in the first angel's message answers the first important question about origins. Although most mainline Christian academic, scientific, and theological circles have endorsed a theistic evolution or progressive creation perspective, Revelation 14:7 encourages a reevaluation of this position.

Addressing the Issue of Separating Scripture From the Word of God

With its implication that we should understand the six-day creation and global flood as actual historical events, Revelation 14:7 also speaks to the hermeneutical issue of whether we should separate the concept "Scripture" from the concept of "Word of God." In 1771 a founding father of the historical-critical method, Johann S. Semler, suggested that "the root of evil (in theology) is the interchangeable use of the terms 'Scripture' and 'Word of God.'"[33] The traditional historical-critical approach believes that we must not equate the two concepts. We cannot freely criticize, alter, or adjust Scripture if we regard it as the literal, truthful word of God in sentence form.

However, if the creative events implied by Revelation 14:7 did occur historically, the passage identifies or equates biblical statements as the Word of God containing historically, ontologically true propositions. Erasing the separation between Scripture and the Word of God overturns a basic working assumption of the historical-critical method. This means, in effect, that contemporary exegetes and theologians are invited to equate the concept "Scripture" and the concept "Word of God."

Postmodernism

Seventh, Revelation 14:7 responds decisively to the heart of postmodernism. Postmodernism insists that objective, unchanging truth might not exist.[34] Rather, postmodernism insists that competing frames of reference endure that need not be reconciled. The result is that different groups live in mutually exclusive thought worlds. By contrast, and given the end-time setting of Revelation 14, verse 7 itself constructs a single six-contiguous-creative-day creation worldview as being valid to the coming of Christ and beyond. As a result, it serves as a single objective overarching truth, or unchanging metanarrative, thus demonstrating that such truth is possible in a postmodern era. This suggests that scientists, theologians, and laypersons may accept the single worldview implied here as the objective historical truth for our postmodern context.

Epistemology and Language Theory

Finally, we may observe an eighth implication involving certain issues raised by epistemology and language theory in the area of religious, theological, and biblical statements. Such highly sophisticated and complicated issues deserve much more attention than we can give here, but a few preliminary observations might be useful. For instance, how might the passage we have been studying help shape an evangelical account of biblical and theological language theory? Nancey Murphy analyzes two popular attitudes in contemporary philosophy of language that attempt to articulate the relationship between science and religion. She distinguishes between referential and expressivist theories of religious discourse. The former, often reflected in conservative evangelical theology employing a foundationalist metaphor,[35] refers to the same world as does scientific discourse. This allows for genuine conflict between the accounts they give.[36]

On the other hand, Schleiermacher's definition of Christian doctrines as "accounts of the Christian religious affections set forth in speech"[37] illustrates the expressivist theory of language. However, his approach effectively historicizes doctrine.[38] This means that an important shift with significant consequences for both science and religion has occurred in the way religious discourse refers to things. Murphy observes that "here religious language expresses religious awareness and may have no reference to the natural world at all, so the very possibility of conflict (or interaction of any sort) with science is foreclosed."[39] Murphy prefers a form of epistemological holism, shaped by Quine's fabric, field, or web of belief's metaphor. In this approach Murphy sees a mutual conditioning of levels of disciplines, rendering the whole free of foundationalism.[40]

How might the claims of Revelation 14:7 interact with the types of discourse mentioned above? On the assumption that the implied claim in verse 7—that God created life on earth during six days of a literal week, is an ontological truth corresponding to George Lindbeck's third sense of the term true,[41] the passage does indeed seem to refer to the same kind of world as scientific language speaks about. If so, our passage may support some form of a carefully nuanced referential theory of religious discourse. However, even then we may still struggle with what appears to be conflict between the claims of verse 7 and some interpretations of science. But despite its problems it might be more inclusive than Murphy's model because the former does not distinguish so radically between the referential intent of the passage (which may seemingly conflict with science) and the theological interpretation.[42] In any case, these brief and tentative reflections will hopefully stimulate discussion and further study between Revelation 14 and epistemology and theological language theory.

This epistemic paradigm for theology seeks to respond to recent criticisms by Mark Noll in his *Scandal of the Evangelical Mind*.[43] Noll laments that contemporary evangelicals continue to cling to a hermeneutic that attempts to arrive at truth by reading Genesis 1-11 in a historical sense.[44] He argues that theology must return to the accommodationist positions of Charles Hodge and

Benjamin B. Warfield. Although they held to biblical inerrancy, they advocated that contemporary evolutionary theory must reinterpret the biblical teaching on the length of creation and the origin of humanity except for the human soul.[45] However, Revelation 14:7 suggests that the opposite is the case. Instead of the evangelical mind scandalizing itself by considering Genesis 1-11 as historically true, the real scandal results from relegating these chapters to the nonhistorical while still trying to use them as a basis of theological truth. The implications of the first angel of Revelation 14 are indeed far-reaching.

Conclusion

The eight implications resulting from the allusion of Revelation 14:7 to Exodus 20:11 (as well as other implications that space does not permit us to develop)[46] show how verse 7 provides a powerful basis for a new, unparalleled Christian unity of several dimensions. In review, the allusion first implies the reality of a six-day creation worldview, and that, in the second place, this worldview is relevant today. Third, instead of the macroevolutionary worldview the biblical worldview serves as the single frame of reference for exegetical, theological, philosophical, and scientific research during the end-time.

Five other implications of the allusion include: the need for a global flood, confirmation of God's beneficent character, a hermeneutic that interprets the early narratives of Genesis in a literal, historical fashion, the acceptance of an overarching metanarrative instead of postmodernism's fractured worldviews, and possibly some form of understanding of religious discourse. The acceptance and implementation of these implications can unify Christian theology and scientific research in profound and healing ways. Christian theology and science can be free from core contradictory theological and scientific pluralism.

For these reasons Revelation 14:7 can serve as the cosmological North Star for Christian theological, scientific, and spiritual unity in a postmodern era. The passage enables us to know, trust, and worship the immeasurably loving God who in six days created the "heaven, and earth, the sea, and the fountains of water."

Epilogue

In a recent *Adventist Review* article entitled "The Final Deception: An Evil, Counterfeit Trinity Is Now Making Ready for War," Jon Paulien contrasts the messages of the three angels of Revelation 14 against the three unclean spirits of Revelation 16:13-16.[47] Paulien presents three concepts relevant to the present chapter. First, since the plagues of Egypt provide the backdrop for Revelation 16, he sees the choice of "frogs" as especially significant. The plague of frogs was the last plague the magicians could counterfeit. It was their final deception. Linking this fact to Revelation 16, Paulien suggests that the imagery of the frogs signals that the message the spirits present is the final end-time deception. Second, they seek to counterfeit God's three messages in chapter 14: "Revelation 16:14 says that these frogs are 'spirits of demons.' They are the demonic counterparts of the three good angels of Revelation 14:6-12. Both groups of angels have a mission to the whole world (Rev. 14:6; 16:14)."[48] In other words, "In the end it will be . . . three angels against three angels. . . . [One group represents] a counterfeit of God's end-time message."[49]

Third, Paulien suggests that the book of Revelation indicates that the end-time encounter between the two groups of ideas will be "a battle between the Scriptures and perception, between reality as experienced by the five senses, and ultimate reality as revealed by God Himself."[50] In fact, it "will be a battle between two truth systems: one will be confirmed scientifically; the other will be confirmed only by Scripture."[51]

Applied to the implications of Revelation 14:7, Paulien's research seems to indicate that both groups of angels might agree that God is the Creator. Moreover, they also will probably support the fact that He created the heaven, the earth, the sea and the springs of waters. However, they might differ regarding the length and method of creation. According to the genuine message of Revelation 14, God brings basic life-forms into existence during six days. By contrast, the demonic counterpart might argue that God creates such things over a period of millions of years through the macroevolutionary processes suggested by conventional scientific wisdom. If so, evangelical scholars can note the apparent demonic promulgation of such a theistic/scientific claim.

In this context, Paulien's third point, that the final encounter involves the issue of Scripture versus perception by the five senses, can be helpful to creation/evolution dialogue. It can forewarn us that in the final confrontation we may not have the full scientific response to the various challenges facing us, whether it involves flood geology or creation in six days. Thus in some respects the evidence of our five senses may appear to point to conventional scientific conclusions. In this case, end-time believers may have to rely wholly upon the Word of God not only regarding matters such as the state of the dead, but also to a wider circle of issues such as the method of creation and the historicity of the biblical flood. But we must keep in mind that such a position of faith does not really pit science against the Word of God. To the contrary, the position encourages believers that when they finally see the "ultimate reality as revealed by God Himself," they will observe a beautiful harmony between the two realms of discourse, one fully understandable and acceptable by both theologian and scientist.

---

[1] Jon Paulien, "Revisiting the Sabbath in the Book of Revelation" (unpublished paper presented at the Jerusalem Bible Conference, June 9-14, 1998). For information regarding such biblical allusions, see Paulien's published doctoral dissertation, *Decoding Revelation's Trumpets: Literary Allusions and the Interpretation of Revelation 8:7-12,* Andrews University Seminary Doctoral Dissertation Series (Berrien Springs, Mich.: Andrews University Press, 1987), Vol. XI.

[2] ———, "Revisiting the Sabbath," p. 10. Regarding the worship of the true God, compare particularly the language of John 17:3 and Acts 4:12.

[3] *Ibid.,* p. 6. Two other reasons serve to establish further the crucial significance of the allusion to the fourth commandment of Exodus 20. First, according to a particular type of apocalyptic historicist interpretation that we will mention later, the allusion becomes the basis for a particular angel's message of Revelation 14:9-12. Second, the allusion implies at a minimum that the fourth commandment within the "commandments of God" is the version in Exodus 20 and not Deuteronomy 5. Thus when the third angel's message says "Here is the perseverance of the saints who keep the commandments of God" (NASB) and the reader wonders which commandments the messenger has in mind, the logical textual answer is the commandments alluded to in the first angel's message, i.e., the Exodus 20 form and not the Deuteronomy version (see note 4).

[4] *Ibid.,* pp. 7-10. Space constraints prevent us from discussing the thematic and structural parallels Paulien has outlined.

In this context it is helpful to notice that the Revelation 14:7 allusion to the fourth commandment of Exodus 20:11 contrasts with the wording of the Sabbath commandment found in Deuteronomy 5:12-14. While Deuteronomy 5 mentions the Sabbath as the seventh day, it does not explicitly designate the time unit of which the Sabbath is the seventh day. It leaves the reader with the question whether the Sabbath is the seventh day of the lunar month, the seventh day of the year, or the seventh day of some other time unit. One needs to refer to Genesis 1 and 2 and to Exodus 20:11 in order to discover biblically that the Sabbath is the seventh day of the weekly time unit established at creation. In light of this consideration it is understandable why in Revelation 14:7 God intentionally focuses attention upon the wording of the fourth commandment of Exodus 20 rather than upon the Sabbath commandment of Deuteronomy 5.

[5] For helpful discussions on worldview see James W. Sire, *The Universe Next Door: A Basic Worldview Catalog* (Downers Grove, Ill.: InterVarsity Press, 1997).

[6] C. H. Dodd, *According to the Scriptures: The Substructure of New Testament Theology* (London: Nisbet and Co., 1952), p. 136.

[7] *Ibid.,* p. 132.

[8] *Ibid.,* p. 75.

[9] *Ibid.,* p. 76.

[10] *Ibid.,* pp. 86, 132.

[11] As has been the experience of other investigators, the general connection between the latter portion of the first angel's message and the language of the fourth commandment has caught my casual attention from time to time. However, not until recently has the implied specific endorsement in Revelation 14:7 of a creation in six days dawned in my thinking. Others, I am sure, have already seen it. Yet the personal discovery of such a connection has been a deeply moving experience. However, it also embarrasses me that I have been blind so long to something that now appears so simple and obvious.

[12] See the helpful discussion of Reader-Response theories in Norman R. Gulley, "Reader-Response Theories in Postmodern Hermeneutics: A Challenge to Evangelical Theology," in *The Challenge of Postmodernism: An Evangelical Engagement,* ed. David S. Dockery (Wheaton, Ill.: Victor Books, 1995), pp. 228-238. Cf. Gulley's "The Prophetic/Servant Function of Biblical and Theological Scholarship" (unpublished paper presented at the meeting of the Adventist Society of Religious Studies in Orlando, Fla., Nov. 20, 1998), p. 2.

[13] Representative historicist studies include volume 4 of LeRoy Edwin Froom's *The Prophetic Faith of Our Fathers* (Washington, D.C.: Review and Herald, 1954) and Ellen G. White, *The Great Controversy* (Mountain View, Calif.: Pacific Press, 1911), pp. 409–491.

[14] See, for example, such representative historicist works as: Siegfried H. Horn and Lynn H. Wood, *The Chronology of Ezra 7* (Washington, D.C.: Review and Herald, 1970); William H. Shea, *Selected Studies on Prophetic Interpretation* (Washington, D.C.: General Conference of Seventh-day Adventists, 1982); Frank B. Holbrook, ed., *Symposium on Daniel* (Washington, D.C.: Biblical Research Institute, General Conference of Seventh-day Adventists, 1986); Frank B. Holbrook, ed., *The Seventy Weeks, Leviticus, and the Nature of Prophecy* (Washington, D.C.: Biblical Research Institute, General Conference of Seventh-day Adventists, 1986); Frank B. Holbrook, ed., *The Sanctuary and the Atonement* (Washington, D.C.: Biblical Research Institute, General Conference of Seventh-day Adventists, 1989); Richard M. Davidson, *Typology in Scripture* (Berrien Springs, Mich.: Andrews University Press, 1981); Ellen G. White, *Christ in His Sanctuary* (Mountain View, Calif.: Pacific Press, 1969); W. E. Read, "The Investigative, or Pre-Advent, Judgment: Does the Bible Reveal the Time for This Phase of the Judgment to Begin?" in Ministerial Association, *Doctrinal Discussions* (Washington, D.C.: Review and Herald, 1961), pp. 53-64; and Uriah Smith, *The Sanctuary and the Twenty-three Hundred Days of Daniel VIII, 14* (Battle Creek, Mich.: Steam Press of the Seventh-day Adventist Pub. Assn., 1877). See Robert T. Pennock, *Tower of Babel* (Cambridge, Mass.: The MIT Press, 1999), p. 17.

[15] A "creative" day is to be distinguished from a "revelational" day. The former means that the items associated with any particular day of creation week mentioned in Genesis 1 were actually created by God on that day during the literal creation week. Otherwise, the days of creation could be interpreted as "revelational" days, meaning that on a particular day of the Genesis creation narrative God revealed to Moses some items on that day that in reality God had taken millions of years to create.

[16] See note 13.

[17] Gertrude Himmelfarb, *Darwin and the Darwinian Revolution* (New York: W. W. Norton, 1959; Norton Library, 1968), pp. 196-198.

[18] In a recent dissertation, Yoshio Murakami analyzes the influence that Ellen G. White's discussion of the Sabbath as presented in the third angel's message of Revelation 14 had upon the mid-to-late-nineteenth-century America. He argues that her views in this regard were especially relevant to her time because "she emphasized the Sabbath as the memorial of *Creation,* in face of a surge of evolution theory, higher criticism, geological science, and other modern thoughts of the day (Yoshio Murakami, "Ellen G. White's Views of the Sabbath in the Historical, Religious, and Social Context of Nineteenth-Century America" [Ph.D. diss., Drew University, 1994], pp. 240, 241).

[19] We should not ignore the criticisms of a global flood, but should place them on the table for honest discussion, as well as the theological implications of dismissing it altogether. Perhaps the best recent summary of what appear to be the greatest difficulties facing the idea of a global flood is Donald U. Wise, "Creationism's Geologic Time Scale," *American Scientist* 86 (March-April 1998): 160-173. See also: Charles C. Gillispie, *Genesis and Geology* (Cambridge, Mass.: Harvard University Press, 1951); David A. Young, *The Biblical Flood* (Grand Rapids: Eerdmans, 1995); Ronald L. Numbers, *The Creationists* (New York: Alfred A. Knopf, 1992); Stephen Jay Gould, *Rocks of Ages: Science and Religion in the Fullness of Life* (New York: The Ballantine Pub. Group, 1999); ed., Robert W. Hanson (*Science and Creation: Geological, Theological, and Educational Perspectives,* American Association for the Advancement of Science: Issues in Science and Technology Series [New York: MacMillan Pub. Co., 1986]); G. Brent Dalrimple, *Radiometric Dating, Geologic Time, and the Age of the Earth,* reprint, 1981, available from U.S. Geological Survey, Menlo Park, Calif.

For a discussion of field evidence consistent with a global flood, see Ariel A. Roth, *Origins: Linking Science and Religion* (Hagerstown, Md.: Review and Herald, 1998), particularly the first four chapters devoted to the geological evidence for a worldwide flood.

The following technical article is representative of recent paleontological studies concluding that aspects of the geologic column are best explained by appealing to some form of episodic aquatic catastrophe: Michael Holz and Mario Costa Barberena, "Taphonomy of the South Brazilian Triassic Paleoherpetofauna: Pattern of Death, Transport and Burial," *Paleogeography, Paleoclimatology,*

Paleoecology 107 (1994): 179-197. The authors conclude that "the catastrophic . . . floods mobilized great quantities of clay and silt. 'Day-by-day sedimentation' is not effective for the fossil preservation in the Triassic environment" (p. 196); William Ryan and Walter Pitman, *Noah's Flood: The New Scientific Discoveries About the Event That Changed History* (New York: Simon and Schuster, 1998). See Ariel Roth's chapter in this book for a discussion of new geological field evidence consistent with mega aquatic catastrophe. A recent edition of *Origins* 24, No. 1 (1997), entitled "Special Edition: The Yellowstone Petrified 'Forests'," is devoted entirely to a definitive discussion by Harold Coffin and Clyde Webster regarding the Yellowstone petrified "forests" issue putatively establishing the aquatic transport model.

As an example of a useful technical exploration by a creationist of issues relating to radiocarbon ages, see Henry F. Pearl, "A Re-Evaluation of Time-Variations in Two Geochemical Parameters of Importance in the Accuracy Radiocarbon Ages Greater Than Four Millennia" (M.A. thesis, Pacific Union College, 1963). In this work, "Appendix B" presents a valuable exposition of H. W. Clark's ecological zonation theory. The scientific research by R. H. Brown into radiocarbon dating represents the most extensive work regarding this issue from a recent creation perspective. See his excellent articles published in the journal *Origins*.

[20] For an insightful exegetical study of the Revelation 14:7 phrase "springs of waters" see Oleg Zhigankov, "Significance of the 'Fountains of Waters' in Revelation 14:7" (paper presented at the GSEM 920 Religious Studies Seminar, Seventh-day Adventist Theological Seminary, Andrews University, Berrien Springs, Mich., Apr. 27, 1999). A revised version of this essay is forthcoming in *Andrews University Seminary Studies*.

In the paper Zhigankov explores the biblical usage and semantic categories of the phrase, and suggests that it carries a double implication in representing both divine blessing and divine cursing, the latter evidenced by the Genesis universal flood. Building upon the work of scholars such as Richard Davidson, Tikva Frymer-Kensky, and Jon Paulien, Zhigankov explores the biblical meaning of the Genesis flood as a global undoing of creation. Then, developing an insight by Paulien, Zhigankov suggests that the reference in Revelation 14:7 to be a global aquatic undoing of creation might constitute an implied warning by John of an impending second global undoing of creation by a different medium—fire.

[21] Compare E. G. White, "Noah's Time and Ours," *Signs of the Times,* Nov. 27, 1884, p. 706.

[22] The Hebrew term for fountain, *ma'yān,* appears to be related to the Hebrew word for eye *'yān,* which, as William Wilson states, is also "a fountain, or orifice through which water comes; or a well, like an eye in the ground" (William Wilson, *New Wilson's Old Testament Word Studies* [Grand Rapids: Kregel Publications, 1987]). As Wilson indicates, the Hebrew word for fountain may be compared to an eye in the ground flowing [tearing] with water. If so, there were symbolically a world abundance of flowing "eyes in the ground" when all the fountains of the deep broke up during the flood (Gen. 7:11). In light of the Hebrew understanding of "fountain" we can raise the following question from a homiletical, figurative, poetic, spiritual, and personification point of view: If another biblical prophet can poetically characterize the mountains as singing for joy (Ps. 98:8), might the prophet in Genesis 7:11 use a term poetically capable of connoting the earth as "weeping" in sorrow for the massive destruction occurring during God's flood?

[23] The author is indebted to Jon Paulien who on April 27, 1999, in a seminary interdisciplinary religious studies seminar, first suggested the possibility of a connection between two global undoings of creation in Revelation 14:7. Paulien proposes that the possible reference to the Genesis flood in the phrase "springs of waters" might also be an implied forward look to another global undoing of creation, this time by fire as John subsequently describes in the book of Revelation.

[24] Holmes Rolston III, "Does Nature Need to Be Redeemed?" *Zygon* 29, No. 2 (June 1994): 212.

[25] Richard Rice, *The Openness of God: The Relationship of Divine Foreknowledge and Human Free Will* (Nashville: Review and Herald, 1980), p. 43. In this work Rice defends human freedom, and the loving character of God in the face of the existence of profound present evil by exploring the epistemological powers of God. Briefly, according to the openness of God paradigm, it was not certain to a God dynamically related to the world that humans would sin and thus introduce evil, hence God is not responsible for the actuality of evil introduced by beings created with the capacity to sin. In this theoretical sense developed here and in later works, Rice preserves both the love of God and human freedom.

In what way the issues of long periods of time and macroevolutionary theory and hence paleo-natural evil may impact the character of a loving God construed along the lines of the openness of God perspective seem to await further clarification. One issue that may need discussion can be stated by the following question: How shall we sustain the goodness of a God whose creation method of choice is to bring into existence lower creatures having no freedom, then expose them to the evolutionary process of suffering, disease, and death over millions of years prior to the appearance of free human beings?

[26] Philip Clayton, "Metaphysics Can Be a Harsh Mistress," *CTNS Bulletin* 18, No. 1 (Winter 1998): 18. In this same context Clayton adds perceptively that "since revelation rules out a pernicious God, it may ultimately be that one must let go of the idea that God directly brings about the details of the evolving biological world" *(ibid.);* cf. Dwight Nelson, *Built to Last* (Nampa, Idaho: Pacific Press, 1998), pp. 64-68.

[27] For an assessment of the theological implications resulting from a Creator-God who is responsible for the paleo-natural evil in the geologic column, see L. James Gibson, "Theistic Evolution: Is It for Adventists?" 64, No. 1 (January 1992), pp. 22-25.

[28] Thane Hutcherson Ury, "The Evolving Face of God as Creator: Early Nineteenth-Century Traditionalist and Accommodationist Theodial Responses in Anglo Religious Thought to Paleo-natural Evil in the Fossil Record," forthcoming Ph.D. diss., Andrews University, p. 11.

[29] "Theodicy" represents a combination of two concepts: "God" and "just, right, or good," and *Merriam Webster's Collegiate Dictionary, Tenth Edition,* defines it as the "defense of God's goodness and omnipotence in view of the existence of evil."

[30] Langdon Gilkey, "Cosmology, Ontology, and the Travail of Biblical Language," *The Journal of Religion* 41, No. 3 (July 1961), p. 204.

[31] For a classic discussion of this distinction, see Krister Stendahl, "Biblical Theology, Contemporary," *Interpreter's Dictionary of the Bible* (New York: Abingdon Press, 1962), vol. 1, pp. 418-432; Wayne A. Meeks, "A Hermeneutics of Social Embodiment," *Harvard Theological Review* 79, Nos. 1-3 (1986): 176-186.

[32] A recent issue of *Adventist Today* (September/October 1998) reports on the Science and Faith Convention held at Andrews University in late July 1998. The journal devotes most of its space to issues of when creation took place. It would be helpful to have another issue address the question of how long Scripture says God took to create.

[33] Johann Salomo Semler, *Abhandlung von freier Untersuchung des Canon* (1771), Vol. I, pp. 13f., 46f., as quoted in Gerhard Maier, *The End of the Historical-Critical Method,* trans. Edwin Leverenz and Rudolf Norden (St. Louis: Concordia, 1977), p. 15.

[34] Among the many useful studies of theology and postmodernism the following merit careful attention: Huston Smith, *Beyond the Post-Modern Mind* (New York: Crossroad Pub. Co., 1982); Diogenes Allen, *Christian Belief in a Postmodern World: The Full Wealth of Conviction* (Louisville: Westminster/John Knox Press, 1989); Stanley J. Grenz, *A Primer on Postmodernism* (Grand Rapids: William B. Eerdmans Pub. Co., 1996); Stanley Hauerwas, Nancey Murphy, and Mark Nation, eds., *Theology Without Foundations: Religious Practice and the Future of Theological Truth* (Nashville: Abingdon, 1994); and Nancey Murphy, *Anglo-American Postmodernity* (Boulder, Colo.: Westview Press, 1997).

For an insightful discussion of a helpful approach to theology in the postmodern era based on the Imre Lakatos "research programmes," see Nancey Murphy, "What Has Theology to Learn From Scientific Methodology?" in *Science and Theology: Questions at the Interface,* ed. Murray Rae, Hilary Regan, and John Stenhouse (Grand Rapids: Eerdmans, 1994), pp. 101-126.

[35] A foundation metaphor of truth/knowledge stands in contrast to Willard Van Orman Quine's fabric, web, or field metaphor of truth/beliefs/knowledge introduced in the early 1950s. Quine, a professor of philosophy at Harvard University, presented his new metaphor in the now-classic article "Two Dogmas of Empiricism," appearing in *From a Logical Point of View: 9 Logico-Philosophical Essays* (Cambridge, Mass.: Harvard University Press, 1993), pp. 20-46. See particularly p. 42.

[36] Nancey Murphy, "Anglo-American Postmodernity: A Response to Clayton and Robbins," in *Zygon* 33, No. 3 (September 1998): 479. Murphy's article is the latest expression of a helpful, ongoing discussion between herself, Philip Clayton (an associate professor and chair of the Philosophy Department at California State University [Sonoma]), Rohnert Park, and J. Wesley Robbins (professor of philosophy at Indiana University, South Bend).

[37] Friedrich Schleiermacher, *The Christian Faith,* ed. H. R. Mackintosh and J. S. Stewart (Philadelphia: Fortress, 1976), p. 76.

[38] For a discussion of Schleiermacher's historicization of doctrine, see John T. Baldwin, "Historicization and Christian Theological Method," *Journal of the Adventist Theological Society* 4, No. 2 (Autumn 1993): 161-171. In his *Brief Outline* Schleiermacher also affects the historicization of doctrine. See Friedrich Schleiermacher, *Brief Outline on the Study of Theology,* trans. Terrence N. Trice (Atlanta: John Knox, 1997).

An account of the profound theological significance of the historicization of nature appears in Stephen Toulmin, "The Historicization of Natural Science: Its Implications for Theology," in *Paradigm Change in Theology* (New York: Crossroad Pub. Co., 1991), pp. 233-241.

[39] Murphy, "Anglo-American Postmodernity: A Response to Clayton and Robbins," p. 479. For a helpful discussion of these two sorts of religious language and Murphy's wholistic proposal, see Nancey Murphy, *Anglo-American Postmodernity: Philosophical Perspectives on Science, Religion, and Ethics* (Boulder, Colo.: Westview Press, 1997), especially chapters 5-9.

[40] ———— , "Anglo-American Postmodernity," pp. 479, 480, and note 4.

[41] For a brief overview of Lindbeck on truth, see Murphy, "Anglo-American Postmodernity," pp. 121, 122.

[42] A helpful discussion of various models of the relationship between theology and science appears in Nile Henrik Gregersen and J. Wentzel va Huyssten, eds., *Rethinking Theology and Science: Six Models for the Current Dialogue* (Grand Rapids: Eerdmans, 1998).

[43] Mark Noll, *The Scandal of the Evangelical Mind* (Grand Rapids: Eerdmans, 1994), pp. 194, 200-208.

[44] *Ibid.,* pp. 133, 188, 189, 196, 199.

[45] *Ibid.,* pp. 184, 206-208.

[46] Other implications of the allusion of Revelation 14:7 to Exodus 20:11 that might be explored, were space available, include concepts such as: the atonement, ethics, the seventh-day Sabbath, the mark of the beast, the foundation of all three messages of Revelation 14, the nature of the fall of Babylon and the contents of its intoxicating wine, and the return of Jesus.

[47] Jon Paulien, "The Final Deception: An Evil, Counterfeit Trinity Is Now Making Ready for War," *Adventist Review,* Oct. 29, 1998, pp. 7-11.

[48] *Ibid.,* p. 10.

[49] *Ibid.*

[50] *Ibid.,* p. 11.

[51] *Ibid.*

CHAPTER 2

THE "DAYS" OF CREATION IN GENESIS 1: LITERAL "DAYS" OR FIGURATIVE "PERIODS/EPOCHS" OF TIME?

Gerhard F. Hasel

John Nevins Andrews, professor of Old Testament and biblical theology, Seventh-day Adventist Theological Seminary, Andrews University, Berrien Springs, Michigan

Abstract

People have debated for centuries the question of whether the six days of creation were actual 24-hour periods of time or only symbolic representations of longer periods of time, perhaps millions of years. During the past century and a half, because of the influence of the theory of evolution and its vast eons of time, the matter has undergone more serious scrutiny.

The following chapter discusses the historical background and the literary nature of the creation account in detail and relates it to a variety of contemporary interpretations. The author concludes with 10 considerations that support the concept of a literal creation week with seven consecutive 24-hour days.

Introduction

The increased focus of recent decades on creationism, "creation-science,"[1] "origin science,"[2] and "theistic science"[3] has created a climate in which old questions have arisen anew with specific focus and additional sophistication. One of those questions concerns the meaning of the term "day" in Genesis 1:1 and 2:3.

The nature of the Genesis account of creation, with its six "days" (Gen. 1:5-31) followed by the "seventh day" (Gen. 2:2, 3), is of special interest, since it is customarily understood to mean one literal week. Such a short time in the creation account has come under debate on the basis of the current naturalistic theory of evolution. The contrast is between the brief period of the creation account and the long ages demanded by naturalistic evolution.

This chapter will seek to accomplish several interrelated tasks: (1) to provide some methodological observations with a brief history of interpretation; (2) to cite representative recent published opinions suggesting that the "days" of creation are long epochs or periods of time and not literal 24-hour days; (3) to present the data in Genesis 1 in relationship with other evidence found in the Old Testament; and (4) to apply to the data of Genesis 1 the standard linguistic and semantic investigations requisite in sound scholarship, based on the best current knowledge.

Methodological Observations and the History of Interpretation

A knowledge of some aspects in the history of interpretation of the "days" of creation in Genesis 1 may prove to be helpful. Historical information assists the modern interpreter to recognize that it is incorrect to suggest that only since the publication of Charles Darwin's epochal work *On the Origin of Species* (1859) have interpreters transposed the Genesis creation "days" into nonliteral periods of time. Earlier extrabiblical considerations led previous scholars to depart from the literal meaning of creation "days."

Some Medieval Understandings of Creation "Days"

The Alexandrian church father Origen (c. A.D. 185-c. 254), an accomplished practitioner and defender of the allegorical method of interpretation,[4] has received credit for being the first to understand the creation "days" in an allegorical and nonliteral manner.[5]

Augustine (A.D. 354-430), the most famous of the Latin fathers, followed Origen in arguing that we should approach the creation "days" allegorically rather than literally.[6] Scholars understand Augustine to teach that God created the world in a single flash of a moment.

At this point it seems appropriate to reflect on some methodological matters. Neither Augustine nor Origen had any evolutionary concept in mind. They took the creation "days" as nonliteral, standing for something else, because it was philosophically mandatory to assign to God creation activity unrelated to human time. Since the "days" of creation are God's work, they argued, such "days" have to be representative of philosophical notions associated with God taken from their philosophical perspectives.

Greek philosophy regards God as timeless. Since the creation "days" are part of divine activity, the two church fathers assumed that they also should be understood in a timeless sense. Philosophy, not scientific speculation, influenced the thinking of Origen and Augustine, leading them to reinterpret the creation "days."

What this approach has in common with modern attempts, which also take

41

the creation "days" to mean something other than what the face value of the terminology seems to suggest, is that both derive from influences outside the biblical text itself. Medieval theologians, who assumed the creation "days" to be nonliteral, based it on nonbiblical, pagan philosophical modes of thinking.

Today still another influence from outside the biblical text leads interpreters to change what seems to be the plain meaning of "days." At present a naturalistically based scientific hypothesis, the modern theory of evolution, prompts such changes.

The Alexandrian allegorical method of interpretation shaped the thinking of medieval Catholic theologians. They adapted the fourfold sense of Scripture for medieval times,[7] one that still has support in current official Roman Catholicism.[8] The three nonliteral meanings of the fourfold sense of Scripture (i.e., allegory, anagogy, and tropology) dominated Christendom for more than a millennium, providing the hermeneutical means for the reinterpretation of the literal sense of the creation "days."

Reformation Understanding of Creation "Days"

The sixteenth-century Reformers agreed that the fourfold sense of Scripture compromised the literal sense of the Bible, making its authority for faith and life null and void. They insisted that the single, true sense of Scripture is the literal sense, the plain meaning of the text.

One of the major achievements of the Protestant Reformation was the return to Scripture itself. It meant that Scripture has no need of an external key for interpretation—whether that key be the pope, the church councils, philosophy, or any other human authority. Scripture's perspicuity became the norm of the day. Protestantism considered a reading from within its own context as paramount. We must not superimpose external meaning on it, as had been the practice during medieval Catholicism. Rather we should approach the Bible in its literal and grammatical sense.[9]

Martin Luther, accordingly, argued for the literal interpretation of the creation account: "We assert that Moses spoke in the literal sense, not allegorically or figuratively, i.e., that the world, with all its creatures, was created within six days, as the words read."[10] The other Reformers understood the creation "days" in the same way. Such literal and grammatical interpretation, sometimes called the historical-grammatical method, remained the norm for biblical interpretation more or less into the nineteenth century.[11]

Changes Under the Influence of Modernism

As the concept of long time periods made its way into the understanding of earth's origins in the wake of the publications of James Hutton (1726-1797) and Charles Lyell (1797-1875), some Christian concordist interpreters started to interpret the Genesis "days" of creation in a nonliteral manner. The Bible itself did not demand it, but rather the new worldview of uniformitarianism and its concept of origins that required long periods of time.

The understanding of the creation "days" as "days of restoration,"[12] "days of revelation,"[13] aside from taking a "day" for an "age" ("day-age" theory) or an epoch/era,[14] goes back to this period and the changes in time frames required by the new geology. A nonliteral reinterpretation of "days" was typical of concordists who had accepted long ages for the origin of earth.[15] In view of such developments, we cannot avoid concluding that the need to provide for geological ages became the catalyst for the reinterpretation of the "days" of creation.

Recent Changes in Interpretation Among Broad Concordists

Broad concordists of the past 10 years have increasingly attempted to interpret the "days" in the Genesis creation account in nonliteral ways, in order to harmonize the long ages called for by the evolutionary theory with the time implications of the biblical record of divine creation in Genesis 1.

It is an acknowledged fact that the long and checkered history of the relationship between science and Scripture has affected the understanding of the Bible.[16] The shift from the Ptolemaic worldview to the Copernican one is probably the most celebrated example.[17]

Christian medieval theologians had adopted the non-Christian Ptolemaic worldview as the correct Christian and biblical view. It conceived of the earth as the center of the solar system, and often of the whole universe itself. Thus it became a first-class dilemma when the heliocentric Copernican worldview became seemingly irrefutable.

From a methodological point of view the interpretational model the scientist uses as the key to understand data observed in nature will predetermine to a large degree the outcome of the enterprise itself, as well as the meaning of data derived from nonnatural sources, including the Bible. Many recognize that "scientific theories do affect biblical interpretation at least to the extent that they become the occasion for reassessing the interpretation of a few passages (Gen. 1, 2, 6-8)."[18] The decisive question, then, is whether the reassessment superimposes a meaning on the biblical text that is alien to Scripture and its own context.

At least two major options seem to present themselves: 1. A reassessment on the basis of "scientific" conclusions could lead to an interpretation of biblical texts appropriate to the framework of the context and intention of the totality of Scripture. In such a case the reassessment does not violate Scripture. 2. Reexamining a biblical passage could likewise produce a conclusion that does not agree with what a current scientific hypothesis holds. Those who accept full biblical authority could reassess the conclusion(s) drawn from the scientific interpretation of natural data. The latter approach, in turn, may affect the scientific theory, or science broadly perceived, "at the very least by leading us to reassess whether all the conclusions drawn from a scientific theory are warranted, or in some cases to ask whether the theory as a whole is suspect."[19]

The Inherent Authority of Scripture

Some have taken the stance that a scientific theory, by its very nature and the breadth of its acceptance, has priority over Scripture.[20] It is far beyond the confines of this chapter to unfold the complexity of such a question. Suffice it to say that if we understand Scripture to be the result of divine revelation and written under inspiration, the Bible will have a dimension of authority not found in the so-called book of nature. Based on that higher level of authority, Scripture can assist us in understanding the book of nature, providing a more comprehensive model of interpretation than we might expect from a purely naturalistic model.

Scripture, if we are to maintain its own integrity, can hardly accommodate every interpretation that science, sociology, history, or any other discipline comes up with. Based on its own nature and authority, the Bible has its own integrity of meaning and its inherent truth claims. They emerge ever more clearly through careful study employing sound methods of interpretation that harmonize with and root themselves in the testimony of Scripture itself. This implies that Scripture's authority resides in itself—it is based in revelation and grounded in inspiration.

Such self-sufficiency of Scripture does not mean that we cannot discuss any question raised by other areas of investigation, such as science, history, or sociology. But a vast difference exists between asking new questions of Scripture and superimposing new meaning on the Bible.

Figurative Interpretations of the Creation "Days"
Representative Arguments for Long Ages

Scholars often clearly state the real purpose of current attempts to interpret the "days" of Genesis 1 in terms other than their face value. A few citations from respected individuals will speak for themselves.

John C. L. Gibson, a British scholar, argues that we should take Genesis 1 as a "metaphor," [21] "story," or "parable," [22] and not as a straightforward record of events of creation. He writes in his 1981 Genesis commentary as follows:

"If we understand 'day' as equivalent to 'epoch' or 'era,' we can bring the sequence of creation in the chapter into relationship with the accounts of modern evolutionary theory, and so go some way towards recovering the Bible's reputation in our scientific age. . . . In so far as this argument begins with an attempt to go beyond the literal meaning and to take the week assigned to creation as a parable of a much longer period, it is to be commended."

In 1983 the German commentator Hansjörg Bräumer stated: "The creation 'day' which is described to contain 'morning and evening' *[sic]* is not a unit of time which can be determined with a watch. It is a divine day in which a thousand years are equal to but yesterday [Ps. 90:4, margin]. Day one in creation is a divine day. It cannot be an earthly day since the temporal measure, the sun, is still missing. It will, therefore, do no harm to the creation account to understand creation in rhythms of millions of years." [23]

D. Stuart Briscoe, an American progressive creationist, addresses the issue in his commentary on Genesis as well:

"The natural scientist talks convincingly in terms of millions of years and evolutionary eras while the Bible believer looks at the six days and wonders what on earth to do. . . . It is not at all unreasonable to believe that 'day' (Hebrew *yôm*), which can be translated quite literally as 'period,' refers not to literal days but to eras and ages in which God's progressive work was being accomplished." [24]

We could endlessly duplicate such explanations. Typically they come from scholars in the concordist camp. More precisely, they belong to the branch of "broad concordists" who in recent times have become associated with progressive creationism. [25]

Analysis and Evaluation of Psalm 90:4 and 2 Peter 3:8

Psalm 90:4. Let us begin with Psalm 90:4. Interpreters have invoked the passage again and again to indicate that the creation "days" are to be nonliteral, standing for long periods/epochs/ages of time. The passage reads: "For a thousand years in Thy sight are like yesterday when it passes by, or [lit."and"] as a watch in the night" (NASB). [26] Of immediate interest is the comparison of the long time period of 1,000 years with but "yesterday" and "a watch of the night." The passage contains a comparative particle in the original Hebrew, rendered into English either as "like" or "as."

From the point of view of Hebrew syntax, the comparative particle serves not only the expression "yesterday" but also the phrase "as a watch in the night," demonstrating that the comparison is not between a "day" being like 1,000 years. A thousand years with God are "like" yesterday, that is, the past day, or "like" "a watch in the night," even a briefer period of time than "yesterday." The point is that God reckons time differently than the way humans do.

Genesis 1 is not interested in depicting how God defines time. The Genesis context of creation speaks of "days" in the sense of creation time during which God made our world and whereby He set the rhythm of the week. Thus Genesis 1 does not explain or address how God calculates time on His scale, but how the creation "days" set the norm for subsequent days in the weekly cycle of time.

Furthermore, Genesis 1 lacks any comparative particle such as "like" or "as" in connection with its usage of "day." The absence in Genesis 1 of a Hebrew comparative expression with either the word "day" or the expression "evening and morning" indicates that the passage intends no such comparison. The issue in Genesis 1 is not one of comparison. Rather it is the amount of time God uses to create the world and whether the time period is identical to the seven-day week, the rhythm of historical time.

From contextual as well as grammatical-syntactical and semantic points of view, the application of Psalm 90:4 to Genesis 1 simply does not work. It lacks any appropriate linguistic and phraseological criteria of comparison. Those who link the two texts ignore contextual, linguistic, and phraseological criteria. In a way, those who relate the "days" of Genesis 1 with the "yesterday" and the "watch of the night" or the 1,000 years in God's scale of time are comparing apples with oranges.

Another approach that some have used in attempting to make the creation "days" into long periods of time is that if one should read the "sixth day as the sixth epoch of creation, this opens the door to some kind of pre-Adamic *homo [sic] sapiens*."[27] In other words, the long-age substitution for a literal "day" does away with the view that Adam and Eve were the first human beings whom God created on earth.

A third difficulty relates to the fact that Psalm 90 is not a creation psalm. Contextually speaking, Psalm 90 does not address the issue of how God regards the "days" of creation, but rather how humans are to regard time when compared to time in the realm of God.

Fourth, Psalm 90 does not even employ the term "day" by itself. It uses it in a linguistic relationship in verse 4 that syntactically joins two words together. The English language has one word for that linguistic relationship, "yesterday." But "yesterday" in Psalm 90:4 is in parallelism with the expression "as a watch in the night," that is, a very short interval of time. It means that the psalm does not compare the 1,000 years simply to a day, but in fact to a shorter interval of time.

In short, Psalm 90:4 does not define the meaning of the designation "day" in Genesis 1. In view of the problems cited and other difficulties,[28] it is not surprising that many of those who currently employ the "day-age theory" as a solution to the tension between science and religion ignore Psalm 90:4. When read on its own terms, the text does not address the issue of the length of the creation "day."

Second Peter 3:8. Broad concordists have also used 2 Peter 3:8, "with the Lord one day is as a thousand years" (NASB), to support the day-age theory. Some have taken it as a "biblical" mathematical equivalent: "one day equals a thousand years" literally. Others regard the 1,000 years to mean an indefinite long period, an age, or the like. In that case, some argue, "one day equals a long period of time" or "one day equals an age."

We should point out that those who invoke this text face several major problems: (1) 2 Peter 3:8 has no creation context; (2) 2 Peter 3:8 has a comparative particle lacking in Genesis 1; (3) 2 Peter 3:8 becomes nonliteral when we take the 1,000 years to mean an "age" or the like; (4) 2 Peter 3:8 reveals that God is not limited to time or subject to it in fulfilling His promises.

Lloyd R. Bailey, a broad concordist himself, clearly expresses the intent of the passage: "The text of 2 Peter (3:8) has been misused by those who would bring it to bear upon the word 'day' in Genesis 1. . . . Rather, the purpose of that text is to point out that 'The Lord is not slow about his promise . . . but is forbearing . . . not wishing that any should perish . . .' (3:9; cf. verse 4). That is, God is not subject to time in the sense that humans are (". . . as some count slowness," verse 9). The intent, then, is to make a statement about God's fidelity to promises, and not to define the meaning of the word 'day' as it is used in Genesis 1."[29]

It seems best to let 2 Peter 3:8 make its own point and not to use it for something topically, contextually, and linguistically unrelated.

"Days of Revelation"?

A few still hold the theory that the creation "days" are actually "days of revelation." The Scottish geologist Hugh Miller made the concept prominent during the nineteenth century.[30] In this century P. J. Wiseman revived it in his 1946 publication *Creation Revealed in Six Days*, later reprinted in 1977.[31]

According to this interpretation, God did not create the world in six days, but He instead "revealed" and explained in six literal days what He had already done over many spans of time. Its proponents take the recurring phrase "and God said" as support for their concept that the "days" of creation are actually "days of revelation." In this theory the world does not require a relatively recent origin nor creation in six literal 24-hour days.

Many have noted that the "days of revelation theory," also called the "vision theory," rests to a large degree upon a "misunderstanding of the word 'made,' in Exodus 20:11,"[32] for which Wiseman claims the meaning "showed."[33] But "showed" is not a valid meaning for the Hebrew term *'asah*. No Hebrew-English dictionary supports such a possible translation. The Hebrew term *'asah,* used more than 2,600 times in the Old Testament, indicates "to make, manufacture, produce, do, etc.,"[34] but never once "to show" in either the Old Testament or in extrabiblical Hebrew.[35] The meaning "to show" evolved for the sake of the theory. In view of this fact, it is not surprising that the "days of revelation theory" has not found much support.[36]

In summary, current broad concordists seek to interpret Genesis 1 in some sort of "figurative, symbolic, or otherwise loose reading—such as the idea that the 'days' of Genesis 1 may be interpreted as long periods of time."[37] Their goal is to accommodate the evolutionary theory's need for long periods of time. Based on this time frame hypothesis, they reinterpret Scripture in ways that they believe will harmonize the claims of both the biblical creation account and naturalistic evolution. Those who seek to adjust Scripture for the sake of concordism are known as broad concordists.

In contrast, strict concordists are scholars of equal erudition and skill. They are also interested in harmonizing science and religion. However, they are unwilling to give the biblical text a "loose reading." They agree that a meaning of a text must rest on the internal criteria of language and its usage according to the commonly accepted standards of linguistics. To them the context of Scripture is primary, and linguistic standards need to follow sound grammatical-syntactical conventions. Thus strict concordists are fully aware of the tensions, but resist forcing a meaning on the biblical text not supported by appropriate linguistic analysis.

The Literary Genre of Genesis 1
Literary Genre/Form Argument

The recent Genesis commentary by evangelical scholar Victor P. Hamilton takes the position that we must regard the "days" of Genesis 1 as nonfigurative and nonmetaphorical, that is, as literal solar days consisting of 24 hours.[38] However, as a broad concordist he is already committed to long ages and remains interested in finding harmony with modern naturalistic science. In order to do so he appeals to "a literary reading of Genesis 1 [which] still permits the retention of 'day' as a solar day of 24 hours."[39] How does he accomplish this?

Hamilton speaks of a "literary reading" of the Genesis creation account. The "literary reading" allows him to understand the "days" of creation "not as a chronological account of how many hours God invested in His creating project, but as an analogy of God's creative activity."[40] In his view the 24-hour "days" in Genesis 1 are but an "analogy" based on a "literary [nonhistorical] reading" of the Genesis creation account.

The "literary reading" view derives from Charles E. Hummel.[41] Hummel argues that even if the passage means the "days" in Genesis 1 to be 24-hour solar days, which he concludes they are, "the question still remains whether the [literary] format is figurative or literal, that is, *analogy* of God's creative activity or a chronological *account* of how many hours he worked."[42] He believes that the "who" and "why," but not the "how," of creation are important (following Bernard Ramm) and that, therefore, the *"analogy . . . provides a model for human work."*[43]

The "analogy" theory involves understanding the literal "day" as "a metaphor" that uses "the commonplace (or commonly understood, if you wish) meaning of a word" (viz. the word "day") "in a figurative manner."[44] The analogy theory removes the schema of six days of work and one day of rest from a chronological piece of information and transforms it into a broad pattern of work-and-rest applicable to humanity.[45]

As appealing as the theory seems to be, it still ignores the contextual and literary problems. We cannot simply take "day" as just analogous for work/rest. Hummel finds himself forced (followed by Hamilton) to redefine the literary genre of Genesis 1 from that of a straightforward creation account to one he designates as a "semipoetic narrative."[46] This falls under the *"historical-cultural"* approach to creation.[47]

It is evident that form criticism and its genre method of interpretation have greatly influenced such broad concordist scholars. Form criticism, a submethod of the historical-critical method, began with Hermann Gunkel at the turn of the century.[48] Gunkel raised the question "Are the narratives of Genesis history or legend?"[49] His premise was that "many things reported in Genesis . . . go directly against our better knowledge."[50] The idea of "our better knowledge" is an admission on Gunkel's part that a naturalistic evolutionary worldview provides the authoritative norm of what is history or legend. Thus he suggested that the literary genre of Genesis is not history, but "legend." Gunkel was the first liberal scholar to assign to the creation account in Genesis a literary genre other than as history in the sense of a factual account. Other liberal scholars, neoorthodox theologians, and now also in part neo-Evangelical broad concordist scholars have followed him.

Although we need not attempt to exhaustively cite the literary genre categories proposed for categorizing Genesis, we should look at some major representative examples. Karl Barth, the father of neoorthodox theology, regards Genesis 1, 2 as "saga"[51] and of course, nonhistorical. S. H. Hooke, the leader of the myth-and-ritual school, says that the Genesis creation account is a "cultic liturgy."[52] Gordon Wenham, a neo-evangelical scholar, believes it to be a "hymn."[53] Walter Brueggemann, a liberal nonconcordist, suggests that it is a "poem."[54] Claus Westermann, a form critic, calls it a "narrative."[55] John H. Stek, a broad concordist, names it a "metaphorical narration."[56] Gerhard von Rad, a tradition critic, designates it as "doctrine."[57] Others hold that it is a "myth,"[58] "parable,"[59] "story," "theology,"[60] "allegory," etc.

We need to make several essential observations in view of the plethora of current opinions on the nature of the literary genre of the Genesis creation account:

1. The obvious consensus is that there is no consensus on the literary nature of Genesis 1. It makes the literary genre approach for a nonliterary reading of Genesis 1 suspect of special pleading.

Since no consensus exists, the careful interpreter will cautiously avoid jumping on the bandwagon of literary genre identification in an attempt to redefine the literal intent of Genesis 1. Form-critical genre description, from its beginning (the time of Gunkel to the present), has sought to remove the text of Genesis 1 from the realm of history and fact.[61]

2. The "literary genre" approach reveals it to be another way, at first used by nonconcordists, to prevent the creation account of Genesis from functioning as an authoritative, literal text, with implications for the relationship of science and the Bible. Noel Weeks has rightly suggested that "the way in which God revealed the history of creation must itself be justified by Scripture"[62] and not by appeal to a form-critical literary genre description from which we have removed any element of historicity.

3. Interpreters following the "literary genre" approach interpret the "days" of creation in a literal and grammatical way. But the use of the "literary genre" approach restricts the meaning of Genesis 1 to a thought form that does not demand a factual, historical reading of what took place. The "literary genre" redefinition of the creation account thus prevents it from informing modern readers on how, in what manner, and in what time God created the world. Instead, it simply wishes to affirm minimalistically that God is

Creator. And that affirmation is meant to be a theological, nonscientific statement, with no impact on how the world and universe came into being and developed subsequently.

As we have seen, the "literary genre" approach employs a literary critical methodology[63] that reduces the creation account to a nonhistorical or non-factual role. In this case it does not matter whether we regard the creation "days" as literal 24-hour days, because the account as a whole, including the creation "days," has a meaning other than a historical or factual one.

Genesis 1: Literal or Figurative?

The question still remains whether the creation account of Genesis 1 is literal or figurative as a whole.[64] Often interpreters take Genesis 1 as part of the larger unit of Genesis 1-11 to determine its nature, purpose, and function. It is an acknowledged fact that the chapters at the beginning of the book of Genesis contain singularities, that is, unrepeated, one-time events that have no immediate analogy in present experience.

How does the modern historian handle such singularities? The standard position of modern historiography rests on the principle of analogy (cf. Ernst Troeltsch), that is, nothing in past experience can be reckoned to be histori-cal except as it corresponds to present experience.[65] Such an approach derives from the notion of the basic uniformity of human experience and historical events.[66] The principle of analogy holds that we can understand the past only by borrowing from the present and applying it to the past. But to consistently do so means that we must deny the historicity and factuality of most of Genesis 1-11, including the creation account of Genesis 1.

Can and should the uniformitarian principle of analogy reign as the supreme norm for understanding the past?[67] "A problem arises when the uni-formity [of past and present] is raised to a universal principle that makes some evidence inadmissible," writes a strong supporter of the principle of analogy and modernistic historiography.[68] His admission of the problem calls for great caution in how we apply the uniformitarian principle of analogy.

Human beings know of many experiences in present reality that are sin-gular and without parallel in the past. For example, a quarter of a century ago the first human beings walked on the moon. That had never happened be-fore. Another example is the use of atomic bombs for the destruction of two Japanese cities in 1945. Such destruction had never happened before and still stands unique to the present. We could mention many other singularities.

Do singularities exist today that are either human-made or part of another order, that is to say, that are real events and situations that have no analogy in the past, thus allowing us to postulate singularities in the past that have no analogy at present? For example, R. G. Collingwood, the famed British philosopher of history, noted that the ancient Romans engaged in population control by exposing newborn infants to die. It is a singularity that has no analogy at present in population control attempts.[69]

When we keep these limitations of the principle of analogy in mind,[70] we recognize that it is not sound to reject the creation account as nonhistorical and nonfactual just because we know of no analogy at present. Genesis 1 contains singularities that may be perceived to be just as real, historical, and factual as the singularities of another kind either in the present or the past.

We have good reasons for maintaining that Genesis 1 is a factual account of the origin of the livable world. The biblical record is accurate, authentic, and historical.

Genesis 1 and Comparative Literature of the Past

From a purely comparative approach of the literary structures, the language patterns, the syntax, the linguistic phenomena, the terminology, and the sequential presentation of events in the creation account, Genesis 1 does not differ from the rest of the book of Genesis[71] or the whole Pentateuch, for that matter.

When we compare it to the hymns in the Bible, we see that the creation account is not a hymn. An examination of the parables, poetry, and cultic liturgy shows that the creation account belongs to none of them. When placed alongside various other kinds of literary forms, we find that the creation account is not a metaphor, story, or the like.

One recent study of the literary form of Genesis 1-11, done on the basis of contemporary Near Eastern literature, has concluded that "we are dealing with the genera of historical narrative-prose, interspersed with some lists, sources, sayings, and poetical lines."[72] It is a fairly good description of the content of Genesis 1.

A detailed study of the literary form of Genesis 1 has concluded that we are dealing with the literary genre of "prose-genealogy."[73] Even Gunkel noted long ago that Genesis is "prose." He observed also that it is "more artistic in its composition and has some sort of rhythmical construction."[74] The nonpoetic nature of Genesis 1 shows that it seeks to be understood in its plain sense as a straightforward and accurate record of creative events.

Comparing the information provided in Genesis 1 with other ancient Near Eastern literature leads to the inescapable conclusion that "Genesis 1 has no parallel anywhere in the ancient world outside the Bible."[75] Genesis 1 is the most cohesive and profound record produced in the ancient world of "how" and "when" and by "whom" and in "what" manner the world came into being. We find no ancient parallel to it in any type of literature. Some have found bits and pieces to echo various cosmogonic myths and speculations, but the biblical creation account as a unit stands unique in the ancient world in its comprehensiveness and cohesiveness.[76]

The Literary Form of Genesis 1 Within Its Biblical Context

It would be helpful to analyze the literary form in distinction to the "literary genre" of form criticism discussed above.

John H. Stek suggests that the "literary type [of Genesis 1], as far as present knowledge goes, is without strict parallel; it is *sui generis.*"[77] We have already noted that the presentation and content of Genesis 1 as a whole has no counterpart in the ancient world.[78] Does that mean, however, that it is *sui generis* in the sense that we should not understand it to be literal in purpose? Surely, as creation itself is unique, so the creation account must of necessity be unique. But it is hardly *sui generis* in an exclusive literary sense that will remove it from communicating on a factual, accurate, and historical level.

Based on its relationship with the remainder of Genesis (and the Bible as a whole), we can properly designate the creation account (Gen. 1:1-2:3) as a historical prose record written in rhythmic style, recording factually and accurately "what" took place in the creation of "the heavens and the earth," depicting the time "when" it took place, describing the processes of "how" God did it, and identifying the divine Being "who" brought it forth. The result of creation week was a perfect, "very good" world with an environment suitable for humanity to live in. This historical prose record of creation reports correctly in specific sequences the creation events within chronological, sequential, and literal "days." These "days" inaugurate the subsequent historical process of time ordered in weekly cycles in which humanity and nature function under God's ultimate control. In this sense, Genesis 1 is the inaugural history[79] of initial beginnings that shapes from creation week onward the subsequent flow of human history.

Literal Interpretation of Creation "Days"

We shall now consider the usage of "day" (Hebrew *yôm*) along major lines of current scholarship. Both liberal and nonliberal scholars have concluded that the word "day" (Hebrew *yôm*) in Genesis 1 must be understood in a literal sense. We will review some of their reasons and provide additional ones.

53

Considerations From Commentaries

The influential Continental liberal Old Testament theologian and exegete Gerhard von Rad states, "The seven days are unquestionably to be understood as actual days and as a unique, unrepeatable lapse of time in the world."[80] Gordon Wenham, a British nonconcordist Old Testament scholar, concludes, "There can be little doubt that here 'day' has its basic sense of a 24-hour period."[81] James Barr, renowned Semitist and Old Testament scholar, notes with a vengeance against figurative interpreters that the creation "days" were six literal days comprising a 144-hour period.[82] Form critic Hermann Gunkel concluded long ago that "the 'days' are of course days and nothing else."[83] We could continue this refrain with many additional voices, all sharing the same nonconcordist position.

Victor P. Hamilton concludes, as do other broad concordist neo-Evangelical scholars, that "whoever wrote Genesis 1 believed he was talking about literal days."[84] John H. Stek, another broad concordist, makes a number of points in his support for literal "days":

"Surely there is no sign or hint within the narrative [of Genesis 1] itself that the author thought his 'days' to be irregular designations—first a series of undefined periods, then a series of solar days—or that the 'days' he bounded with 'evening and morning' could possibly be understood as long aeons of time. His language is plain and simple, and he speaks in plain and simple terms of one of the most common elements in humanity's experience of the world. . . . In his storying of God's creative acts, the author was 'moved' to sequence them after the manner of human acts and 'time' them after the pattern of created time in humanity's arena of experience."[85]

Numerous scholars and commentators, regardless of whether they are concordist or nonconcordist, have concluded that the creation "days" cannot be anything but literal 24-hour days. They are fully aware of the figurative, nonliteral interpretations of the word "day" in Genesis 1 that attempt to harmonize the biblical account with the long ages demanded by the evolutionary model of origins. Yet they insist on the ground of careful investigations of the usage of "day" in Genesis 1 and elsewhere that the true meaning and intention of a creation "day" is a literal day of 24 hours.

Considerations From Lexicography

The most widely recognized Hebrew lexicons and dictionaries of the Hebrew language published in the twentieth century affirm that the designation "day" in Genesis 1 seeks to communicate a 24-hour solar day. A prestigious recently published lexicon refers to Genesis 1:5 as the first scriptural entry for the definition of "day of 24 hours" for the Hebrew term *yôm* ("day").[86] Holladay's Hebrew-English lexicon follows suit with "day of 24 hours."[87] The Brown-Driver-Briggs lexicon, the classical Hebrew-English lexicon, also regards the creation "day" of Genesis 1 as a regular "day as defined by evening and morning."[88]

Lexicographers of the Hebrew languages are among the most qualified of Hebrew scholars. We expect them to give great care in their definitions and also usually to indicate alternative meanings, if warrant exists. None of the lexicographers have departed from the meaning of the word "day" as a literal day of 24 hours for Genesis 1.

Considerations From Dictionaries

Magne Saeboe writes in the acclaimed *Theological Dictionary of the Old Testament* that "day" *(yôm)* in Genesis 1 has a literal meaning in the sense of "a full day."[89] He does not even consider another meaning or alternative.

Ernst Jenni, an acclaimed twentieth-century Hebrew scholar, states in the most widely used theological dictionary of the Hebrew language that we must understand "day" in the Genesis creation account in its literal meaning as a "day of 24 hours in the sense of an astronomical or calendrical unit of time."[90]

Considerations Based on Semantics

The field of semantics in linguistic study refers to what scholars call signification.[91] It deals with the issue of "the accurate evaluation of the meaning of expressions [words, phrases, clauses, sentences, etc.] which have actually been used."[92]

Semantics calls for attention to the crucial question of the exact meaning of the Hebrew word *yôm*. Could the designation "day" in Genesis 1 possibly have a figurative meaning in the chapter? Or should we understand it on the basis of the norms of semantics as a literal "day"? The matter of semantics is particularly important in view of the fact that the Hebrew term *yôm* has a large variety of meanings, including extended meanings such as "time," "lifetime," and so on. Is it possible to import an extended meaning from the rest of the Old Testament into Genesis 1? Could this not solve the problem of the conflict between a short creation week and the long ages called for by naturalistic evolution?

As we have already observed, the Hebrew term *yôm*, in its variety of forms, can also mean a time or period of time (Judges 14:4), and in a more general sense, "a month [of] time" (Gen. 29:14), "two years [of] time" (2 Sam. 13:23; 14:28; Jer. 28:3, 11), and "three weeks [of] time" (Dan. 11:2, 3).

In the plural form it can indicate a "year" (1 Sam. 27:7), a "lifetime" (Gen. 47:8), and so forth. Any good lexicon will provide a comprehensive listing of the various possibilities.[93]

It is important to keep in mind that "the semantic content of the words can be seen more clearly in their various combinations with other words and their extended semantic field."[94]

What are the semantic-syntactical guidelines for extended, nonliteral meanings of the Hebrew term *yôm?* Such usages of the term *yôm* always occur in connection with prepositions,[95] prepositional phrases with a verb, compound constructions, formula, technical expressions, genitive combinations, construct phrases, and the like.[96] In other words, extended, nonliteral meanings of the Hebrew term have special linguistic and contextual connections that indicate clearly that the writer intends a nonliteral meaning. If such special linguistic connections are absent, the term *yôm* does not have an extended, nonliteral meaning, but rather its normal value of a literal day of 24 hours.

In view of the wealth of ways Scripture employs this Hebrew term, it is imperative to study how Genesis 1 handles *yôm* so that we can compare it with other usages. Does this biblical chapter contain the needed indicators by which we can clearly recognize *yôm* to have either a literal or nonliteral meaning? How does Genesis 1 employ the term? Does it appear together with combinations of other words, prepositions, genitive relations, construct state, and the like, as mentioned previously, that would indicate a nonliteral meaning? It is exactly these kinds of semantic-syntactical combinations that inform us what the biblical writer intended with the term.

Let us present the facts of the usage of the term *yôm,* "day," in Genesis 1, as any scholar who knows Hebrew can describe them:

1. The term *yôm* always appears in the singular.

2. The term *yôm* always accompanies a numeral. In Genesis 1:5 it is a cardinal and elsewhere in Genesis 1:1–2:3 it is always an ordinal. We will examine this below.

3. The term *yôm* never combines with a preposition, genitive combination, construct state, compound construction, or the like. Always it appears as a plain noun.

4. The term *yôm* consistently gets defined by a temporal phrase in the preceding sentence: "And there was evening and there was morning." This clause serves in a defining function for the word "day."

5. The complementary creation account of Genesis 2:4-25 contains a nonliteral, figurative meaning of the singular of the term *yôm,* "day" (Gen.

2:4). But it employs the semantic-syntactical conventions known from the remainder of the Old Testament to indicate such a meaning.

Let us note the criteria employed in Genesis 2:4. The noun *yôm* accompanies the preposition *be* to read *beyôm*. Second, the passage uses it in a construct relation with the infinitive form of *'asah,* "to make." It reads literally, "in the day of making." The combination of the singular with a preposition in construct with an infinitive[97] makes this combination a "temporal conjunction"[98] that serves as a "general introduction of time."[99]

The last part of Genesis 2:4 reads literally, "In [the] day of the Lord God making the earth and heaven." Proper English calls for the literal "in [the] day of," which is syntactically a temporal conjunction that serves as a general introduction of time, to be rendered with "when." The sentence then reads, "When the Lord God made . . ." It is a clear-cut case of an extended, nonliteral use of *yôm* in the creation account of Genesis 2:4-25 and shows that the contrary usage of *yôm* in Genesis 1, without any expected qualifier that marks it as a nonliteral use, has a literal meaning. The term *yôm* in Genesis 1 has no prepositions. Nor does it appear in a construct relation, and it does not have the syntactical indicator we would expect of an extended, nonliteral meaning. Thus in Genesis 1 *yôm* can mean only a literal "day" of 24 hours.

In short, the semantic-syntactical usages of *yôm,* "day," in Genesis 1, when compared with semantic-syntactical usages and linguistic connections of the same term in other Old Testament passages that do give it an extended meaning, do not allow it here to mean a long period of time, an age, or the like. The Hebrew language—its grammar, syntax, and linguistic structures, as well as its semantic usage—allows for only the literal meaning of "day" for the creation "days" of Genesis 1.

Considerations Based on Singular Usage

The Hebrew term *yôm* appears in the Hebrew Old Testament 2,304 times,[100] of which 1,452 usages occur in the singular.[101] The five books of Moses (Pentateuch) have it 668 times, and the book of Genesis employs it 152 times.[102] Genesis has the singular form of "day" 83 times, with the remainder in the plural.

As Genesis enumerates the six "days" of creation it uses "day" consistently in the singular. One plural usage appears in the phrase "for days and years" in Genesis 1:14 (NASB), which is, of course, not a creation "day." Such a plural application in verse 14 hardly enters the discussion of making creation "days" long periods of time since calendrical usage of "days and years" keeps it literal itself. Without doubt, verse 14 means literal days of

24-hour days, just as we likewise understood the "years" as literal ones.

The additional appearances of "day" in the singular in Genesis 1 occur in verses 5 and 16. "And God called the light day *[yôm]*" (verse 5, NASB) and God made the "greater light to govern the day" (verse 16, NASB). Verse 5 employs the term in the sense of the literal daylight period of the 24-hour day, in contrast to the night part, "the night" (verse 16), of the same segment of time.[103] Both "day" and "night" make a "full day."[104]

We have to recognize the fact that the term *yôm* in every one of the six days has the same connection: (a) it is used as a singular; (b) it has a numeral; and (c) it is preceded by the phrase "There was evening and there was morning." This triple interlocking connection of singular usage, joined by a numeral, and the temporal definition of "evening and morning" keeps the creation "day" the same throughout the creation account. It also reveals that "time is conceived as linear and events occur within it successively."[105] To depart from the numerical consecutive linkage and the "evening–morning" boundaries would take extreme liberty with the plain and direct meaning of the Hebrew language.[106]

Considerations Based on Numeral Usage

The six creation "days" in each instance have an accompanying numeral in the sequence of 1 to 6 (Gen. 1:5, 8, 13, 19, 23, 31). The day following the "sixth day," the "day" on which God rested, Scripture designates as "the seventh day" (Gen. 2:2 [two times], 3).

What seems of significance is the sequential emphasis of the numerals 1-7 without any break or temporal interruption. This seven-day schema, the weekly pattern of six workdays followed by "the seventh day" as rest day, interlinks the creation "days" as normal days in a consecutive and noninterrupted sequence.

When the Old Testament employs *yôm* together with a numeral (150 times) it refers invariably to a literal day of 24 hours. The only exception in numbers of 1-1,000 appears in an eschatological text in Zechariah 14:7. Translators have rendered the Hebrew expression *yôm 'echad* in verse 7 into English in a variety of ways: "for it will be a unique day" (*New American Standard Bible,* New International Version); "and there shall be continuous day" (New Revised Standard Version); "it will be continuous day" (Revised English Bible); or "and the day shall be one."[107] The "continuous day," or "one day," of the eschatological future will be one in which the normal rhythm of evening and morning, day and night, will change so that in that eschatological day there shall be "light even at the evening" (verse 7).

Scholars generally acknowledge that this is a difficult text in the Hebrew language, and we can hardly use it to change the plain usage in Genesis 1.[108]

Considerations Based on Article Usage

The Hebrew has "day" without the article in each instance of each creation day, except in the cases of "the sixth day" (Gen. 1:31, Hebrew *yôm hashshishî*) and "the seventh day" (Gen. 2:2).[109]

Scholars note from time to time that the first "day" of Genesis 1:5 in Hebrew reads literally "one day,"[110] because we have the cardinal number "one" used with "day." Some have interpreted the lack of the definite article to mean that all creation "days" (except "the sixth day," which has the article) will allow "for the possibility of random or literary order as well as a rigidly chronological order."[111] But it is a rather shaky interpretation, one that we cannot support from any semantic-syntactical point of view.

We need to understand the syntax of the Hebrew text and interpret the passage accordingly without violating the internal structure of the Hebrew language. The recent research grammar by Bruce K. Waltke and M. O'Connor points out that the indefinite noun *yôm* with the indefinite cardinal numeral for "one" (Hebrew *'echad*) in Genesis 1:5 has "an emphatic, counting force" and a "definite sense" in addition to having the force of an ordinal number that we must render as "the first day."[112]

Such syntactical observations of the Hebrew language remind us that "the first day" and "the sixth day" of the creation week are meant to be definite in the sense that they have the article by syntactical rule or by writing (not to speak of "the seventh day," which we will consider below). The first and last creation "days" are definite by syntax or writing, the first by syntactical function, and the last by the usage of the article. One observation emerges—such definite usage of the first and last day of creation forms a literary device, an *inclusio,* that frames the six creation "days" with definite or articular days. This usage seems to limit the debate whether the "days" of Genesis 1 have either a random order or chronological order.[113]

The opposite is actually the case. Since the first and sixth days are definite, providing a clear boundary, the whole series of days must be chronological and sequential, forming an uninterrupted six-day period of literal 24-hour days of creation. Thus the definite use of the first and sixth days, respectively, mark and frame the six-day sequence into a coherent sequential and chronological unit of time that will repeat itself during each successive week.

"The seventh day" also has the Hebrew article. Since "the first day" (verse 5) is definite as well as "the sixth day" (verse 31), it forms a larger unit. It is the unit of six workdays followed by "the seventh day" (Gen. 2:2, 3), the day of rest. In this way the sequence of six workdays find their goal and climax chronologically and sequentially in "the seventh day," making together the weekly cycle with the day of rest being the "seventh day" of the week.

The larger unit of literal time accordingly consists of the divinely planned unit of the "six-plus-one schema," "six" workdays followed in an uninterrupted manner and in sequence by "the seventh day" of rest. God divinely planned and ordained the uninterrupted sequence as the rhythm of the time for each following week.

Considerations Based on the "Evening-Morning" Boundary

The Genesis creation account not only links each day to a sequential numeral, but also sets the time boundaries by "evening and morning" (verses 5, 8, 13, 19, 23, 31). The rhythmic boundary phrase "and there was evening and there was morning" provides a definition of the creation "day." The creation "day" consists of "evening" and "morning," and is thus a literal "day."

The term for "evening" (Hebrew *'ereb*)[114] covers the dark part of the day in a *pars pro toto* (meaning that a part [in this case, the "evening"] stands for the whole dark part of the day) usage (cf. "day-night" in Genesis 1:14). The corresponding term "morning" (Hebrew *boqer*) is also *pars pro toto* "for the entire period of daylight."[115] We should note that the "evening-morning" expression must have the same signification in every one of its six usages.[116] Thus "evening and morning" is a temporal expression defining each "day" of creation as a literal day. It cannot be made to mean anything else.

Considerations Based on Pentateuchal Sabbath Passages

Another kind of internal evidence the Old Testament gives for the meaning of days derives from two Sabbath passages in the Pentateuch that refer back to the creation "days." They inform the reader how God understood the creation "days."

The first passage forms part of the fourth commandment God spoke on Mount Sinai: "Six days you shall do all your labor . . . , but the seventh day is a sabbath of the Lord your God. . . . For in six days the Lord made the heavens and the earth, . . . and rested on the seventh day; therefore the Lord blessed the sabbath day and made it holy" (Ex. 20:9, 11, NASB).

"These words" Yahweh Himself speaks (verse 1). The linkages to creation appear in the wording ("seventh day," "heaven and earth," "rested," "blessed," "made it holy") and in the "six-plus-one" schema (see also Deut. 5:13, 14).[117] Evidently the Ten Commandments take the creation "day" as "a regular day"[118] of 24 hours and demonstrate that the weekly cycle is a temporal creation ordinance.

The passage provides both an internal Pentateuchal and wider Old Testament guideline on how God, the giver of the "Ten Words," understands the creation "day." The divine speech that promulgates the Sabbath commandment regards the "six days" of creation to be sequential, chronological, and literal.[119]

The argument that the relationship of the fourth commandment is only an "analogy" or "archetype" in the sense that humanity's rest on the seventh day ought to be like God's rest in creation[120] has its basis in reductionism and an impermissible change of imagery. Terence Fretheim noted that the commandment does not use analogy or archetypal thinking, but that its emphasis is "stated in terms of the imitation of God or a divine precedent that is to be followed: God worked for six days and rested on the seventh, and therefore you should do the same."[121]

The second Pentateuchal Sabbath passage is Exodus 31:15-17, again spoken by God Himself. It has several terminological linkages with Genesis 1 and is conceptually and thematically related to it. The passage has to be understood to mean that the creation "day" was a literal one and that it was sequential and chronological. The weekly Sabbath for God's people is thus based on imitation and example, for "in six days the Lord made heaven and earth, but on the seventh day He ceased from labor, and was refreshed" (verse 17, NASB).

God was refreshed because He delighted in His completed work of creation. Humanity will also be refreshed and experience delight when it keeps the "seventh day" as Sabbath (verse 15).

The "sign" nature of the Sabbath in verse 15 reveals that the Sabbathkeeper follows the divine Exemplar. He Himself observed "the seventh day" that humans who belong to Him will imitate. They will do so in the same rhythm of the literal weekly cycle of six workdays followed chronologically and sequentially by "the seventh day" as a day of rest and refreshment, just as their Creator had done during creation week.

Considerations Based on Sequence of Events

The creation of vegetation with seed-bearing plants and fruit trees took place on the third day (Gen. 1:11, 12). Much vegetation needs insects for pollination. God did not create insects, though, until the fifth day (verse 20). Plants requiring insects for pollination would face a serious problem should the creation "day" consist of long ages or aeons. They could not have survived an "age" or "aeon" without being able to reproduce themselves. In addition, "consistency of interpretation in the 'day-age theory' would demand a long period of light and darkness during each of the ages. This would quickly be fatal to both plant and animal life."[122]

It seems that the biblical writer expects us to understand the creation "day" as a literal day and not as a long period of time, whether ages, periods, or aeons.

Although such arguments may not be decisive, they nevertheless point in the same direction as the linguistic and semantic points found in the Hebrew text itself.

Conclusion

This chapter investigated the meaning of creation "days." It has considered key arguments in favor of a figurative, nonliteral meaning of the creation "days" and found them to be wanting on the basis of genre investigation, literary considerations, grammatical study, syntactical usages, and semantic connections. The cumulative evidence, based on comparative, literary, linguistic, and other considerations, converges on every level, leading to the inescapable conclusion that the designation *yôm,* "day," in Genesis 1 means consistently a literal 24-hour period.

The author of Genesis 1 could not have produced more comprehensive and all-inclusive ways to express the idea of a literal "day" than the ones chosen. The complete lack of indicators such as prepositions, qualifying expressions, construct phrases, semantic-syntactical connections, and so on indicates that we cannot possibly take the designation "day" in the creation week to be anything other than a regular 24-hour day. The combinations of the factors of articular usage, singular gender, semantic-syntactical constructions, time boundaries, and so on corroborated by the divine promulgations in such Pentateuchal passages as Exodus 20:8-11 and Exodus 31:12-17, suggest uniquely and consistently that the creation "day" is meant to be literal, sequential, and chronological in nature.

---

[1] The designation "creation-science" has been defined by Louisiana law (Senate Bill No. 86, 1981) as follows: "'Creation-science' means the scientific evidences for creation and inferences from those scientific evidences." A similar wording had appeared shortly before in the Arkansas Bill (Act 590) of Mar. 19, 1981. For details, see Norman L. Geisler, *The Creator in the Courtroom* (Milford, Mich.: Mott Media, 1982), pp. 5, 224. Phillip E. Johnson (*Darwin on Trial,* 2d ed. [Downers Grove, Ill.: InterVarsity, 1993], p. 4, n. 1) states that "'creation science' refers to young-earth, six-day special creation."

[2] This designation is preferred and argued for by Norman L. Geisler and J. Kerby Anderson, *Origin Science: A Proposal for the Creation-Evolution Controversy* (Grand Rapids: Baker, 1987).

[3] The significant volume of essays edited by J. P. Moreland (*The Creation Hypothesis: Scientific*

Evidence for an Intelligent Designer [Downers Grove, Ill.: InterVarsity, 1994]) uses the designation "theistic science" as opposed to "naturalistic science," the common notion of science that rules out the God hypothesis from the start. "Theistic science" is a "research program . . . that, among other things, is based on two propositions: 1. God, conceived of as a personal, transcendent agent of great power and intelligence, has through direct primary causation and indirect secondary causation created and designed the world for a purpose and has directly intervened in the course of its development at various times. . . . 2. The commitment expressed in proposition 1 can appropriately enter into the very fabric of the practice of science and the utilization of scientific methodology" (pp. 41, 42). The remainder of the seminal essay by J. P. Moreland in the above volume ("Theistic Science and Methodological Naturalism," pp. 41-66) elaborates this definition.

[4] Frederic W. Farrar, *History of Interpretation* (Grand Rapids: Baker, 1866, 1961), pp. 187-203.

[5] The decisive section from Origen's *On First Principles: Book Four* (excerpt quoted in Karlfried Froehlich, trans./ed., *Biblical Interpretation in the Early Church* [Philadelphia: Fortress, 1984], p. 63) noted that the days of creation cannot be understood to be literal, just as it "is foolish enough to believe that, like a human farmer, God planted a garden to the east of Eden and created in it a visible, physical tree of life." See also Terence E. Fretheim, "Were the Days of Creation Twenty-four Hours Long?" in Ronald R. Youngblood, ed., *The Genesis Debate: Persistent Questions About Creation and the Flood* (Nashville: Thomas Nelson, 1986), pp. 12-35.

[6] Augustine *The City of God* 11. 4. 6, 7.

[7] The fourfold sense of Scripture consists of the following: (1) the literal sense; (2) the allegorical (spiritual-mystical) sense; (3) the anagogical (future) sense; and (4) the tropological (moral) sense. See Farrar, p. 205.

[8] The new *Catechism of the Catholic Church,* published in English in 1994, states: "According to an ancient tradition, one can distinguish between two *senses* of Scripture: the literal and the spiritual, the latter being subdivided into the allegorical, moral [tropological], and anagogical senses. The profound concordance of the four senses guarantees all its richness to the living reading of Scripture in the Church." Later on the same page affirms: "It is the task of exegetes to work, according to these rules, toward a better understanding and explanation of the meaning of Sacred Scripture" (*Catechism of the Catholic Church* [Vatican City: Libreria Editrice Vaticana, 1994], p. 33).

[9] See: (a) Robert M. Grant, *A Short History of the Interpretation of the Bible* (New York: Macmillan, 1963), pp. 128, 129; (b) Emil G. Kraeling, *The Old Testament Since the Reformation* (New York: Schocken Books, 1969), pp. 9-32; (c) John Rogerson, Christopher Rowland, and Barnabas Lindars, *The Study and Use of the Bible,* vol. 2 of *The History of Christian Theology* (Grand Rapids: Eerdmans, 1988), pp. 77-95.

[10] Martin Luther, *Lectures on Genesis: Chapters 1-5, Luther's Works* (St. Louis: Concordia, 1958), 1:5. Later Luther, in commenting on the phrase "evening and morning," states that the creation day "consists of twenty-four hours" (1:42).

[11] The development of the historical-critical method from the late seventeenth century onward until its full maturity at the end of the nineteenth century did not decisively change the interpretation of the creation "days." The reason for this is that the biblical text was now seen as an artifact of the past that has no direct relationship to the belief systems of the present.

[12] The Scottish theologian Thomas Chalmers (1780-1847) has received credit for being the first proponent of the view that the six creation "days" are actually "days of reconstruction," giving rise to the "ruin-reconstruction hypothesis" (see W. Hanna, ed., *Select Works of Thomas Chalmers* [Edinburgh: T. Constable and Co., 1855], vol. 5, pp. 146-150). This hypothesis has found strong defenders, such as George H. Pember (*Earth's Earliest Ages,* 2nd ed. [London: Hodder and Stoughton, 1907]) and more recently A. C. Custance (*Without Form and Void* [Brookville, Ont.: by the author, 1970]). The most detailed and scholarly critique of the "ruin-reconstruction hypothesis" has been produced by Weston W. Fields, *Unformed and Unfilled: The Gap Theory* (Phillipsburg, N.J.: Presbyterian and Reformed Pub. Co., 1978). See also Henri Blocher, *In the Beginning: The Opening Chapters of Genesis* (Downers Grove, Ill.: InterVarsity, 1984), pp. 41-43.

[13] While not the first to claim that the days of creation are actually six days of revelation and not days of creation, the Scottish geologist Hugh Miller (1802-1856) was the foremost nineteenth-century author to proclaim the idea (Francis Haber, *The Age of the World: Moses to Darwin*

[Baltimore: Johns Hopkins University Press, 1959], pp. 236, 237). In this century P. J. Wiseman, the father of the famous Assyriologist Donald Wiseman, propounded the view. More on this later.

[14] The "day-age" theory originated in the eighteenth century and came to prominence in the nineteenth century through the writings of geologists James D. Dana and J. W. Dawson. See Bernard Ramm, *The Christian View of Science and Scripture,* 2nd ed. (Grand Rapids: Eerdmans, 1971), p. 211; and Haber, pp. 122, 123, 199, 200, 255.

[15] For a view of these ideas, see Thomas A. McIver, "Creationism: Intellectual Origins, Cultural Context, and Theoretical Diversity" (Ph.D. diss., University of California at Los Angeles, 1989), pp. 450-495.

[16] Among the many studies that have explored the subject, see Charles Coulston Gillispie, *Genesis and Geology: A Study in the Relations of Scientific Thought, Natural Theology, and Social Opinion in Great Britain, 1790-1850* (New York: Harper Torchbooks, 1959); R. Hooykaas, *Religion and the Rise of Modern Science* (Grand Rapids: Eerdmans, 1972).

[17] Some illuminating recent publications on this shift include Richard J. Blackwell, *Galileo, Ballarmine, and the Bible* (Notre Dame, Ind.: University of Notre Dame Press, 1991); Charles E. Hummel, *The Galileo Connection: Resolving Conflicts Between Science and the Bible* (Downers Grove, Ill.: InterVarsity, 1986); William John Hausmann, *Science and the Bible in Lutheran Theology* (Washington, D.C.: University Press of America, 1978).

[18] Vern S. Poythress, *Science and Hermeneutics: Implications of Scientific Method for Biblical Interpretation* (Grand Rapids: Zondervan, 1988), p. 24.

[19] *Ibid.*

[20] The ultimate conclusion about the final norm for scientific views and religious faith probably rests on the basis of the conviction, or presupposition, of the interpreter's stance on the authority levels of science and faith. We will also have to contend that science is constantly in flux and makes no absolute claims.

[21] John C. L. Gibson, *Genesis, the Daily Study Bible* (Edinburgh: Saint Andrew Press, 1981), vol. 1, p. 56.

[22] *Ibid.,* p. 55.

[23] Hansjörg Bräumer, *Das erste Buch Mose.* Wuppertaler Studienbibel, Kapital 1-11 (Wuppertal: R. Brockhaus Verlag, 1983), p. 44.

[24] D. Stuart Briscoe, *Genesis, Communicator's Commentary* (Waco, Tex.: Word Books, 1987), p. 37.

[25] Note the very useful discussion of the various groups and definitions of concordism by John T. Baldwin, "Inspiration, the Natural Sciences, and a Window of Opportunity," *Journal of the Adventist Theological Society* 5, No. 1 (1994): 131-154, esp. 139-143; Davis A. Young, "The Discovery of Terrestrial History," in Howard J. Van Till, Robert E. Snow, John H. Stek, and Davis A. Young, eds. *Portraits of Creation: Biblical and Scientific Perspectives on the World's Formation* (Grand Rapids: Eerdmans, 1990), p. 27, n. 2; Clark Pinnock, "Climbing Out of a Swamp: The Evangelical Struggle to Understand the Creation Texts," *Interpretation* 43, No. 2 (1989): 143-155.

[26] For example, Derek Kidner, *Genesis: An Introduction and a Commentary* (Chicago: InterVarsity, 1967), p. 56.

[27] Victor P. Hamilton, *The Book of Genesis: Chapters 1-17,* New International Commentary of the Old Testament (Grand Rapids: Eerdmans, 1990), p. 54.

[28] For a critique of other aspects of the "day/age theory," see Lloyd R. Bailey, *Genesis, Creation, and Creationism* (New York/Mahwah, N.J.: Paulist Press, 1993), pp. 125-128.

[29] *Ibid.,* p. 126.

[30] See note 13 above; cf. Carl F. H. Henry, *God Who Stands and Stays,* vol. 6 of *God, Revelation, and Authority* (Waco, Tex.: Word Books, 1983), vol. 2, p. 112.

[31] Reprinted in P. J. Wiseman, *Clues to Creation in Genesis,* ed. Donald J. Wiseman (London: Marshall, Morgan & Scott, 1977), pp. 109-207.

[32] Kidner, p. 54.

[33] Wiseman, pp. 132, 133.

[34] William L. Holladay, Jr., *A Concise Hebrew and Aramaic Lexicon of the Old Testament* (Grand Rapids: Eerdmans, 1971), pp. 284, 285; Francis Brown, S. R. Driver, and Charles A. Briggs, *A Hebrew and English Lexicon of the Old Testament* (Oxford: Clarendon Press, 1974), pp. 793-795. See

also Helmer Ringgren, *"'asah,"* in G. Johannes Botterweck and Helmer Ringgren, eds. *Theologisches Wörterbuch des Alten Testaments* (Stuttgart: W. Kohlhammer, 1987), vol. 6, pp. 413-432.

[35] Marcus Jastrow, *Dictionary of the Targumim, the Talmud Babli and Yerushalmi, and the Midrashic Literature* (New York: Pardes Pub. House, 1943), vol. 2, pp. 1124, 1125.

[36] A recent exception is Duane Garrett (*Rethinking Genesis: The Sources and Authorship of the First Book of the Pentateuch* [Grand Rapids: Baker, 1991], pp. 192-194), who recognizes that Wiseman's "presentation was somewhat confused, however, and did not persuade many" (p. 193, n. 12). Garrett seeks to bolster the idea of "days" as "seven days of divine revelation to Moses" with form-critical arguments, an attempt quite problematical in itself.

[37] Young, p. 27, n. 2.

[38] Hamilton, pp. 54, 55.

[39] *Ibid.,* p. 55.

[40] *Ibid.,* pp. 55, 56.

[41] Hamilton, p. 56, n. 1, refers to C. E. Hummel, "Interpreting Genesis 1," *Journal of the American Scientific Affiliation* 38 (1986): 175-186.

[42] Hummel, *The Galileo Connection,* p. 214.

[43] *Ibid.,* p. 215.

[44] *Ibid.*

[45] *Ibid.,* pp. 213-216.

[46] *Ibid.,* p. 214.

[47] *Ibid.,* p. 213.

[48] See the recent translations of Gunkel's major study, Hermann Gunkel, *The Folktale in the Old Testament,* trans. Michael D. Rutter (Sheffield: Almond Press, 1987). Patricia G. Kirkpatrick provides excellent analyses and critiques of form criticism in *The Old Testament and Folklore Study* (Sheffield, Eng.: JSOT, 1987). Also Garrett, pp. 35-50.

[49] Hermann Gunkel, *The Legends of Genesis: The Biblical Saga and History* (New York: Schocken Books, 1964), p. 1.

[50] *Ibid.,* p. 7.

[51] See the penetrating discussion of Jerome Hamer, *Karl Barth* (Westminster, Md.: Newman Press, 1962), pp. 119-122.

[52] S. H. Hooke, *Middle Eastern Mythology* (Baltimore: Penguin Books, 1963), pp. 119-121.

[53] Gordon J. Wenham, *Genesis 1-15, Word Biblical Commentary* (Waco, Tex.: Word Books, 1987), vol. 1, p. 10.

[54] Walter Brueggemann, *Genesis: A Bible Commentary for Teaching and Preaching* (Atlanta: John Knox, 1982), p. 26.

[55] Claus Westermann, *Genesis 1-11: A Commentary* (London: SPCK, 1984), p. 80.

[56] John H. Stek, "What Says Scripture?" in *Portraits of Creation,* p. 236.

[57] Gerhard von Rad, *Genesis: A Commentary* (Philadelphia: Westminster, 1972), p. 65.

[58] At present Conrad Hyers, *The Meaning of Creation: Genesis and Modern Science* (Atlanta: John Knox, 1984), pp. 93-114; Susan Niditch, *Chaos to Cosmos: Studies in Biblical Patterns of Creation* (Chico, Calif.: Scholars Press, 1985); and many others. Scholars have a most difficult time defining what they mean by "myth." G. B. Caird (*The Language and Imagery of the Bible* [Philadelphia: Westminster, 1980], pp. 219-224) has identified nine different definitions of myth, and John W. Rogerson (*Myth in Old Testament Interpretation* [Berlin: W. de Gruyter, 1974], pp. 274-278) has pointed to 12 aspects of myth. Genesis 1-11 is removed from the concept of myth (see Benedikt Otzen, Hans Gottlieb, and Knud Jeppesen, *Myths in the Old Testament* [London: SCM, 1980]).

[59] Gibson, p. 55; Donald D. Evans, *The Logic of Self-involvement* (London: SCM, 1963), pp. 242-252.

[60] J. A. Thompson, "Genesis 1-3. Science? History? Theology?" *Theological Review* 3 (1966): 25.

[61] The genre/form approach so widely used today, especially by critical scholars but also employed for other reasons by some evangelicals to Genesis 1, is formally identical or closely associated with the demythologization program of Rudolph Bultmann. He demythologizes the New Testament at any place where it does not conform to the modern worldview. Thus he approaches the Resurrection narrative in such a way that the Resurrection never took place in a literal sense.

Evangelicals have to be aware that they cannot demythologize Genesis 1 without carrying it over to the New Testament.

[62] Noel Weeks, "The Hermeneutical Problem of Genesis 1-11," *Themelios* 4, No. 1 (1978): 14.

[63] See Norman C. Habel, *Literary Criticism of the Old Testament* (Philadelphia: Fortress, 1971), pp. 69, 70.

[64] We do not address the question of a structural interpretation of Genesis 1 by the method of structuralism that seeks to expose the alleged deep structures of a text. The subsequent method of deconstructionalism in linguistics "is an attempt to undermine the reader's expectations that a text will communicate some independently existing truth, by showing that author and reader alike are caught in the system of constraints imposed by the linguistic and literary system to which they belong, and are capable of communicating or receiving only such meanings as the system makes possible" (John Barton, "Structuralism," *Anchor Bible Dictionary,* ed. David N. Freedman [New York: Doubleday, 1992], vol. 6, p. 215; cf. Jonathan D. Culler, *The Pursuit of Signs: Semiotics, Literature, Deconstruction* [Ithaca, N.Y.: Cornell University Press, 1981]). Just as deconstructionism denies to any text a fixed and stable meaning, so "reader-response criticism" gives up the idea of a fixed meaning of a text as well (see J. Severino Croatto, *Biblical Hermeneutics: Toward a Theory of Reading as the Production of Meaning* [Maryknoll, N.Y.: Orbis Books, 1987]; Edgar V. McKnight, *The Postmodern Use of the Bible: The Emergence of Reader-oriented Criticism* [Nashville: Abingdon, 1988]).

[65] Paul D. Hanson, "Theology, Old Testament," *Harper's Dictionary of the Bible,* ed. Paul Achtemeier (San Francisco: Harper & Row, 1987), p. 1059: "We have already observed that every scholarly endeavor inevitably is based upon presuppositions. This is already true on the level of the descriptive task with which OT theology begins. For example, the scholar who accepts Ernst Troeltsch's 'analogy principle' (i.e., to be credible, a happening recorded in a historical source must have parallels in modern experience) will dismiss all reconstructions of the Exodus from Egypt or the resurrection of Jesus, which defy explanation within the nexus of cause and effect as understood by modern science, whereas others may not be so bound."

[66] Van A. Harvey, *The Historian and the Believer* (New York: Macmillan, 1966), pp. 43-64.

[67] Edward H. Carr, *What Is History?* (Baltimore: Penguin Books, 1964), pp. 87-108.

[68] Edward Krentz, *The Historical-Critical Method* (Philadelphia: Fortress, 1975), p. 57.

[69] R. G. Collingwood, *The Idea of History* (London: Oxford University Press, 1956), p. 240.

[70] For a critique of the principle of analogy, see T. Peters, "The Use of Analogy in Historical Method," *Catholic Biblical Quarterly* 35 (1973): 473-482; Wolfhart Pannenberg, *Questions in Theology* (Philadelphia: Westminster, 1970), vol. 1, pp. 39-53.

[71] See the classical study by William Henry Green, *The Unity of the Book of Genesis* (1895 reprint) (Grand Rapids: Baker, 1979).

[72] Walter C. Kaiser, "The Literary Form of Genesis 1-11," in J. Barton Payne, ed., *New Perspectives on the Old Testament* (Waco, Tex.: Word Books, 1970), p. 61.

[73] Jacques B. Doukhan, *The Genesis Creation Story: Its Literary Structure,* Andrews University Seminary Doctoral Dissertation Series (Berrien Springs, Mich.: Andrews University Press, 1978), vol. 5, p. 182.

[74] Gunkel, *Legends,* p. 38.

[75] Garrett, p. 192.

[76] Gerhard F. Hasel, "The Polemical Nature of the Genesis Cosmology," *Evangelical Quarterly* 46 (1974), pp. 81-102, pointed out a number of explicit and implicit polemical emphases in Genesis 1. This fact does not diminish in the least the biblical author's intention to write an account that has a literal intent to provide factual and historical information.

[77] Stek, p. 241.

[78] Hummel, *The Galileo Connection,* p. 216: "Genesis 1 contrasts sharply with the cyclical, recurring creations described by Israel's pagan neighbors."

[79] It is neither "metahistory," which is removed from real history, nor "salvation history," which never happened in the way it is written in the Old Testament. Cf. Robert Gnuse, *Heilsgeschichte as a Model for Biblical Theology* (Lanham, Md.: University Press of America, 1989).

[80] Von Rad, p. 65.

[81] Wenham, p. 19.

[82] James Barr, *Fundamentalism* (Philadelphia: Westminster, 1978), pp. 40-43.

[83] Hermann Gunkel, *Genesis Übersetzt und Erklärt* (Göttigen: Vandenhoeck and Ruprecht, 1901), p. 97.

[84] Hamilton, p. 53.

[85] Steck, pp. 237, 238.

[86] Benedikt Hartmann, Philippe Reymond, and Johann Jakob Stamm, *Hebräisches und Aramäisches Wörterbuch der Hebräischen Sprache* (Leiden: E. J. Brill, 1990), p. 382. Hereafter cited as *HAL*. Its predecessor, i.e., by Ludwig Koehler and Walter Baumgartner, *Lexicon in Veteris Testamenti Libros* (Leiden: E. J. Brill, 1958), p. 372, reads "day (of 24 hours)" for the creation day.

[87] William H. Holladay, *A Concise Hebrew and Aramaic Lexicon of the Old Testament* (Grand Rapids: Eerdmans, 1971), p. 130.

[88] Brown, p. 398.

[89] Magne Saeboe, *"yôm,"* in *Theological Dictionary of the Old Testament,* ed. G. Johannes Botterweck and Helmer Ringgren (Grand Rapids: Eerdmans, 1990), vol. 6, p. 23.

[90] Ernst Jenni, "jom Tag," in *Theologisches Handwörterbuch zum Alten Testament,* ed. Ernst Jenni and Claus Westermann (Zurich/Munich: Theologischer Verlag, 1971), vol. 1, p. 709.

[91] James Barr, *The Semantics of Biblical Language,* 3rd ed. (London: SCM, 1991), p. 1.

[92] *Ibid.*

[93] *HAL,* pp. 382-384; Brown, pp. 398-401.

[94] Saeboe, p. 14.

[95] *Ibid.,* p. 15: "In the Hebrew OT, 1,057 (45.9 percent) involve a preposition (esp. with the singular)."

[96] *Ibid.,* pp. 14-20.

[97] E. Kautzsch and A. E. Cowley, eds., *Gesenius' Hebrew Grammar,* 2nd ed. (Oxford: Clarendon Press, 1910), p. 347, § 114e: "This use of the infinitive construct is especially frequent in connection with *be* or *ke* to express time-determinations (in English resolved into a temporal clause . . .)."

[98] Westermann, p. 198.

[99] Saeboe, p. 15.

[100] *Ibid.,* p. 13; Jenni, p. 708.

[101] Jenni, p. 707, notes that the Old Testament uses only four nouns more often.

[102] *Ibid.,* p. 708.

[103] Stek, p. 237, is correct in noting that each "day" of creation has to be the same since the "evening and morning" time expression and the numeral is in each instance identical. In other words, each creation "day" is of equal length. From this he shows that it is not defensible to argue that the first three "days" were long periods of time while the remaining "days" were 24-hour days. Edward J. Young argued the latter position in his *Studies in Genesis One* (Philadelphia: Presbyterian and Reformed Pub. House, 1964), p. 104, and has found a recent supporter in R. Clyde McCone ("Were the Days of Creation Twenty-four Hours Long?" [*The Genesis Debate,* p. 24]).

Young and his followers seek to separate the lengths of creation days because they claim that the sun and moon had not been created yet until the fourth day. The question really is whether that is the case. It seems likely that on the fourth day God appointed the sun and moon to rule the day and night, respectively. This appointment to the ruling function does not mean that the sun and moon did not exist before then. It is possible that they were not visible to the human eye before the fourth day. Some have for this reason suggested that there may have been a vapor or cloud cover over the ground until the fourth day.

[104] Saeboe, pp. 22, 23.

[105] Bruce K. Waltke, *"yôm,* day, time, year," in *Theological Wordbook of the Old Testament,* ed. R. Laird Harris (Chicago: Moody, 1980), p. 371.

[106] Hamilton, p. 54.

[107] Ralph L. Smith, *Micah-Malachi, Word Biblical Commentary* (Waco, Tex.: Word Books, 1984), p. 277.

[108] The other exception is with numbers above 1,000 in the apocalyptic text of Daniel 12:11, 12 with the reference to 1290 "days" and the 1335 "days." We observe some differences from Genesis 1. In both instances Daniel 12 employs the plural form of "days" in contrast to Genesis 1. In Genesis 1 the "day" refers to what has happened in the past, while in Daniel 12 "days" refers to a prophetic time in the future. The context of all other prophetic time predictions in the book of

Daniel makes it clear that in prophetic perspective each time element, whether "times" (Dan. 4:16, 23, 25, 32), "time, times and half a time" (Dan. 7:25, NIV), "evenings and mornings" (Dan. 8:14, NIV), "weeks" (Dan. 9:24), and respectively, "days" (Dan. 12:11, 12), stand for other realities in real historical time. In other words, in Daniel the year/day principle is at work each time a time prophecy is provided. The Danielic apocalyptic context is different than the creation context of Genesis 1. Time at the beginning, in creation, is not identical with predictive time, which has its fulfillment in the historical future. Genesis 1 has nothing really predictive. The latter is a prose record of the past and not an apocalyptic prophecy of the future. Such content and contextual perspectives do not warrant a departure from the plain meaning in the Genesis creation account.

[109] In Genesis 1:31 the Hebrew has an article both before *yôm* and the numeral, while in Genesis 2:3 the article appears only before the numeral following the noun *yôm*. According to Hebrew syntax, the article in the latter case makes the word that the numeral qualifies articular.

[110] Ronald F. Youngblood, *The Book of Genesis,* 2nd ed. (Grand Rapids: Baker, 1991), p. 26. Westermann, p. 76, actually translates "one day."

[111] *Ibid.*

[112] Bruce K. Waltke and M. O'Connor, *An Introduction to Biblical Hebrew Syntax* (Winona Lake, Ind.: Eisenbrauns, 1990), p. 274. The translation "day one" is syntactically not correct even though the cardinal is used here. In clauses of the type of Genesis 1:5 the cardinal serves effectively as an ordinal number (Nahum M. Sarna, *Genesis,* Jewish Publication Society Torah Commentary [Philadelphia: Jewish Publication Society, 1989], pp. 8, 353).

[113] Youngblood, p. 26.

[114] See Herbert Niehr, *"'ereb,"* *Theologisches Wörterbuch zum Alten Testament,* vol. 6, pp. 359-366.

[115] M. Barth, *"boqer,"* *Theological Dictionary of the Old Testament,* vol. 2, p. 225.

[116] Werner H. Schmidt, *Die Schöpfungsgeschichte der Priesterschrift,* 2nd ed. (Neukirchen-Vluyn: Neukirchener Verlag, 1967), p. 68.

[117] See Niels-Erik A. Andreasen, *The Old Testament Sabbath: A Tradition-Historical Interpretation,* Society of Biblical Literature Dissertation Series No. 7 (Missoula, Mont.: Society of Biblical Literature, 1972), pp. 174-202; Gerhard F. Hasel, "The Sabbath in the Pentateuch," *The Sabbath in Scripture and History,* Kenneth A. Strand, ed. (Washington, D.C.: Review and Herald, 1982), pp. 21-43; "Sabbath," *The Anchor Bible Dictionary,* pp. 849-856; Gnana Robinson, *The Origin and Development of the Old Testament Sabbath: A Comprehensive Exegetical Approach* (Frankfurt: Peter Lang, 1988), pp. 139-142, 296-301.

[118] Schmidt, p. 68, n. 5.

[119] See also Weeks, p. 18: "The commandment loses completely its cogency if they [the 'days'] are not taken literally."

[120] Blocher, p. 48; see also Henricus Renckens, *Israel's Concept of the Beginning: The Theology of Genesis 1-3* (New York: Herder & Herder, 1964), pp. 98-100.

[121] Fretheim, p. 20.

[122] Bailey, p. 126.

CHAPTER 3

GENESIS 2:
A SECOND CREATION ACCOUNT?[1]

Randall W. Younker
Seventh-day Adventist Theological Seminary
Andrews University

Introduction

Even to the casual reader, the conclusion of the first chapter of Genesis gives the impression of a completed creation: "And God saw every thing that he had made, and, behold, *it was* very good. And the evening and the morning were the sixth day. Thus the heavens and the earth were finished, and all the host of them. And on the seventh day God ended his work which he had made; and he rested on the seventh day from all his work which he had made. And God blessed the seventh day, and sanctified it: because that in it he had rested from all his work which God created and made" (Gen. 1:31-2:3).

Several verses in the second chapter of Genesis, however, appear to list four things that God had *not yet* created, thus perplexing some readers. After reiterating in Genesis 2:4 that the Lord God had finished making "the earth and the heavens," verse 5 goes on to say that He had *not yet* made: (1) the "shrub of the field"; (2) the "plant of the field"; (3) "a man to work the ground"; and (4) "rain to water the earth." Does not chapter 1 clearly depict the creation of human beings and plants prior to the end of that first week of creation? Do we have a contradiction between chapters 1 and 2?

Before we answer such questions, however, it is necessary to digress for a moment. Historical-critical scholarship has long held that the first two chapters of Genesis contain two different and somewhat contradictory creation stories.[2] Such scholars regard the first account as consisting of Genesis 1:1-2:4a, and generally assume it to have been written by, or derived from, "priestly" authors or sources somewhere between the seventh and fifth centuries B.C. Historical-critical scholars refer to this hypothetical author or source as P (for "priestly"). Genesis 2:4b-25, according to the same scholars, represents a second creation account that, although it appears second in the order of our present Bibles, is thought to have been written earlier by either a hypothetical author or derived from a source named J (J derives from the name of God, Jehovah, but scholars usually refer to it as the "Yahwist" source), or it represents the combined work of two authors or sources, E (J still referring to the "Yahwist" and E to the "Elohist"). Critical scholars have generally assumed that the Yahwist lived in Judah and wrote his portion of Scripture c. 950 B.C., while the Elohist lived in Ephraim (or northern kingdom) and made his contribution to the scriptural tradition c. 850 B.C.

Some of the evidence offered as proof of the priestly authorship of Genesis 1:1–2:4a involves the careful organization of the chapter. God does creation in uniform blocks of time—in six 24-hour days. The language is concise and ends the discussion of each day in a similar orderly fashion: "and there was evening and morning, day [fill in the number] . . ." The priestly author, however, supposedly employed a more impersonal view of God—not surprising since the priests would want people to maintain a proper distance, reverence, and respect for the Deity. Thus chapter 1 refers to God as *Elohim,* or simply, God. By contrast, critical scholars believe the hypothetical author of Genesis 2:4b–25, the Yahwist, intended to portray a more "personal" picture of God. Thus the Yahwist has God down on His hands and knees, so to speak, forming the first man with His own hands and breathing His breath directly into the being's nostrils. God here receives a personal name. He is not simply *Elohim* (God), but rather is *Yahweh* (Lord) or *Yahweh-elohim* (Lord God).

It is beyond the scope of this chapter to deal with all the claims of the historical critics concerning the first two chapters of Genesis. A number of scholars have examined the various arguments that two or more authors or sources lie behind the composition of Genesis 1 and 2 and have not found them compelling.[3] For example, we can illustrate the use of different divine names for the same Deity within the same text (such as *Elohim* and *Yahweh* in Genesis 1 and 2) from extrabiblical Near Eastern documents. Similarly, the stylistic differences between chapters 1 and 2 are not necessarily atypical in ancient Near Eastern literature and can be explained as reflecting the different subject matter within each chapter. The focus of this brief study is, rather, on the alleged contradiction between Genesis 1 and 2 that some presume to be the result of the different authorships of the two chapters—the idea that Gen. 1:1–2:4a contains one creation story written by a priestly author (or authors) writing sometime between the seventh and fifth centuries B.C. and that Genesis 2:4b–25 reflects a second creation story composed by a Yahwist author c. 950 B.C. (or later).

Obviously, such an assumption raises a lot of questions for those who have traditionally held a high view of Scripture. Such a perspective not only necessarily denies a Mosaic authorship c. 1450 B.C., it also leaves open the question of divine inspiration and the historicity of the Genesis creation account, as well as the general overall reliability of Scripture. The critical view of a noninspired, non-Mosaic authorship of Genesis has certainly not been the traditional view of either Jews or Christians. As Dillard and Longman point out, early Jewish and Christian tradition virtually unanimously ascribed Genesis to Moses.[4] Support for a Mosaic authorship appears in Ecclesiasticus 24:23, Philo, Josephus, the Mishnah, and the Talmud. The numerous references by the apostles and Christ to various portions of Genesis that they specifically ascribe to Moses (e.g., Rom. 4:17; Gal. 3:8; Heb. 4:4; James 2:23) have been particularly authoritative for Bible-believing Christians. Especially interesting are Jesus' comments in His dialogue with the Pharisees about the permissibility of divorce (Matt. 19; Mark 10). In His response, Jesus asked, "What did Moses command you?" (Mark 10:3, NIV). When they replied by quoting Deuteronomy 24:1-4, Jesus countered by citing Genesis 1:27 and Genesis 2:24 (Mark 10:6-9; Matt. 19:4, 5). Clearly, Jesus' counterargument, derived from Genesis 1:27; 2:24, rested on the assumption of a Mosaic authorship of the passages—an understanding His antagonists shared—otherwise, His argument would have lacked authority.

Adventists have also long accepted the Mosaic authorship of Genesis.[5] Ellen G. White wrote that while Moses sojourned in Midian, "Here, under the inspiration of the Holy Spirit, he wrote the book of Genesis."[6] Based on both the internal evidence of Scripture, including the inferred and explicit testimony of the apostles and Jesus, as well as the understanding of Ellen White and the Adventist pioneers, the overwhelming majority of Adventists have understandably been reluctant to adopt a view that would deny a God-inspired, Mosaic authorship of Genesis, including the first two chapters. But what does one do, then, with the apparent contradictions between Genesis 1 and 2 that some scholars attribute to different authors or sources? The answer, I would suggest, is to take a closer look at the text, as, indeed, many scholars have done.

A Closer Look at the Text

Anyone who carefully reads the first chapter of Genesis can readily see that the account of the seven days of creation does not really end at verse 31 of chapter 1. Rather the description of God's activities during this first week of the world's history actually continues into the first few verses of chapter 2. Most scholars and advanced students of the Bible realize that the original authors of the biblical text did not create the chapter and verse divisions. These originated much later and often break the text in an arbitrary fashion. Indeed, to compensate for such arbitrary organization, many modern English translations indicate where the actual, natural break occurs by placing a gap or a heading between 2:4a and 2:4b—right in the middle of this verse![7]

The theme of chapter 2, therefore, properly begins at 2:4, and as noted above, the first point this new section makes is that there were four things that did *not yet* exist after God had completed the earth and the heavens—the shrub of the field, the plant of the field, the human being to till the soil, and rain. How is it that these four things did *not yet* exist after God announced His creation complete? Are they, especially the plants and man, somehow different than those mentioned in chapter 1? If so, how and why did these things come into existence? The answer to such questions is the point of chapter 2.

Hebrew Terms for Vegetation in Genesis 1 and 2

Although most scholars who have studied the first two chapters of Genesis appear to have assumed that the words and phrases for plants or vegetation used in Genesis 1:11, 12 and Genesis 2:5 carry the same meaning, the fact is that the Hebrew terms employed in the two chapters are not the same! Genesis 1:11, 12 actually reads: "Let the earth produce vegetation *(deshe)*: seed-bearing plants *('esev matsry' tsr')* [according to its kind], and fruit-bearing fruit trees *('es pry asa pry)* with seed "according to its kind." Genesis 2:5, on the other hand, reads that prior to man's creation there was no shrub of the field *(siah ha-sadeh)* and no plant of the field *('esev ha-sadeh)* "had yet sprung up." Even those who cannot read Hebrew can see that the words are not identical.

However, we can still ask, Do the Hebrew botanical expressions *siah ha-sadeh* and *'esev ha-sadeh* of Genesis 2:5 mean the same thing as the terms that occur in Genesis 1:11, 12? It appears that many commentators have assumed so. Dillman (1892), for example, argued that the *"siah of the field"* and the *"'esev ha-sadeh"* of Genesis 2:5 represented the two major plant categories of the botanical world and thus stood for the plant kingdom in its entirety. Other commentators have generally followed a similar approach.

However, as Cassuto has shown, a closer reading of the text reveals that the botanical terms of Genesis 1:11, 12 and Genesis 2:5 do not have identical meanings. The Genesis 2 word *siah* appears only two other times in the Hebrew Bible—Genesis 21:15 and Job 30:4, 7, while the full expression *siah ha-sadeh* is unique, occurring only in Genesis 2:5. The contexts of both Genesis 21:15 and Job 30:4, 7 make it clear that the *siah* is a xerophyte, that is, a plant adapted to dry or desert environments. As such, it is most likely a spiny or thorny plant. Such an understanding of the *siah* receives support from Genesis 3:18. The text couples the expression *'esev ha-sadeh* ("plant of the field") with "thorns and thistles" *(weqos we-dardar),* rather than *siah ha-sadeh,* as was the case in Genesis 2:5. Apparently the writer intended "thorns and thistles" as a parallel expression for the earlier *siah ha-sadeh.* The apparent substitution of *siah ha-sadeh* for "thorns and thistles" in Genesis 3:18, along with the contexts of Genesis 21:15 and Job 30:4, 7, thus make it most likely that we should understand the *siah* to be a thorny xerophyte.

According to M. Zohary, an Israeli botanist, more than 70 species of spiny plants grow in Israel.[8] Scripture mentions 20 of them, although no other plant group is so frequently misidentified and arbitrarily translated. Such plants, while essential to the fragile ecosystems of dry desert regions, agriculturalists generally classify as intrusive, "obnoxious" plants. They are not the type of plant that a farmer of the ancient Near East would deliberately cultivate in his garden, nor were such plants likely included among the species God planted in the garden east in Eden, which was filled with all sorts of "trees that were pleasing to the eye and good for food" (Gen. 2:8, 9, NIV). Thus one of the plants that did *not yet* exist as we begin the narrative of Genesis 2:4b was the thorny xerophyte—the agriculturist's bane. What is the point the author is trying to make here? To better understand, we first go on to the next plant that was *not yet*—the "plant of the field."

Plant of the Field

While the other botanical term in Genesis 2 *('esev,* plant) is fairly common in the Hebrew text, it appears in the full expression *'esev hassadeh* ("plant of the field") only in Genesis 2:5 and Genesis 3:18. Cassuto points out that Genesis 3:18 specifically designates "plants of the field" as the food Adam will have to eat as a result of his sin and that he will obtain them only through "painful toil" and the "sweat of [his] brow." In other words, "plants of the field" are those plants grown through the labor humanity became burdened with *because of the fall into sin.* As Cassuto observes, "these species did not exist, or were not found in the form known to us until after Adam's transgression, and it was in consequence of his fall that they came into the world and received their present form."[9] The fact that Genesis 3:19 explicitly states that these plants were used to make *bread* would indicate that the expression "plants of the field" specifically refers to wheat, barley, and other similar grains. Raising such crops requires the "tilling of the ground," another inherent feature of such plants specifically mentioned in the text.

Taken together, then, these two botanical terms—"shrub of the field" and "plant of the field"—encompass not the entire plant kingdom, as Dillman assumed, but rather that part of the plant kingdom that the cultivator is particularly concerned with—food crops and weeds. Wenham notes that part of the distinction between *siah* (thistle?) and *'esev* (grain?) within the context of Genesis 2 lies in whether human beings can eat them or not.[10]

No Man to Till the Ground

The necessity of human labor in the production of the "plant of the field" leads to the next item that did *not yet* exist—someone to till the ground. Again some scholars have assumed that Genesis 2:5 contradicts chapter 1 because, while the first chapter depicts the creation of human beings on the sixth day, Genesis 2:5 seems to imply that God had not yet brought man into existence after "the earth and heavens were made." However, this results from an oversimplified reading of the text that ignores the critical modifier "to till the ground."

It is important to observe that God did not intend the being He created in Genesis 1:26-30 to work the ground in the fashion described in Genesis 3. Rather, he was to "rule over the fish of the sea and the birds of the air . . . over all the creatures that move along the ground" (NIV). Further, God had given him "every seed-bearing plant on the face of the whole earth and every tree that has fruit with seed in it" (NIV) for food. The passage says nothing of deriving food from "working the ground."

A being who "works the ground" does not come into view until *after* Adam's fall. Then, *because of Adam's sin,* God tells him, "Cursed is the ground because of you; through painful toil you will eat of it [the ground] all the days of your life" (Gen. 3:17). Thus like the "plant of the field" of Genesis 2:5, the "man to work the ground" does not exist until *after* the fall and only as a direct result of sin (note also that Cain, also described as one who "worked the soil" [Gen. 4:2, NIV], was the first murderer).

Genesis 2:5, therefore, is not claiming that human beings did not yet exist after God had made the earth and heavens. Rather it is speaking of the absence of a *sinful* person (i.e., one who must work the ground for food). Such an individual would not enter the scene until after the fall, an event not discussed until chapter 3. Genesis 2 thus sets the stage for what comes later in Genesis 3.

Support for such an interpretation appears in ancient Mesopotamian primeval histories. The Sumerian account of creation, the so-called Eridu Genesis, tells us that the gods immediately forgot about humans after creating them, leaving the humans miserable.[11] Specific indications of their condition include the absence of irrigation canals (no water for crops), seeder plows (no grains), and domesticated animals (no wool for clothes—people were naked). One goddess, Nintur, remembers humanity, however, and solves their dilemma by providing "culture" that included the "gifts" of cities, cult places, and kings. The kings will make the common people "work like cattle," dredging canals and growing crops. As a result, humans were no longer miserable. It is interesting to compare the biblical attitude about "culture" with the Sumerian. In Genesis kings, cities, the need to wear clothing, and the requirement to irrigate and work the ground for food receive a negative slant. The origin of cities, kings, the necessity to wear animal skins, and to work the ground by irrigating and plowing are the direct result of sin. Prior to sin, it was God who took care of all human needs—He was not a God who forgot His people or left them to their own devices. Rather He provided everything they had to have! The Sumerian version of creation, however, views the same items—kings, cities, animal clothing, and tilling the ground—positively and as gifts from the gods/goddesses. Several scholars have commented on the polemic nature of Genesis in contrast to Mesopotamian "primeval histories."

Some have pointed out that in Genesis 2:15 prefall human beings were to "work the garden," and thus Genesis 2:5 simply anticipates the activity described in the later verse. Indeed, the Hebrew word for "work" is the same in both verses *(eved)*. However, working a garden is not the same as working the ground. Whereas the English word "garden" evokes images of neatly hoed rows of carrots, radishes, turnips, etc., the Hebrew word for garden *(gan)* has a wider meaning. Although archaeological and ethnographic evidence suggests that vegetables often played an important role in the diet of people of the ancient Near East, people did not think highly of vegetable gardening.[12] Indeed, the Old Testament refers to a vegetable garden *(gan yaraq)* only once (1 Kings 21:2). Rather the ancient Hebrew *gan* (usually translated as garden) was generally understood to be an enclosed, nonirrigated fruit tree orchard or vineyard, and was considered a possession of great value. Even though both orchard and field cultivation are initially highly labor intensive, once an orchard matures it provides a high, stable yield for a minimum amount of labor.[13] Field cultivation, on the other hand, continues to be more labor intensive on an annual basis.[14] Hence, people considered healthy, mature orchards as prized possessions. That the garden of Eden was a fruit tree orchard is clear from Genesis 2:9, which specifically mentions that it contained "all kinds of trees" "good for food." When ancient Israelites heard or read that God gave Adam a *gan,* or orchard, they recognized it as a truly wonderful gift, suitable even for a king.

Finally, we should remember that Genesis 3 explicitly associates the expression of "working the ground" with the entrance of sin. Rather than laboring in the garden which God provided, and then eating the fruits of its trees, sinful human beings must now obtain their subsistence by the sweat of their brows through the working of the ground.

Rain

The final thing that Genesis 2:5 indicates did *not yet* exist after God finished the earth and the heavens is rain. Following the same pattern clearly set for the three previous categories, it is logical to assume that rain does not make its appearance until *after* the entrance of sin. That is indeed the case. However, unlike the first three items that appear immediately after humanity's fall, Scripture does not mention rain until Genesis 7:3, 12, at the commencement of the flood, although the context clearly indicates that rain too comes as a consequence of sin.

Although the thorny shrubs, cultivated plants, and the act of cultivation were immediate judgments brought upon human beings for their sin, God permitted the human race to continue living. The final judgment of rain arrives only after antediluvian humanity's condition worsens to the point that God regrets giving them a second chance and determines to terminate the rebellious members of the human race. Rain makes its entrance into the world, not as a water source for agriculture, but as an agent of God's judgment.

Conclusion

A closer reading of the text suggests that chapter 2 does not offer a creation account that contradicts chapter 1. Rather, the point of the introductory verses of chapter 2 is to explain the origin of four things that did not form part of the original sin-free creation described in chapter 1. The four things included: (1) thorns, (2) agriculture, (3) cultivation/irrigation, and (4) rain. Chapter 2 informs the reader that each one directly resulted from the entrance of sin. Genesis 3:17, 18 introduces thorns, plants requiring cultivation, and a human race that must work the ground for its food as curses or judgments immediately after the fall. Although Scripture does not mention rain until the flood, rain too represents a curse—a judgment against humanity's sin. Thus, rather than a contradiction of chapter 1, the early verses in chapter 2 actually serve as a bridge between the perfect creation of chapter 1 and the introduction of sin into the world in chapter 3. Chapter 2:4b-7 essentially asks the ancient Hebrews how these four undesirable elements of their lives—(1) the need to deal with thorny plants, (2) the annual uncertainty and hard work of the grain crop, (3) the need to undertake the physically demanding plowing of the ground, and (4) the dependence on the uncertain, but essential, life-giving rain—come to be part of humanity's lot?

After posing his vexed question in Genesis 2:4b-7, the author proceeds to answer it, beginning in verse 2:8, by recapping in more detail the creation of the original sin-free human being who would bring about the conditions that would result in the four things that *were not yet*. The remainder of chapter 2 thus leads naturally and directly into chapter 3, with its description of the fall and the events that led to how things got the way they are now—an account that actually continues right through to the flood account.[15]

If one were to argue that Genesis 1 and 2 were the result of different authors, it should not be done on the basis of the alleged contradictions of Genesis 2:4b-7. The verses actually tend to support the unified and integrated nature of the early chapters of Genesis.[16]

---

[1] This essay is an expanded version of an earlier paper appearing in the author's book *God's Creation* (Nampa, Idaho: Pacific Press, 1999).

[2] For typical historical-critical approaches, see A. Dillman, *Genesis, Critically and Exegetically Expounded* (Edinburgh: T & T Clark, 1897); J. Skinner, *A Critical and Exegetical Commentary on Genesis* (Edinburgh: T & T Clark, 1930); E. A. Speiser, *Genesis: A New Translation With Introduction and Commentary* (New York: Doubleday, 1964); G. von Rad, *Genesis* (Westminster, 1961); C. Westermann, *Genesis: A Commentary* (Augsburg, 1984-1986).

[3] O. T. Allis, *The Five Books of Moses* (Presbyterian and Reformed, 1943); U. Cassuto, *The Documentary Hypothesis*, trans. I. Abrahams (Jerusalem: Magnes, 1961); K. Kitchen, *Ancient Orient and Old Testament* (Downers Grove, Ill.: InterVarsity, 1967); G. J. Wenham, "The Date of Deuteronomy: Linchpin of Old Testament Criticism: Part II," *Themelios* 11 (1985): 3-18; I. M. Kikawada and A. Quinn, *Before Abraham Was: The Unity of Genesis 1-11* (Nashville: Abingdon, 1985); R. N. Whybray, *The Making of the Pentateuch: A Methodological Study* (Sheffield, Eng.: JOST, 1987).

[4] R. B. Dillard and T. Longman III, *An Introduction to the Old Testament* (Grand Rapids: Zondervan, 1994), p. 39.

[5] See F. D. Nichol, ed., *The Seventh-day Adventist Bible Commentary* (Washington, D.C.: Review and Herald, 1953), vol. 1, pp. 201-203.

[6] E. G. White, *Patriarchs and Prophets* (Mountain View, Calif.: Pacific Press, 1958), p. 251.

[7] Not all scholars agree that the division should occur between 2:4a and 2:4b. Victor Hamilton separates the two chapters between 2:3 and 2:4. He bases his conclusion on the assumption that the expression "these are the generations" (Hebrew *toledot*) always appears at the beginning of a literary unit as a superscription, not at its end. Moreover, John Skinner points out that the *toledot* formula is always followed by the genitive of the progenitor, never of the progeny. As Hamilton points out, "the phrase *the generations of the heavens and the earth* describes not the process by which the heavens and earth are generated, but rather, that which is generated by the heavens and the earth. Quite obviously this would be a most inaccurate description of the process of creation as delineated in 1:1-3." See V. Hamilton, *The Book of Genesis Chapters 1-17* (Grand Rapids: Eerdmans, 1990), p. 151; J. Skinner, *A Critical and Exegetical Commentary on Genesis* (Edinburgh: T & T Clark, 1930), p. 41.

[8] Michael Zohary, *Plants of the Bible* (New York: Cambridge Press, 1982), p. 153.

[9] Cassuto, p. 102.

[10] Wenham, p. 58.

[11] T. Jacobsen, "The Eridu Genesis," *Journal of Biblical Literature* 100 (1981): 513-529.

[12] Borowski cites two texts in support of his conclusion. Proverbs 15:17 reads "Better a meal of vegetables *[aruhat yaraq]* where there is love than a fattened calf with hatred" (NIV). The second is the story of Daniel. It gives the impression that people did not consider vegetables as nutri-

tious as other foodstuffs. Borowski suggests that the underdeveloped state of horticulture may be behind the Israelite attitude that held vegetables in low regard. See O. Borowski, *Agriculture in Iron Age Israel* (Winona Lake, Ind.: Eisenbrauns, 1987), p. 101. See also D. Hopkins, *The Highlands of Canaan* (Sheffield, Eng.: Almond Press, 1985), p. 243.

[13] Hopkins, p. 227.

[14] *Ibid.,* p. 214.

[15] Thus I believe that scholars like Kikawada and Quinn, Kitchen, and others (see n. 2) are correct in seeing all of Genesis 1-11 as a single literary unit.

[16] For a good overview of these issues and a similar conclusion, see Nichol, pp. 201-203.

CHAPTER 4

BIBLICAL EVIDENCE FOR THE UNIVERSALITY OF THE GENESIS FLOOD

Richard M. Davidson

Seventh-day Adventist Theological Seminary

Andrews University

Conflicting Schools of Interpretation

One of the most controversial aspects of the flood narrative concerns the extent of the Genesis flood itself. Commentators have taken three major positions: (1) the traditional, that asserts the worldwide nature of the deluge; (2) limited or local flood theories that narrow the scope of the flood story to a particular geographical location in Mesopotamia; and (3) a nonliteral (symbolic) interpretation that suggests that the flood story is a nonhistorical account written to teach theological truth.

Against the third position, the nonhistorical, we must note the evidences within the biblical account affirming the historical nature of the flood. In the literary structure of the flood story,[1] the genealogical frame or envelope construction (Gen. 5:32; 9:28, 29) plus the secondary genealogies (Gen. 6:9, 10; 9:18, 19) indicate that the biblical author intends the account as factual history. The use of the genealogical term *tôl*ᵉ*dôt* ("generations," "account") in the flood story (Gen. 6:9), as throughout Genesis (13 times, structuring the whole book), reveals that the author regarded his story to be as historically veracious as the rest of Genesis.[2] Walter Kaiser analyzes the literary form of Genesis 1-11 and concludes that we must take this whole section of Genesis as "historical narrative prose."[3]

A number of references in the book of Job may allude to the flood (Job 9:5-8; 12:14, 15; 14:11, 12; 22:15-17; 26:10-14; 28:9; 38:8-11).[4] The historical occurrence of the flood is part of the saving/judging acts of God, and the theological arguments of later biblical writers employing flood typology assume its historicity and build on it.[5]

Thus according to the biblical writers, far from being a nonhistorical, symbolical, or mythical account written only to teach theological truths, the flood narrative seeks to accurately record a real, literal, historical event.

For evangelical Christians who take seriously the biblical record and accept the historicity of the flood account, the question still remains whether we should regard the event described as a local and limited flood or as a global cataclysm.

The limited flood theories rest primarily on scientific arguments that present seemingly difficult geological, biological, and anthropological problems for a global flood.[6] Since the scientific argumentation is outside the scope of this chapter, I can only suggest that such problems are not insurmountable given the supernatural nature of the flood. Numerous recent scientific studies provide a growing body of evidence for diluvial catastrophism instead of uniformitarianism.[7]

The local flood theories further assert that we should interpret the terminology describing the extent of the flood in a relative and not an absolute global sense. Such theories regard the various seemingly universal terms as implying only a limited locality, indicating universality within the writer's worldview, but a limited scope in terms of our modern worldview.[8] We will take up this issue in the next section.

The traditional conservative understanding of the flood narrative is that Genesis 6–9 describes a worldwide deluge. We should note that it is also the view of the majority of liberal-critical commentators on Genesis 6–9, although they regard the biblical view as borrowed from other ancient Near Eastern accounts and not historical.[9]

The thesis of this chapter is that only the traditional position of a literal, global flood does full justice to the biblical data, and such a universal interpretation is crucial for flood theology in Genesis and for the theological implications drawn by later biblical writers.

Biblical Terminology in Genesis 6–9 Indicating Universality

Perhaps the most important kind of biblical evidence for a universal flood is the specific all-inclusive terminology found within the Genesis account itself. The late Gerhard Hasel provided a careful treatment of it in three studies in the publication *Origins*,[10] and therefore I need not go into detail here. Eight different terms or phrases in Genesis 6–9, most echoing their counterparts in the worldwide creation account of Genesis 1 and 2, indicate universality.

First, the term *hā'āres* "the earth," occurring 46 times in the flood narrative (Gen. 6:12, 13, 17, etc.), always without any accompanying genitive of limitation, clearly parallels the usage of the same term in the account of worldwide, universal creation in Genesis 1:1, 2, 10. (While Scripture may at times elsewhere employ the term without a genitive and still in context limit its scope to a certain "land," the explicit link to creation in the flood account [see especially Gen. 6:6, 7] clearly gives a universal context for its usage in Genesis 6-9.)

Some have argued that if Moses had wished to indicate the entire world, he would have used the Hebrew term *tēḇēl*, which means the world as a whole, or dry land in the sense of continents. The flood narrative never uses it. But we should point out that *tēḇēl* never appears in the entire Pentateuch, including the creation account. In fact, nowhere do the narrative portions of the Hebrew Bible contain it, but only poetic texts (39 times), usually as a poetic synonym in parallel with *hā'āreṣ* "the earth." Thus this argument from silence does not adequately consider the contextual and poetic use of terminology, and therefore carries little weight.

A second expression, *'al-pᵉnê kol-hā'āreṣ*, "upon the face of all the earth" (Gen. 7:3; 8:9), clearly alludes to the first occurrence of the same phrase in the universal context of creation (Gen. 1:29; cf. verse 2 for a related universal expression), and thus implies a universality of the same dimension as in creation also here, that is, the entire surface of the global mass. While the shortened expression "all the earth" *(kol-hā'āreṣ)* by itself may have a limited meaning elsewhere when indicated by the immediate context (see Ex. 10:5, 15; Num. 22:5, 11; 1 Kings 4:34; 10:24; 2 Chron. 36:23; Gen. 41:57), the immediate context of the flood story is the universal sinfulness of the human beings whom God had made and created (Gen. 6:6, 7) to have dominion over "all the earth" (Gen. 1:26), and the succeeding context is the worldwide dispersal of humanity after the Tower of Babel "upon the face of all the earth" (Gen. 11:4, 8, 9). In each of the four occurrences of the phrase "upon the face of all the earth" in Genesis outside the flood story (Gen. 1:29; 11:4, 8, 9), it clearly has the sense of the entire land surface of the globe, and nothing in the flood narrative restricts such universality. (We should also note that the one place in Genesis where in context a similar phrase "upon all the face of the earth" is not global [the famine mentioned in Genesis 41:56], the Hebrew has a change in word order from elsewhere in Genesis *['al-kol pᵉnê hā'āreṣ]*).

Third, the phrase *pᵉnê hā'aḏāmāh*, "face of the ground" (five times in the flood narrative, Gen. 7:4, 22, 23; 8:8, 13), occurs in parallel with universal terms we have just noted, "the earth" (Gen. 7:23) and "face of the whole earth" (Gen. 8:9). "Face of the ground" likewise harks back to its first usage in the universal context of creation (Gen. 2:6).

Fourth, the term *kol-bāśār* "all flesh," occurs 12 times in Genesis 6-9

(Gen. 6:12, 13, 17, 19; 7:16, 21; 8:17; 9:11, 15, 16, 17). The word *kol,* "all," (which can occasionally express less than totality if the context demands) when used before an indeterminate noun with no article or possessive suffix, as here in Genesis 6-9, indicates totality. God's announcement to destroy "all flesh" (Gen. 6:13, 17) and the narrator's comment that "all flesh" died (Gen. 7:21, 22) except the inhabitants of the ark indicate worldwide destruction. The one occurrence of *kol* plus the determinate noun *hābāśār,* "all the flesh" (in Gen. 7:15), likewise indicates totality as well as unity.

Fifth, "every living thing" *(kol-hāhay)* of all flesh (Gen. 6:19) is another expression of totality. In Genesis 7:4, 23 the similar term *kol-hay*ᵉ*qûm* means literally "all existence." The term acquires further universal dimensions by the addition of the clause harking back to creation—"all existence *that I have made*" (Gen. 7:4)—and by the exclusive statement: "Only Noah and those who were with him in the ark remained alive" (verse 23). As Hasel puts it, "There is hardly any stronger way in Hebrew to emphasize total destruction of 'all existence' of human and animal life on earth than the way it has been expressed. The writer of the Genesis flood story employed terminology, formulae, and syntactical structures of the type that could not be more emphatic and explicit in expressing his concept of a universal, worldwide flood."[11]

Sixth, the phrase "under the whole heaven" *(tahat kol-hāšśāmāyim),* (Gen. 7:19) appears six times in the Old Testament outside of the flood narrative, and always with a universal meaning (see Deut. 2:25; 4:19; Job 28:24; 37:3; 41:11; Dan. 9:12). For example, Scripture uses the phrase to describe God's omniscience: "For He looks to the ends of the earth, and sees under the whole heavens" (Job 28:24, NKJV). Again it depicts God's sovereignty: "Whatsoever is under the whole heaven is mine" (Job 41:11). (Note that the usage in Deuteronomy 2:25, describing "the nations under the whole heaven," receives further qualification and limitation from the phrase "who shall hear the report of you" [NKJV], and thus is potentially universal and not an exception to the universal sense.)

The phrase "under the whole heaven" or "under all the heavens" also universalizes the phrase "under heaven" (Gen. 6:17) in this same flood context. The word "heaven" by itself can have a local meaning (e.g., 1 Kings 18:45), but here the context is global. Ecclesiastes, which contains numerous allusions to creation, likewise utilizes the term "under heaven" with a universal intention (Eccl. 1:13; 2:3; 3:1; cf. the parallel universal expression "under the sun" in Eccl. 1:3, 9; 2:11, 17; etc.).

In the flood account "under the whole heaven" forms part of two forceful verses describing the extent of the flood: "And the waters prevailed so mightily upon the earth that all the high mountains under the whole heaven were covered; the waters prevailed above the mountains, covering them fifteen cubits deep" (Gen. 7:19, 20, RSV). Critical scholar John Skinner notes that Genesis 7:19, 20 "not only asserts its [the flood's] universality, but so to speak proves it, by giving the exact height of the waters above the highest mountains."[12]

We cannot simply explain the biblical language here in terms of a local sky, and certainly cannot refer to the local mountains being covered by snow, as some proponents of a local flood have suggested. H. C. Leupold points out that the writer of verse 19 is not content with a single use of *kol* ("all") in "all the high mountains," but "since 'all' is known to be used in a relative sense, the writer removes all possible ambiguity by adding the phrase 'under all the heavens.' A double 'all' *(kol)* cannot allow for so relative a sense. It almost constitutes a Hebrew superlative. So we believe that the text disposes of the question of the universality of the Flood."[13]

Seventh, Hasel devoted an entire scholarly article to the phrase "all the fountains *[ma'yᵉnot]* of the great deep *[tᵉhôm rabbāh]*" (Gen. 7:11; 8:2) and showed how it is linked with the universal "deep" *(tᵉhôm)* or world-ocean in Genesis 1:2 (cf. Ps. 104:6: "Thou didst cover it [the earth] with the deep *[tᵉhôm]* as with a garment; the waters stood above the mountains" [RSV]). The "breaking up" and "bursting forth" (i.e., geological faulting) of not just one subterranean water spring in Mesopotamia, but of *all* the "fountains" of the great deep, coupled in the same verse with the opening of the windows of the heavens, far transcends a local scene. Hasel concludes that "the bursting forth of the waters from the fountains of the 'great deep' refers to the splitting open of springs of subterranean waters with such might and force that together with the torrential downpouring of waters stored in the atmospheric heavens a worldwide flood comes about."[14]

Eighth, in another article, Hasel shows how the Hebrew Bible reserved a special term, *mabbûl,* that in its 13 occurrences refers exclusively to the worldwide Genesis flood (12 occurrences in Genesis, once in Psalm 29:10). The word may have derived from the Hebrew root *ybl,* "to flow, to stream." The term *mabbûl,* which the flood narrative usually associates with *mayim,* "waters," seems to have become "a technical term for waters flowing or streaming forth and as such designates the flood (deluge) being caused by waters. . . . *Mabbûl* is in the Old Testament a term consistently employed for the flood (deluge) that was caused by torrential rains and the bursting forth of subterranean waters."[15] This technical term clearly sets the Genesis deluge apart from all local floods. Psalm 29:10 utilizes it to illustrate Yahweh's universal sovereignty over the world at the time of the Noahic flood: "The Lord sat enthroned at the Flood, and the Lord sits as King forever" (NKJV).

Summarizing the evidence of the technical terminology Scripture uses to depict the extent of the flood in Genesis 6-9, Hasel writes: "The Genesis flood narrative provides ample evidence of being an account which is to be understood as a historical narrative in prose style. It expects to be taken literally. There is a consistent and overwhelming amount of terminology and formulae . . . which on the basis of context and syntax has uniformly indicated that the flood story wants to be understood in a universal sense: the waters destroyed all human and animal plus bird life on the entire land mass of the globe. To read it otherwise means to force a meaning on the carefully written and specific syntactical constructions of the original language which the text itself rejects."[16]

Other Biblical Evidence for a Universal Flood

Many additional lines of biblical evidence converge in affirming the universal extent of the flood and also reveal the theological significance of such a conclusion. We will summarize 14 points that emerge from the biblical text.

First, key terms and motifs in Genesis 6-9 converge to make a major theological statement: the Noahic flood is nothing less than the cosmic/universal undoing or reversal of creation. Numerous biblical scholars have recognized this highly significant theological point of the flood narrative. Tikva Frymer-Kensky describes the flood as "the original, cosmic undoing of creation."[17] Elsewhere she writes: "The flood was an undoing of creation: the cosmic waters overwhelmed the earth, coming through the windows of the sky and the fountains of the great deep beneath the earth (7:11; cf. 8:2). Thus, return to the primeval watery condition set the stage for a new beginning for the world."[18] According to John Skinner, "the flood is a partial undoing of the work of creation."[19] Similarly, Nahum Sarna writes that "the flood is a cosmic catastrophe that is actually the undoing of creation. . . . The 'floodgates of the sky' are openings in the expanse of the heavens through which water from the celestial part of the cosmic ocean can escape onto the earth. In other words, creation is being undone, and the world returned to chaos."[20] Claus Westermann speaks of the "invasion of chaos into the created order; the flood assumed cosmic proportions."[21] Umberto Cassuto points out that at the high point of the flood, "we see water everywhere, as though the world had reverted to its primeval state at the dawn of creation, when the waters of the deep submerged everything."[22] David Clines uses the apt term *bouleversement*, or "reversal" of creation, to depict the theological significance of the flood.[23] For Joseph Blenkinsopp, "the deluge is an act of uncreation, undoing the work of separation by returning everything to the primeval, watery chaos from which the created order first arose."[24]

Gerhard von Rad vividly underscores the universal implications of this undoing or reversal of creation: "We must understand the flood, therefore, as a catastrophe involving the entire cosmos. When the heavenly ocean breaks forth upon the earth below, and the primeval sea beneath the earth, which is restrained by God, now freed from its bonds, gushes up through yawning chasms onto the earth, then there is a destruction of the entire cosmic system, according to biblical cosmology. The two halves of the chaotic primeval sea, separated—the one up, the other below—by God's creative government (ch. 1:7-9), are again united; creation begins to sink into chaos. Here the catastrophe, therefore, concerns not only men and beasts . . . but the earth (chs. 6.13; 9.1)—indeed, the entire cosmos."[25] Only a cosmic/universal flood can theologically encompass the cosmic/universal reversal or undoing of creation described in Genesis 6-9.

Second, the trajectory of major themes in Genesis 1-11—creation, fall, plan of redemption, spread of sin—is universal in scope and calls for a corresponding universal judgment. We have already noted in reference to specific flood terminology the numerous allusions to the universal context of creation. The creation of "the heavens and the earth" certainly is not local in scope, according to Genesis 1, 2.

Likewise, the fall of humanity in Adam and Eve led to the sinful condition of the entire human race *(hā'ādām)*, not just the inhabitants of Mesopotamia (see Gen. 6:5, 11; Rom. 3:19; 5:12). Again, the protoevangelium (first gospel promise) outlined in Genesis 3:15 involves the universal moral struggle between the spiritual descendants (or "seed") of the serpent and the spiritual descendants ("seed") of the woman, culminating in the victory of the representative Messianic seed over the serpent.[26] The biblical plan of redemption is certainly universal in scope.

In a similar way, humanity's sinful condition described at the time of the flood includes more than those living in the Fertile Crescent. From *God's* perspective, not simply from the culturally conditioned local view of the narrator, we have the results of the divine investigative judgment: "And God saw that the wickedness of man *(hā'ādām)*, (humankind) was great in the earth, and that every imagination of the thoughts of his heart was only evil continually" (Gen. 6:5). Such universal sinfulness naturally calls for universal judgment.

Third, the divine purpose given for sending the flood makes explicit its universal scope: "And the Lord said, 'I will destroy man [*hā'ādām*, humanity] whom I have created from the face of the earth; both man and beast, creeping thing and birds of the air, for I am sorry that I have made them'" (verse 7, NKJV). Nothing less than a complete destruction of the human race (except for Noah, verse 8) seems envisaged. Given the length of time from creation (more than 1,650 years minimum), the longevity of the antediluvians (nearly 1,000 years), and God's command at creation to "fill the earth" (Gen. 1:28, NKJV), it is highly unlikely that the preflood population would have stayed only in Mesopotamia. Thus the destruction of humanity would necessitate more than a local flood.

Fourth, the genealogical lines from both Adam (Gen. 4:17-26; 5:1-31) and Noah (Gen. 10:1-32; 11:1-9) are exclusive in nature, indicating that as Adam was father of all preflood humanity, so Noah was father of all postflood humanity. From the descendants of Noah "the nations spread abroad on the earth after the flood" (Gen. 10:32, RSV). The Tower of Babel incident accelerated humanity's dispersal across the globe (Gen. 11:1-19).

Striking extrabiblical evidence that all human races, and not just those of the Fertile Crescent, have their origin in the descendants of Noah comes from the amazing prevalence of ancient flood stories throughout the world. Scholars have collected more than 230 different flood stories from among the most diverse peoples of the earth.[27] A worldwide flood appears as the most frequently given cause for past universally destructive calamities in the folk literature of antiquity.[28]

A remarkable number of both the oral and written traditions agree upon the basic points of the biblical account: a great flood as a result of divine judgment against human sin destroyed all humanity, and a single man and his family or a few friends survived the deluge in a ship or other seafaring vessel. The stories nearest to the area of the dispersion from Babel share the most details with the biblical account.[29] This vast body of ancient witnesses to a worldwide deluge offers powerful testimony to the historicity and universality of the biblical flood.

Fifth, God gives the same inclusive divine blessing to be fruitful, multiply, and fill the earth to both Adam and Noah (Gen. 1:28; 9:1), presenting still another linkage between universal creation and the flood, between the original beginning and the "new beginning." As the human race at creation flows from Adam and Eve, so the postdiluvial humanity comes through Noah.

Sixth, the covenant (Gen. 9:9, 10) with its rainbow sign (verses 12-17), has a clear link to the extent of the flood and thus includes the whole earth (verses 13-17). If only a local flood had occurred, then the covenant would be only a limited covenant, and the rainbow sign of "the all-embracing universality of the divine mercy"[30] would lose its meaning.

Seventh, the viability of God's promise (Gen. 9:15; cf. Isa. 54:9) and the integrity of God in keeping His promise is wrapped up in the worldwide extent of the flood. We cannot underscore this point too heavily: if Genesis 6-9 describes only a local flood, then God has broken His promise every time another local flood happens! The only way we can see God's promise not to send another flood to destroy every living thing (Gen. 8:21) as being kept is if the flood was a universal one that destroyed the whole human race outside the ark.

Eighth, the enormous size of the ark detailed in Genesis 6:14, 15 and the stated necessity for saving all the species of animals and plants in the ark (verses 16-21; Gen. 7:2, 3) all support the concept of a global flood. A massive ark filled with representatives of all nonaquatic animal/plant species would be unnecessary if it were only a local flood, for they could have survived elsewhere in the world. Yet the biblical record insists that God brought the animals into the ark to preserve representatives of all of the various kinds of life-forms (Gen. 6:19, 20).

As a matter of fact, if God intended only a local flood, the building of any ark at all, even for Noah and his family, would have been superfluous—God could simply have warned Noah and his family in time to escape from the coming judgment, just as He did with Lot in Sodom. But the point of the ark narrative is that there was no other way of escape. In the midst of the flood "only Noah and those who were with him in the ark remained alive" (Gen. 7:23, NKJV).

Ninth, the covering of all the high mountains by at least 15 cubits (Gen. 7:19, 20) could not involve simply a local flood, since water seeks its own level across the surface of the globe. Even one high mountain covered in a local Mesopotamian setting would require that same height of water everywhere on the planet's surface.

In this connection we note that it is not necessary to postulate the existence of mountains as high as Mount Everest at the time of the flood, and thus to require water covering the earth to a depth of six miles, as some proponents of a local flood suggest would be necessary.[31] The antediluvian mountains were quite possibly much lower than at present. Passages in the books of Job and Psalms may well refer to the process of postdiluvian mountain uplift (see Job 9:5; 28:9; and Ps. 104:7, 8).

Proponents of a local flood often argue that a worldwide deluge would imply "that the earth's surface was completely renovated during the flood year" and thus "prediluvian topography would have been exceedingly different from postdiluvian topography." This implication, they claim, conflicts with biblical evidence that "strongly suggests that prediluvian geography did basically resemble postdiluvian geography."[32] They particularly cite the topographical descriptions of the Garden of Eden: the lands of Havilah and Cush, and the four rivers, two of which (the Tigris and the Euphrates) were familiar to the readers of Genesis in Moses' time.

What they do not recognize, however, is that although there are some similarities between the prediluvian and postdiluvian topography, we would find more differences than similarities. Two of the rivers mentioned apparently no longer existed in Moses' time. Scripture mentions the Pishon and Gihon in terms of where they used to flow, in the postdiluvian areas of Havilah and Cush respectively. The other two rivers—the Tigris and Euphrates—Scripture describes as coming from a common source in the Garden of Eden, certainly far different from their present courses. Thus the topographical descriptions in the early chapters of Genesis harmonize with a worldwide flood.

Tenth, the duration of the flood makes sense only with a universal flood. The deluge of rain from above and water from the fountains of the deep below continued 40 days (Gen. 7:17), and all the highest mountains still remained covered five months after the flood began. The tops of the mountains did not appear until after seven months, and the floodwaters had not dried up enough for Noah to leave the ark until one year and 10 days had passed (see verse 11; Gen. 8:14). Such lengths of time seem commensurate only with a global and not a local flood.

Eleventh, the text describes the receding of the water (Gen. 8:3) by Hebrew phrases that, in parallel with similar phraseology and grammatical construction for the "to and fro" motion of the raven (verse 7), should be translated as "going and retreating"[33] and imply oscillatory water motion lasting for 74 days (see verses 3-5). The waters rushing back and forth similar to ocean tidal movement as the overall level gradually decreased supports a global interpretation such as "the oceanic energy impulse model of the flood,"[34] but is incongruous with a local flood theory.

Twelfth, the New Testament passages concerning the flood all employ universal language: "swept them *all* away" (Matt. 24:39, RSV); "destroyed them *all*" (Luke 17:27, RSV); "he did not spare the ancient *world,* but preserved Noah . . . with seven other persons, when he brought a flood upon the *world* of the ungodly" (2 Peter 2:5, RSV); "a few, that is, eight persons, were saved through water" (1 Peter 3:20, RSV); Noah "condemned the *world*" (Heb. 11:7, RSV). A local flood would not have ended the antediluvian world. As Archer states, "we have the unequivocal corroboration of the New Testament that the destruction of the human race at the time of the flood was total and universal."[35]

Thirteenth, the New Testament flood typology assumes and *depends upon*

not only the historicity but also the universality of the flood to argue theologically for an imminent worldwide judgment by fire (2 Peter 3:6, 7). Peter
argues that just as a worldwide judgment by water caused the unbelieving antediluvian world to perish, so in the antitype there must be a universal end-
time judgment by fire, bringing about the destruction of the ungodly.[36]

Fourteenth and last, out of the cosmic reversal of creation—the first point
noted above—proceeds a cosmic new beginning. As Clines states it, "the 'uncreation' which God has worked with the flood is not final; creation has not been
permanently undone. Old unities of the natural world are restored (8:22), and the
old ordinances of creation are renewed (9:1-7)."[37] Jacques Doukhan has shown
the precise literary parallels between the successive stages of "re-creation" in the
aftermath of the flood (Gen. 8; 9) and the seven days of creation in Genesis 1; 2:

1. The wind over the earth and waters (Gen. 8:1; cf. Gen. 1:2).
2. Division of waters (Gen. 8:1-5; cf. Gen. 1:6-8).
3. Appearance of plants (Gen. 8:6-12; cf. Gen. 1:9-13).
4. Appearance of light (Gen. 8:13, 14; cf. Gen. 1:14-19).
5. Deliverance of animals (Gen. 8:15-17; cf. Gen. 1:20-23).
6. Animals together with human beings, blessing, food for human beings,
image of God (Gen. 8:18-9:7; cf. Gen. 1:24-31).
7. Sign of covenant (Gen. 9:8-17; cf. Gen. 2:1-3).[38]

Thus in the overarching literary structure of the "re-creation" in the
flood narrative, the detailed parallels with the cosmic creation account of
Genesis 1, 2 underscore the universal dimension of the flood.

Conclusion

In conclusion, the question of the extent of the Genesis flood is not just
a matter of idle curiosity, with little at stake for Christian faith. For those who
see the days of creation in Genesis 1 as six literal 24-hour days,[39] a universal
flood is an absolute necessity to explain the existence of the geological column (see chapter 5). A literal creation week is inextricably linked with a
worldwide flood.

But a universal flood is crucial not only in seeking to reconcile science
and Scripture. It is also pivotal in understanding and remaining faithful to the
theology of Genesis 1-11 and the rest of Scripture.

The many links with the universal creation in Genesis 1 and 2 that we have
noted in this study not only support the global nature of the flood, but serve to
theologically connect protology (creation) and eschatology (judgment/salva-
tion) in the opening chapters of Scripture. The flood is an eschatological step-
by-step "uncreation" of the world and humanity followed by a step-by-step

"re-creation" of the new world. "Thus," writes Von Rad, "the story of the flood—and this is theologically the most important fact—shows an eschatological world judgment. . . . The world judgment of the flood hangs like an iron curtain between this world age and that of the first splendor of creation."[40]

The theology of the global flood is, therefore, the pivot of a connected but multifaceted universal theme running through Genesis 1-11 and constituting an overarching pattern for the whole rest of Scripture: worldwide creation revealing the character of the Creator and His original purpose for creation; humanity's turning away from the Creator and the universal spread of sin, ending in the universal "uncreation" through universal eschatological judgment; and re-creation, in the eschatological salvation of the faithful covenant remnant and the universal renewal of the earth.

[1] See William H. Shea, "The Structure of the Genesis Flood Narrative and Its Implications," *Origins* 6 (1979): 8-29.

[2] Jacques B. Doukhan, *The Genesis Creation Story: Its Literary Structure* (Berrien Springs, Mich.: Andrews University Press, 1978), pp. 167-220.

[3] Walter C. Kaiser, Jr., "The Literary Form of Genesis 1-11," in J. Barton Payne, ed., *New Perspectives on the Old Testament* (Waco, Tex.: Word, Inc., 1970), pp. 48-65.

[4] See Henry M. Morris, *The Remarkable Record of Job: The Ancient Wisdom, Scientific Accuracy, and Life-changing Message of an Amazing Book* (Grand Rapids: Baker, 1988), pp. 26-30.

[5] See Richard M. Davidson, *Typology in Scripture: A Study of Hermeneutical "Typos" Structures* (Berrien Springs, Mich.: Andrews University Press, 1981), pp. 326, 327.

[6] See Donald C. Boardman, "Did Noah's Flood Cover the Entire World? No," in Ronald F. Youngblood, ed., *The Genesis Debate: Persistent Questions About Creation and the Flood* (Grand Rapids: Baker, 1990), pp. 210-229; Arthur C. Custance, *The Flood: Local or Global?* (Grand Rapids: Zondervan, 1979), pp. 15-27; Derek Kidner, *Genesis: An Introduction and Commentary,* in D. J. Wiseman, ed., *Tyndale Old Testament Commentaries* (Downers Grove, Ill.: InterVarsity Press, 1967), pp. 93-95; T. C. Mitchell, "Flood," in *The New Bible Dictionary,* 2nd ed. (Downers Grove, Ill.: InterVarsity Press, 1993), pp. 380-383; Bernard Ramm, *The Christian View of Science and Scripture* (Grand Rapids: Eerdmans, 1954), pp. 232-249; Davis A. Young, *Creation and the Flood: An Alternative to Flood Geology and Theistic Evolution* (Grand Rapids: Baker, 1977), pp. 171-210.

[7] See Harold G. Coffin and Robert H. Brown, *Origin by Design* (Washington, D.C.: Review and Herald, 1983); Alfred M. Rehwinkel, *The Flood in the Light of the Bible, Geology, and Archaeology* (St. Louis: Concordia Pub. House, 1951); Ariel A. Roth, "Are Millions of Years Required to Produce Biogenic Sediments in the Deep Ocean?" *Origins* 12 (1985): 48-56; "Catastrophism—Is It Scientific?" *Ministry,* July 1986, pp. 24-26; "Those Gaps in the Sedimentary Layers," *Origins* 15 (1988): 75-85; *Origins: Linking Science and Scripture* (Hagerstown, Md.: Review and Herald, 1998); John C. Whitcomb, *The World That Perished,* rev. ed. (Grand Rapids: Baker, 1988); John C. Whitcomb and Henry M. Morris, *The Genesis Flood: The Biblical Record and Its Scientific Implications* (Philadelphia: Presbyterian and Reformed Pub. Co., 1961).

[8] See Boardman, pp. 223-226; Custance, pp. 15-27; Kidner, pp. 93-95; Ramm, pp. 241, 242.

[9] See Gerhard F. Hasel, "The Biblical View of the Extent of the Flood," *Origins* 2 (1975): 78 and note 16 for bibliography of representatives of this position: Fohrer, Koehler, Noth, Procksch, Skinner, Sarna, Speiser, Von Rad, Vriezen, Zimmerli, etc. We will cite some of them as well as other more recent representatives of the view later.

[10] Gerhard F. Hasel, "The Fountains of the Great Deep," *Origins* 1 (1974): 67-72; "The Biblical View of the Extent of the Flood," pp. 77-95; "Some Issues Regarding the Nature and Universality of the Genesis Flood Narrative," *Origins* 5 (1978): 83-98.

[11] ———, "The Biblical View of the Extent of the Flood," p. 86.

[12] John Skinner, "A Critical and Exegetical Commentary on Genesis," in *The International Critical Commentary on the Holy Scriptures of the Old and New Testaments,* 2nd ed. (Edinburgh: T & T Clark, 1930, 1956), vol. 1, p. 165.

[13] H. C. Leupold, *Exposition of Genesis* (Grand Rapids: Baker, 1942), pp. 301, 302.

[14] Hasel, "The Fountains of the Great Deep," p. 71.

[15] ———, "Some Issues Regarding the Nature and Universality of the Genesis Flood Narrative," pp. 92, 93.

[16] ———, "The Biblical View of the Extent of the Flood," p. 87.

[17] Tikva Frymer-Kensky, "Pollution, Purification, and Purgation in Biblical Israel," in Carol L. Meyers and M. O'Connor, eds., *The Word of the Lord Shall Go Forth: Essays in Honor of David Noel Freedman in Celebration of His Sixtieth Birthday* (Winona Lake, Ind.: Eisenbrauns, 1983), p. 410.

[18] ———, "The Flood," in Paul J. Achtemeier, ed., *Harper's Bible Dictionary* (San Francisco: Harper and Row, 1985), p. 312.

[19] Skinner, p. 164.

[20] Nahum M. Sarna, *Genesis,* The JPS Torah Commentary (Philadelphia/New York/Jerusalem: Jewish Publication Society, 1989), pp. 48, 84.

[21] Claus Westermann, *Genesis 1-11: A Commentary,* trans. John J. Scullion (Minneapolis: Augsburg, 1974/1984), p. 434.

[22] Umberto Cassuto, *A Commentary on the Book of Genesis,* trans. Israel Abrahams (Jerusalem: Magnes Press, 1964), p. 97.

[23] David J. A. Clines, "Noah's Flood: I: The Theology of the Flood Narrative," *Faith and Thought* 100, No. 2 (1972, 1973): 128-142; cf. Michael Fishbane's reference to Job 3:1-13 in similar language as "a systematic *bouleversement,* or reversal, of the cosmicizing acts of creation described in Gen. 1-2:4a" (Michael Fishbane, "Jeremiah 4:23-26 and Job 3:3-13: A Recovered Use of the Creation Pattern," *Vetus Testamentum* 21 [1971]: 153).

[24] Joseph Blenkinsopp, *The Pentateuch: An Introduction to the First Five Books of the Bible* (New York: Doubleday, 1992), p. 83.

[25] Gerhard von Rad, *Genesis: A Commentary,* rev. ed. (Philadelphia: Westminster, 1972), p. 128.

[26] See O. Palmer Robertson, *The Christ of the Covenants* (Grand Rapids: Baker, 1980).

[27] See James G. Frazer, *Folklore in the Old Testament: Studies in Comparative Religion* (London: MacMillan, 1918), vol. 1, pp. 105-361; Byron C. Nelson, *The Deluge Story in Stone: A History of the Flood Theory of Geology* (Minneapolis: Augsburg, 1931).

[28] Stith Thompson, *Motif-Index of Folk-Literature: A Classification of Narrative Elements in Folktales, Ballads, Myths, Fables, Medieval Romances, Exempla, Fabiaux, Jest-Books, and Local Legends* (Bloomington, Ind.: Indiana University Press, 1955), vol. 1, pp. 182-194.

[29] See Alexander Heidel, *The Gilgamesh Epic and Old Testament Parallels* (Chicago: University of Chicago Press, 1946); Thorkild Jacobsen, "The Eridu Genesis," *Journal of Biblical Literature* 100 (1981): 513-529; W. G. Lambert and A. R. Millard, *Atrahasis: The Babylonian Story of the Flood* (London: Oxford University Press, 1969).

[30] Franz Delitzsch, "Genesis," in Carl F. Keil and Franz Delitzsch, *Biblical Commentary on the Old Testament: The Pentateuch,* trans. James Martin (Grand Rapids: Eerdmans, 1888, 1976), vol. 1, pp. 289, 290.

[31] See Ramm, p. 242.

[32] Young, p. 210.

[33] See Steven A. Austin, "Did Noah's Flood Cover the Entire World? Yes," in Ronald F.

Youngblood, ed., *The Genesis Debate: Persistent Questions About Creation and the Flood* (Grand Rapids: Baker, 1990), p. 218; Hasel, "Some Issues Regarding the Nature and Universality of the Genesis Flood Narrative," p. 93.

[34] Austin, p. 218.

[35] Gleason L. Archer, Jr., *A Survey of Old Testament Introduction,* rev. ed. (Chicago: Moody Press, 1985), p. 208.

[36] Davidson, pp. 326, 327.

[37] Clines, p. 138.

[38] Jacques B. Doukan, *Daniel, the Vision of the End* (Berrien Springs, Mich.: Andrews University Press, 1987), pp. 133, 134; cf. Warren A. Gage, *The Gospel of Genesis: Studies in Protology and Eschatology* (Winona Lake, Ind.: Carpenter Books, 1984), pp. 10-20.

[39] Gerhard F. Hasel, "The 'Days' of Creation in Genesis 1: Literal 'Days' or Figurative 'Periods/Epoch' of Time?" *Origins* 21, No. 1 (1994): 5-38.

[40] Von Rad, pp. 129, 130.

CHAPTER 5

THE GRAND CANYON AND THE GENESIS FLOOD

Ariel A. Roth
Loma Linda, California
Geoscience Research Institute

Introduction

The Grand Canyon of the Colorado River (Figures 1-3) has been described as one of the world's grandest natural architectural masterpieces. President Theodore Roosevelt, who helped establish the United States National Park System, of which the Grand Canyon is a part, declared that the Grand Canyon is "the one great sight which every American should see." Some have not been that impressed, calling it just a bad case of soil erosion, or commenting that once you get there, there is nothing to do but turn around and go back home. The latter comment gives a false impression because more than 4 million people visit the canyon every year. No one can stand on its edge and not be at least awed by its size. Pictures offer but a poor substitute for the experience of actually seeing it.

The Colorado River winds its way for 275 miles (446 kilometers) through the region of the canyon, dropping about 2,000 feet (610 meters) in the process. The Grand Canyon is much deeper in the mid region where the river cuts through a broad dome, scores of miles wide, called the Kaibab-Coconino Uplift. Here the canyon reaches a depth of 1.1 miles (1.8 kilometers) from rim to river, and a maximum width of nearly 20 miles (30 kilometers). The size is impressive, although some of the transverse gorges of the Himalayas reach nearly three times the depth of the Grand Canyon.[1] However, what is especially important about the canyon is how well it so openly exposes many important geologic features beneath its rim. Rightfully some have identified it as the geologic showcase of the world.

Although the size of the canyon itself is most impressive, the extremely parallel nature of the rock layers and how small the Colorado River is as it courses its way through the huge canyon (Figure 1) also greatly impress the visitor. Two main aspects of this landscape generate important questions: (1)

How did the layers get there? and (2) How was the canyon cut? Many mysteries still lie hidden in the canyon rocks, but geologists have uncovered a significant amount of data on both questions.

Figure 1

View to the northeast of the eastern region of the Grand Canyon. The light strips in the bottom of the gorge are the Colorado River flowing toward the west (left). The sedimentary layers below the dark arrow on the left are Precambrian, while the dominantly parallel layers in the cliff to the right are Phanerozoic.

The Standard Geologic Interpretation for the Formation of the Grand Canyon Rock Layers

Most geologists believe that the rock layers of the Grand Canyon, and most other major sedimentary layers of the earth, formed during a period of many millions of years. For instance, geologists commonly represent the strikingly horizontal layers of the canyon as having taken more than 300 million years for their deposition. Scientists have extensively studied these layers, and the geologic literature covering them is vast.[2]

Geologists have postulated various ancient environments for the deposition of the layers. They consider the lowest widespread layer (just above the arrow in Figure 1) to represent a combination of shallow marine and river deposits, although some evidence suggests that the strata formed in deeper water.[3] Researchers interpret the layers above this, up to well past the middle of the canyon wall, as having been deposited mainly in a marine environment, with seas repeatedly advancing and retreating over the area, while occasionally rivers deposited sediments in the environment. In this segment of the layers one finds an upward trend toward less marine and more terrestrial environments.

Figure 2

View of the Grand Canyon looking to the north from the South Rim. The three arrows designate where major portions of the geologic column are missing between the layers. The Colorado River, which is not visible, runs from the right to the left in the deep Inner Gorge, seen in the middle of the picture. Part of a large side canyon extending to the north appears in the distance below the central part of the horizon line.

One of the most striking rock units of the canyon is the light-colored Coconino Sandstone occurring near the top of the canyon (just above the top arrow in Figure 2). Traditionally geologists have interpreted it as the product of an ancient desert dune environment, although some have questioned the idea.[4] From the top of the Coconino Sandstone to the rim of the canyon the layers are thought to have been deposited for millions of years in a marine or near marine type of environment. Conventional geology suggests that slow erosional processes during millions of years carved out the canyon.

The Recent Creation Described in the Bible and the Standard
Long Age Geologic Interpretation of the Grand Canyon:
The Biblical Flood Connection

Many worldviews circulate about origins. Two of the most important and well-defined ones are the evolutionary model endorsed by most scientists and the creation model based on the biblical account of beginnings. A number of intermediate views do exist between creation and evolution,[5] but they tend to be less defined since we have no data from authoritative sources such as nature (science) or the Bible that directly support such intermediate concepts. Because such ideas tend to be on the speculative side, we will restrict our discussion to the two main concepts: creation and evolution.

The two concepts could hardly be more different from each other. Creation posits a recent event in which God makes life and its world stage in six literal days just a few thousand years ago. Evolution proposes that simple life originated by itself a few billion years ago and that simple life developed by naturalistic means into advanced forms—including human beings—by a slow and gradual evolutionary process that took hundreds of millions of years. No supreme being participated in the process.

Each model has contrasting interpretations of the formation of the Grand Canyon and about the origin of life-forms. Evolutionists interpret the fossil sequence we find as we go up through the layers as reflecting slow evolutionary changes, while most creationists interpret the same fossil sequence as representing different kinds of created organisms transported and buried by the worldwide flood[6] described in the early part of the Bible.

To the creationist the flood is the event that reconciles the presence of the different kinds of organisms in the geologic layers of the Grand Canyon (and of the world) with a six-day creation week. Few appreciate the fact that without the flood to account for most of the different kinds of fossils we find in the rock layers of the earth, we cannot account for the creation week described in the Bible. For instance, in the lower layers of the canyon we find a variety of marine fossils. Higher up in the mid region we encounter some plant fossils not represented in the lower layers. If one puts hundreds of millions of years between the time of origin of the marine and plant fossils, as evolution suggests, then God did not create all living organisms during six days, as described in the Bible. On the other hand, if the fossil-bearing layers resulted from the biblical flood that buried many of the different kinds of the organisms God brought into being during creation week (Gen. 1; Ex. 20:11; 31:17), the fossil record and creation week do correlate. Hence our interpretation of the canyon has significance for our worldview about origins.

A Creationistic Interpretation of the Grand Canyon

Most of the widespread layers of rock that we see in the canyon consist of various sediments cemented together, hence geology calls them sedimentary rocks. Such rocks sometimes contain quite abundant fossils. Water most often transports the sediments that solidify to produce sedimentary rocks. However, even scientists who believe in creation do not usually interpret all the layers in the canyon as originating during the flood. In the canyon's lowest portions, especially toward the eastern end, we find thick strata (layers) of sedimentary rocks that have very few or questionable fossils in them. These are part of the lower rock layers we call Precambrian. (You can see them in Figure 1 as the layers below the arrow.) Flood geologists usually consider Precambrian rocks to have existed before the biblical flood. The layers above the Precambrian are designated as Phanerozoic. They contain many more fossils and in the canyon region are strikingly parallel in arrangement (Figures 1, 2). Only the lower half of the Phanerozoic appear in the Grand Canyon. Just beyond the canyon, especially to the north and east, we encounter thick sedimentary layers that lie above the rock layer that forms the rim of the canyon. These thick layers represent a significant portion of the upper part of the Phanerozoic. Flood geologists regard most of the Phanerozoic as having been deposited during the biblical worldwide flood. We will discuss later some suggested creationistic mechanisms for cutting the canyon.

Questions About the Biblical Flood Interpretation of the Grand Canyon

1. The Abundance of Sediments

In the context of the biblical flood, one of the most obvious questions is how all the thick sedimentary layers could get deposited in a single event such as the Genesis flood that lasted only a year. Also, as referred to above, beyond the canyon region we find layers of sediment thicker than the horizontal ones seen in the canyon itself. They lie above those we see in the Grand Canyon. That is a lot of sediment to account for in a one-year flood. However, one needs to keep in mind that: (1) under rapid catastrophic conditions sediments can deposit at the rate of feet per second; (2) many flood geologists do not consider the lowest sedimentary layers in the Grand Canyon to have been lain down during the flood; and (3) in terms of thickness of sediments the canyon region is not at all typical. Here the layers are several times as thick as the average over the earth. Some regions of the world have virtually no sediments at all. Actually, the average thickness of the sedimentary layers resulting from the flood would form only a very thin veneer (a few hundred meters) on the earth's surface. Proportionately, on an ordinary 12-inch (30-centimeter) globe the thickness would be less than one fourth that of an ordinary sheet of paper!

2. Karst Surfaces

Another question some have posed for those who believe in a recent creation relates to the top of the Redwall Limestone that forms a prominent vertical cliff in the midregion of the layers of the canyon (just above the lowest arrow in Figure 2). In places the top surface of that limestone is irregular. Many geologists have interpreted it as an ancient "karst" surface that would normally require many years for erosion.[7] The term karst comes from the Karst region of the Adriatic coast where the limestone has been eroded into a characteristic irregular surface. Limestone quite easily dissolves, which is the reason we often find cavities (Figure 3) and even large caves in it. One of the ancient erosional channels found in the Redwall Limestone is 400 feet (122 meters) deep, and many smaller grooves and cavities exist near the top of the Redwall.[8] How could such irregularities form if the layers of the Grand Canyon had to be all laid down during a one-year flood, as suggested by the biblical model? We need to keep two things in mind: (1) a worldwide flood

Figure 3

An example of a cavity dissolved in limestone (Edwards Limestone) in central Texas. Note that the roof of the cavity, about a meter across, has not collapsed yet.

Figure 4

A collapsed area (collapsed breccia) at the top of the Redwall Limestone in the Grand Canyon. The light-colored rocks are from the Redwall Limestone, while the darker ones are from the overlying Watahomigi Formation. The larger block of Watahomigi in the middle of the figure is about 30 centimeters across. The presence of blocks of Watahomigi suggests that the Watahomigi was laid down before solution of the limestone and its collapse took place.

would have had plenty of high-energy water activity to cut a few channels in the top of the Redwall Limestone (a layer of sediment that may not even have been very hard then), and (2) it appears that some of the irregularities developed after the layers that rest over the limestone had already been laid down, hence they could have formed during the thousands of years after the flood. The evidence for this is that in places we find blocks from the layers above the limestone that have collapsed into the cavities dissolved out of the Redwall Limestone (Figure 4). If the cavities had formed before the layers above them, as assumed for a real karst surface, the cavities would have been first filled in with sediments, not with hard blocks of rock from the layers above (strata not yet formed). It appears that at least some cavities eroded after the layers above the Redwall Limestone had been laid down.[9] A traditional geologist has challenged the usual karst interpretation for a similar situation to the north of the Grand Canyon region, but at the same location in the geologic column.[10] He states: "In my opinion, the late Mississippian karst story in the Rocky Mountains is completely fallacious." This geologist believes that the so-called karst features developed much later. The interpretation of ancient karst surfaces is subject to reevaluation.

Questions About the Standard Long Age Interpretation of the Grand Canyon Rock Layers

It is frequently claimed that we do not find traces of a global deluge in the geologic record. In this section we review features of the geological column exposed in the Grand Canyon and in the surrounding regions with this question in mind. The following five lines of geological field evidence reveal conditions and states consistent with what we would expect in and or subsequent to an aquatic catastrophe of biblical proportions.

1. Widespread Sedimentary Layers

The layers of rock exposed by the canyon seem unusually widespread and horizontal (Figure 2). In some cases this widespread pattern involves more than meets the eye. For instance, on the basis of fossils and other characteristics, geologists commonly divide the Redwall Limestone, forming the single steep cliff mentioned above, into four units lying one above the other. Many of the other major rock units are subdivided into widespread subunits. More than a century ago Clarence Dutton, one of the leading pioneers of geology in the United States, studied the Grand Canyon district and commented that *"the strata of each and every age were remarkably uniform over very large areas, and were deposited very nearly horizontally. . . . Nowhere have we found thus far what may be called local deposits, or such as are restricted to a narrow belt or contracted area."* [11]

Some local deposits like those found at the top of the Redwall Limestone have been described since C. E. Dutton's original survey of the Grand Canyon area, but they are small. The overall pattern of widespread horizontal sedimentary units (Figures 1 and 2) seems to be more consistent with rapid widespread catastrophic flood deposition than slow deposition during hundreds of millions of years.

2. Cracks at the Top of the Hermit Shale Filled With Coconino Sandstone

The dark-colored formation called the Hermit Shale lies just below the light-colored Coconino Sandstone referred to above. The top arrow in Figure 2 indicates the contact between the two. Throughout the canyon region we find fine elongated vertical cracks in the Hermit Shale filled with sand grains from the Coconino (Figure 5). Some of the cracks are as much as 23 feet (7 meters) deep. We might wonder if the presence of such cracks in the Hermit Shale does not require that the Hermit Shale had first dried out before the deposition of the Coconino, thus posing a problem for a flood

Figure 5

Cracks in the dark Hermit Shale of the Grand Canyon filled in with sand from the lighter-colored overlying Coconino Sandstone seen in the top of the picture. Note that the white sandstone in the crack to the left has caused some discoloration of the surrounding rock. Only part of a filled crack can be seen toward the right. The cracks are more than a meter deep.

model. That is not necessarily the case, because cracks can form underwater in soft mud as a result of the cohesion of clays as the process of dewatering (removing the water from the clay) takes place. The presence of the cracks actually seems to pose a problem for the long geological ages model, especially since traditional geology assumes that a gap of several million years exists between the Hermit and the Coconino.[12] How could the cracks in the Hermit remain open for millions of years until the Coconino spread over it? Any rain or strong winds carrying sediments during that time would tend to fill them up. What we have here seems to fit well with rapid action. A possible scenario is that the Coconino covered the Hermit soon after its formation, then the shrinkage cracks formed because of dewatering of the Hermit, and the still-soft Coconino sediments oozed into the cracks as they developed.

3. The Scarcity of Erosion Where Significant Portions of the Geologic Column Are Missing

When we look at the flat-lying Phanerozoic layers of the Grand Canyon, we do not realize that according to the standard geologic interpretation major parts of the geologic column, representing millions of years, are missing between some of these layers. The way one knows that such layers are absent is that strata containing the appropriate fossils of the geologic column absent in the Grand Canyon occur elsewhere in the world. During those assumed gaps of millions of years when allegedly no deposition took place, we would expect erosion to create major valleys and canyons.[13] However, we do not find such expected erosional features in the layers at the time gaps in the Grand Canyon. No place on the surface of the earth exists where we would *not* expect either erosion or deposition during such long periods of time. If deposition did occur, then there would be no gap in the geologic column. But if deposition ceased, we would expect significant erosion over such long periods of time, and as a result the layers of the Grand Canyon should not appear so parallel to each other as they now appear.

The three arrows in Figure 2 point to significant gaps in the layers estimated (from top to bottom) at approximately 6, 14, and 100 million years. Notice that the underlying layers appear essentially free of erosion. The top arrow points to the gap between the Coconino and Hermit, discussed above (see also Figure 5). In referring to the gap at the middle arrow, a geologist comments: "Contrary to the implications of McKee's work, the locations of the boundary between the Manakacha and Wescogame formations [where the gap is] can be difficult to determine, both from a distance and from close range."[14] Referring to some localities of the very long lower gap, another geologist states: "Here, the unconformity [gap], even though representing more than 100 million years, may be difficult to locate."[15] Such quotations suggest that at some locations along the gaps there is no sharp contact demarcation between the lower and upper layers. Long periods of time would produce a lot of weathering and erosion of the rock layers, but that is not what we see.

In addition, these gaps, which represent absent layers according to traditional geology, present difficulties in light of conventional geological erosion rates. The canyon itself is an example of the dramatic effects of deep erosion. Average present rates of erosion for the region around the Grand Canyon would wash away a layered formation as deep as the canyon in less than 12 million years. According to the standard geologic time scale, then, both the canyon and the rock layers that form it should have vanished long ago.[16] While geologists disagree as to how the Grand Canyon itself eroded into existence, the geologist Lucchitta suggests that "most of the canyon cutting occurred in the phenomenally short time of 4 to 5 million years."[17] His claim raises the following question. If most of the huge canyon formed in just 4 or 5 million years, why do we not find similar massive erosional cuts in the hypothesized exposed underlying flat surfaces that would have been subject to erosion forces for more than 100 million years in those areas where a part of the geologic column is now missing? The discrepancy between the expected erosion during the postulated millions of years and what we actually see suggests that those millions of years never took place. The geological conditions recorded in the exposed rock layers of the Grand Canyon favor the rapid deposition that we would assume during the biblical flood.

4. The Lack of Food for Animals in the Coconino Sandstone

The lower half of the Coconino Sandstone contains hundreds of well-defined animal footprint trackways, probably made by amphibians or reptiles. The surprising thing is the lack of plant fossils. Aside from the footprints, the only other fossils that have been reported are those of a few worm tubes and invertebrate trackways.[18] If normal geological forces deposited the Coconino during millions of years, as the standard geologic interpretation assumes, what nourishment existed for the animals who made all these trackways? We have no evidence for the presence of plant food. If sedimentation preserved simple footprints, we would also expect to find the imprints or casts of roots, stems, and leaves of plants—if they were ever present. Other examples of incomplete ecological systems in the fossil record are known.[19]

Almost all of the trackways in the Coconino indicate that the animals were going uphill. Furthermore, good evidence indicates that the trackways formed underwater instead of the usual interpretation that they were made on desert dunes.[20] Is it possible that animals seeking to escape the waters of the flood formed all those trackways? The bodies of the animals themselves could have been swept away by flood activity. That may be why we don't find them. On the other hand, in the context of the standard interpretation of slow geologic processes, we would expect to have at least the imprints of the roots of the plants on which the animals had to feed, but they appear to be absent.

5. Megatrends in Paleozoic Paleocurrents Across North America

Art Chadwick has verified the stable southwesterly pattern of Paleozoic depositional paleocurrents across North America. Paleocurrents can tell us the direction of flow as sediments were being deposited by moving water. Concerning this point, he writes: "During the Paleozoic, in sharp contrast to Mesozoic, Cenozoic and Precambrian tendencies, clear and persistent continent-wide trends are normative. Sediments moved generally from east and northeast to west and southwest across the North American Continent. This trend persists throughout the Paleozoic and includes all sediment types and depositional environments."[21]

An important implication of this discovery is that the Paleozoic directional flow across North America challenges the traditional local basinal sedimentalign interpretation of geologists, where we would expect depositional flow in all directions. A general unidirectional paleocurrent depositional flow tended southwest all across North America throughout the Paleozoic Era. The Paleozoic paleocurrent data implies the presence at times of an aquatic flow in the Paleozoic Era in North America including the Grand Canyon region, equal to what might be described as an ocean. Such a phenomenon is consistent with what we would expect in a flood of the magnitude described in Genesis 6-9.

Taken together, these five lines of evidence indicate how the canyon and the surrounding areas reveal geological traces consistent with a global flood.

How Was the Grand Canyon Cut?

The question of the formation of the Grand Canyon turns out to be extremely complex. Although geologists have studied the matter intensely for more than a century, no simple answer or consensus seems in sight. The details of the discussions are beyond the scope of our brief survey, but are well summarized in the professional geologic literature.[22] The cutting of the canyon is an unsolved mystery sometimes referred to as the "canyon conundrum."[23]

Among the vexing problems that the canyon poses is the fact that the Colorado River, which courses through the canyon, cuts right through a broad dome instead of going around it. We would not expect that a river would go up over a dome instead of skirting it. A related problem is the question of the past location and age of the river. Was it present before the dome formed? Evidence for an ancient Colorado River is notoriously sparse, especially for the region west of the canyon. Some have suggested that in the past on the east side of the dome the river came from the northwest to the edge of the dome and then went to the southeast toward the Gulf of Mexico without ever traversing through the dome itself. Others have postulated that the dome eventually eroded from the west to join the Colorado River from the east, but without much of a source of water to cut a deep gorge through the dome this seems unlikely. Some geologists have hypothesized that on the west side the river may have left the canyon region, going to the northwest before eventually changing its course and heading toward the southwest where we now find it. Also puzzling are the huge side canyons found especially on the north side of the canyon (Figure 2, far side). Such side canyons, ending up in the high region of the dome, have virtually no streams to erode them.

The canyon itself is huge. Erosion had to remove some 950 cubic miles (4,000 cubic kilometers) of sediment to produce it. Yet even that is but a fraction of the erosion evident in the surrounding region, for the layers mentioned earlier that must have been above those now exposed in the canyon.[24] The erosion of these now absent layers forms a broad valley more than 125 miles (200 kilometers) wide that lies above the canyon. It probably took the removal of 15 to 30 times as much sediment to form the broad valley above the canyon as was involved in the carving of the canyon itself. Dutton[25] called the erosion of this broad valley "the great denudation." According to standard geologic interpretations, the great denudation would have been a slow process of broadening of the valley over time as the valley walls retreated laterally during the slow erosion. But this does not seem to be the case. The sides of the broad valley do not have active talus (debris) at the base of the cliffs, as we would expect from such a slow process. The sides of the broad valley are clean as though the valley had been catastrophically washed out. Clean edges are more like what one would assume from the runoff of the waters of the flood than from a gradual weathering process.

What forces excavated the canyon? Although we don't know for sure, we do know that the standard slow model poses a number of questions. It is also of interest that the lore of local Indian tribes reflects more rapid erosional action. One writer, in referring to it, comments that "the Navajo, the Hualapai and the Havasupai still believe that the river is the runoff from a great flood that once covered the earth."[26] Some scientists who believe in the biblical account of beginnings also suggest that the carving of the canyon and the surrounding region is the result of the runoff of the waters of the worldwide biblical flood. They have suggested two biblically based models. One model[27] proposes that at the end of the flood a lot of water had become ponded to the east of the Grand Canyon region. It eventually breached a natural dam on the west side of the trapped water and a great volume of water flowed to the west, cutting the canyon.

A second model proposes that the erosion cut the canyon while the region was still under water, that is below the surface of the floodwaters, as they retreated to the west. The second model might explain the origin of the many side canyons. Underwater erosion in the ocean is a common phenomenon. Many underwater canyons exist along the edge of our continental shelves. A submarine canyon, the Monterey Canyon, located off the coast of California, is as deep and as wide as the Grand Canyon. We may not know exactly how the Grand Canyon was carved, but the action of the receding waters of the biblical flood presents some strong possibilities.

Conclusions

The Grand Canyon has much to say about the past history of life on earth. People have interpreted this fascinating exposure of eroded rocks in a variety of ways. The standard view, accepted by most scientists, proposes that its formation involved many millions of years. However, a number of questions arise when we consider specific details. On the other hand, the biblical model implying rapid formation of the rock layers and of the probable underwater excavation of the canyon answers some of the questions posed by the standard model. While the Grand Canyon still hides many mysteries, and we still have much to learn about it, it also provides evidence that supports the truthfulness of the biblical account of the worldwide flood.

These encouraging conclusions have important connections with other chapters in this volume. With a global flood producing the major portions of the geologic column subsequent to the creation week, the Bible student may confidently believe the historicity of the six-day creation week and the origin of the human race by a loving personal Creator. Thus an important connection exists between, for example, the research by Hasel and Younker regarding the six-day creation, the relationship between Genesis 1 and 2, respectively, and flood research. We cannot regard the former to be literally true apart from the historical reality of a global flood. This illustrates the crucial connection between the flood and the truthfulness of the six-day creation week.

---

[1] D. N. Wadia, *Geology of India,* 4th ed. (New Delhi: Tata McGraw-Hill, 1975), p. 27.

[2] Three useful summaries are S. S. Beus and G. H. Billingsley, "Paleozoic Strata of the Grand Canyon, Arizona," in D. P. Elston, G. H. Billingsley, and R. A. Young, eds., *Geology of Grand Canyon, Northern Arizona (With Colorado River Guides)* (Washington, D.C.: American Geophysical Union, 1989), pp. 122-235; S. S. Beus and M. Morales, eds., *Grand Canyon Geology* (Flagstaff, Ariz.: Museum of Northern Arizona Press, 1990), pp. 83-245; T. D. Ford, "The Grand Canyon of the Colorado," *Geology Today,* Mar.-Apr. 1994, pp. 57-62.

[3] E. G. Kennedy, R. Kablanow, and A. V. Chadwick, "A Reassessment of the Shallow Water Depositional Model for the Tapeats Sandstone, Grand Canyon, Arizona: Evidence for Deep Water Deposition," *Geological Society of America Abstracts With Programs* 28, No. 7 (1996): A-407; E. D. McKee and C. E. Resser, *Cambrian History of the Grand Canyon Region* (Carnegie Institution of Washington Publication, 1945), p. 563.

[4] L. R. Brand, "Footprints in the Grand Canyon," *Origins* 5 (1978): 64-82; L. R. Brand and T. Tang, "Fossil Vertebrate Footprints in the Coconino Sandstone (Permian) of Northern Arizona: Evidence for Underwater Origin," *Geology* 19 (1991): 1201-1204.

[5] A. A. Roth, "Implications of Various Interpretations of the Fossil Record," *Origins* 7 (1980): 71-86; "How to Invalidate the Bible-unconsciously: Some Thoughts on Pluralism About Origins," *Adventist Perspectives* 2, No. 2 (1988): 122-127.

[6] R. M. Davidson, "Biblical Evidence for the Universality of the Genesis Flood," *Origins* 22: (1995): 58-73.

[7] See J. N. Jennings, "Karst Landforms," *American Scientist* 71 (1983): 578-586.

[8] See G. H. Billingsley and E. D. McKee, "The Supai Group of Grand Canyon: Pre-Supai Buried Valleys," in E. D. McKee, ed., *The Supai Group of Grand Canyon, U.S. Geological Survey Professional Paper* 1173 (1982): 137-147; G. H. Billingsley and S. S. Beus, "The Surprise Canyon Formation—An Upper Mississippian and Lower Pennsylvanian Rock Unit in the Grand Canyon, Arizona," *U.S. Geological Survey Bulletin* 1605-A (1985): A27-A33; S. S. Beus, "A Geologic Surprise in the Grand Canyon," *Arizona Bureau of Geology and Mineral Technology Footnotes* 16, No. 3 (1986).

[9] See also N. Eberz, "Redwall Limestone Karst and Colorado River Evolution During Late Tertiary, Grand Canyon National Park, Arizona," *Geological Society of America Abstracts With Programs* 27, No. 6 (1995): A-211.

[10] L.W.D. Bridges, "Rocky Mountain Laramide-Tertiary Subsurface Solution Versus Paleozoic Karst in Mississippian Carbonates," *Wyoming Geological Association Guidebook* (1982): 251-264.

[11] C. E. Dutton, "Tertiary History of the Grand Cañon District," *U.S. Geological Survey Monograph* 2 (1882).

[12] R. C. Blakey, "Supai Group and Hermit Formation," in S. S. Beus and M. Morales, eds., *Grand Canyon Geology* (Flagstaff, Ariz.: Museum of Northern Arizona Press, 1990), pp. 147-182; R. C. Blakey, "Stratigraphy and Geologic History of Pennsylvanian and Permian Rocks, Mogollon Rim Region, Central Arizona and Vicinity," *Geological Society of America Bulletin* 102 (1990): 1189-1217. Figure 1 in "Supai Group" and Figures 4 and 16 in "Stratigraphy" would suggest about 6 million years.

[13] A. A. Roth, *Origins: Linking Science and Scripture* (Hagerstown, Md.: Review and Herald, 1998), pp. 222-229.

[14] Beus and Morales, p. 158.

[15] *Ibid.*, p. 111.

[16] A. A. Roth, "Some Questions About Geochronology," *Origins* 13 (1986): 59, 64-85.

[17] I. Lucchitta, "Development of Landscape in Northwest Arizona: The Country of Plateaus and Canyons," in T. L. Smiley, J. D. Nations, T. L. Péwé, and J. P. Schafer, eds., *Landscapes of Arizona: The Geological Story* (Lanham, Md.: University Press of America, 1984), pp. 269-301.

[18] L. T. Middleton, D. K. Elliott, and M. Morales, "Coconino Sandstone," in Beus and Morales, pp. 183-202; E. Spamer, "Paleontology in the Grand Canyon of Arizona: 125 Years of Lessons and Enigmas From the Late Precambrian to the Present," *The Mosasaur* 2 (1984): 45-128.

[19] A. A. Roth, "Incomplete Ecosystems," *Origins* 21 (1994): 51-56, A. A. Roth (1998): 219-222.

[20] Brand; Brand and Tang.

[21] Arthur V. Chadwick, "Megatrends in North American Paleocurrents," *Society of Economic Paleontologists: Symposium on Paleogeography and Paleoclimatology: Meeting Abstracts* 8 (1993): 58.

[22] Beus and Morales; D. L. Babenroth and A. N. Strahler, "Geomorphology and Structure of the East Kaibab Monocline, Arizona and Utah," *Geological Society of America Bulletin* 56 (1945): 107-150; C. S. Breed, "A Century of Conjecture on the Colorado River in Grand Canyon," *Four Corners Geological Society Guidebook* (1969), pp. 63-68; D. P. Elston and R. A. Young, "Development of Cenozoic Landscape of Central and Northern Arizona: Cutting of Grand Canyon," in D. P. Elston, G. J. Billingsley, and R. A. Young, eds., *Geology of Grand Canyon, Northern Arizona (With Colorado River Guides)* (Washington, D.C.: American Geophysical Union, 1989), pp. 145-165; W. L. Graf, R. Hereford, J. Laity, and R. A. Young, "Colorado Plateau," in W. L. Graf, ed., *Geomorphic Systems of North America* (Geological Society of America Centennial Special), vol. 2 (1987), pp. 259-302; C. B. Hunt, "Grand Canyon and the Colorado River, Their Geologic History," in W. J. Breed and E. Roat, eds., *Geology of the Grand Canyon,* 2nd ed. (Flagstaff, Ariz.: Museum of Northern Arizona Press, 1976), pp. 129-141; C. R. Longwell, "How Old Is the Colorado River?" *American Journal of Science* 244 (1946): 817-835; I. Lucchitta, "History of the Grand Canyon and of the Colorado River in Arizona," in Beus and Morales (1990), pp. 311-332; Lucchitta, "Development of Landscape in Northwest Arizona: The Country of Plateaus and Canyons"; I. Lucchitta, "Early History of the Colorado River in the Basin and Range Province," *Geologic Society of American Bulletin* 83 (1972): 1933-1948; R. J. Rice, "The Canyon Conundrum," *The Geographical Magazine* 55 (1983): 288-292.

[23] Rice.

[24] T. A. Dumitru, I. R. Duddy, and P. F. Green, "Mesozoic-Cenozoic Burial, Uplift, and Erosion History of the West-Central Colorado Plateau," *Geology* 22 (1994): 499-502.

[25] Dutton, pp. 61-77.

[26] R. Wallace, *The Grand Canyon, the American Wilderness Series* (Alexandria, Va.: Time-Life Books, 1973), p. 99.

[27] S. A. Austin, ed., *Grand Canyon: Monument to Catastrophe* (Santee, Calif.: Institute for Creation Research, 1994), pp. 92-107.

CHAPTER 6

THE GEOLOGIC COLUMN AND CALVARY: THE RAINBOW CONNECTION—IMPLICATIONS FOR AN EVANGELICAL UNDERSTANDING OF THE ATONEMENT

John T. Baldwin
Seventh-day Adventist Theological Seminary
Andrews University

T he notion of [the] traditional view of redemption as reconciliation and ransom from the consequences of Adam's fall is nonsense for anyone who knows about the evolutionary background to human existence in the modern world."[1]

"The penalty of man's transgression was borne by a divine Substitute. . . . The death of Christ on the cross of Calvary is our only hope in this world, and it will be our theme in the world to come."[2]

What do stacked fossiliferous sedimentary layers have to do with the shed blood of Christ? Nothing?[3] Everything? Some *tertium quid?* Can such apparently disparate topics possibly have any relationship? Or as Schleiermacher implies in his famous 1829 pact with science,[4] should the theologian let the rocks do their thing and let Christ do His own work? Must the Christian scholar relinquish all attempts to harmonize geology and theology because Athens and Jerusalem cannot speak to one another in this instance? If aspects of how we account for basic portions of the construction of the fossil-bearing portion of the geologic column actually impinge on a central point of theology, can the Christian investigator simply ignore the difficulty?

The problem this chapter addresses is the question whether the geologic column, as science usually interprets it, has any relevance to the causal connection between sin and death, the basic precondition of any substitutionary theory of the atonement. Regarding the latter notion Nigel M. de S. Cameron writes: "It is a fundamental presupposition of our evangelical understanding of the atonement, such that if the sin–death causality be undermined, the efficacy and indeed the rationale of blood atonement is destroyed."[5]

Cameron's statement implies that if for some reason the geologic column shows that death is not in some way causally related to sin as being the wage of sin, it nullifies Jesus' death. His death is then no longer the wage of sin, and hence carries no atoning value.

This chapter addresses four aspects of the question. First, it summarizes the historical background and relevant aspects of the conventional scientific interpretation of the geological column. Second, it notes selected responses of early Christian geologists and leading contemporary Christian theologians to the geologic column. Third, it briefly considers relevant portions of Romans 5 and 8 concerning the origin of death in view of the most recent biblical scholarship. Finally, it describes and evaluates the interconnections between the forming of the geologic column and the forgiving power of the blood of Christ, noting recent responses by Christian theologians and geologists to the conventional scientific view.

The Conventional Scientific Interpretation of the Geologic Column

Christianity continues to stagger as a consequence of the publication of three older but formative books: James Hutton's *Theory of the Earth* (1795), Charles Darwin's *Origin of Species* (1859), and *Essays and Reviews* (1860).[6] The convergence of these three epoch-making volumes unsettled faith in the literal interpretation of the Genesis account of the creation and the flood narratives in the minds of many Christian theologians and geologists. Hutton introduced into geology the concept later known as "deep time," which, as Stephen Jay Gould aptly declares, is the "notion of an almost incomprehensible immensity [of time], with human habitation restricted to a millimicrosecond at the very end!"[7] Darwin posited a naturalistic method by which new and different species originate apart from the creative acts of God. In *Essays and Reviews* leading theologians and biblical scholars reinterpreted the Genesis creation and flood narratives, for example, as poetry and not as historically factual narratives. They did so to accommodate the biblical materials to the revolutionary cosmological claims made by Hutton, Darwin, and others. Does the doctrine of the atonement remain unaffected by such major theological accommodations to contemporary geological and evolutionary theory? We turn now to a consideration of the deposition of the geologic column itself.

Today few, whether special creation scientists, theistic evolutionists, progressive creationists, or conventional geologists, seriously question the reality of the geologic column.[8] All concur that the continents consist largely of crustal material composed of fossil-laden sedimentary layers stacked in a pre-dictable order. Simpler life-forms are found at the bottom of the column, and the more complex life-forms continue to appear higher in the column, with the remains of homo sapiens only at the top of the column (see Figure 1).[9] However, special creation offers scientists and theistic evolutionists funda-mentally differing explanations of how the geologic column formed and con-trasting views regarding the ages of the various layers of sedimentary rock.

Reflecting conventional geological consensus, Gould states that the geo-logic column began to grow on our 4.5 billion-year-old planet about 3.75 billion years ago, as reflected in the oldest sedimentary rocks represented by the Isua series of western Greenland.[10] The important point to notice is that the geologic column supposedly developed in increments over deep time and not all at once, albeit with local catastrophic jerkiness. Thus the bottom lay-ers of the column were once the only layers existing. Nothing rested above them. These bottom layers, therefore, lay exposed to weathering processes for millions of years. In time new sediments became deposited upon the bottom layers. The more recently deposited layers, in turn, lay at the surface for mil-lions of years until additional layers covered them. The entire process pro-ceeded for 3.75 billion years until we have the present geologic column. The strata are revealed most strikingly in the side exposures of the Grand Canyon in Arizona. Some fossilization occurred throughout the 3.75 billion-year ac-cumulation, but most took place only during the past 570 million years, com-mencing with the Cambrian explosion of life-forms.

What implication does this reading of how the geologic column devel-oped have for the Christian gospel? The most important biological puzzle of the column impinging upon atonement theology is the presence of death for seeming millions of years prior to the first human sin. The remains of both an-cient and recent animal forms litter the geologic column. In addition to the normal causes of death, we see in the geologic column perhaps seven distinct universal events of mass extinction.[11] The most famous of the mass extinctions was the demise of the dinosaurs, which, according to conventional geology, occurred about 65 million years ago at the boundary between the Cretaceous and the Tertiary, now known as the famous KT boundary (see Figure 1).

However, the largest mass extinction event appears lower in the column at the boundary between the Permian and Triassic, a period geologists date about 240 million years ago. University of Chicago geologist and paleontol-ogist David M. Raup estimates the marine species loss in this one profound mass destruction event at 96 percent.[12] Scientists interpret such events as vital to any evolutionary process. Without death and the mixing of the gene pool through sexual reproduction, nothing would change in nature. Thus the life-and-death cycle is necessary to the success of the biological kingdom. The countless fossils in the column seem to suggest that death has been an actuality for millions of years before the first human sin, thus appearing to undermine any causal link between sin and death. The theological implication of the conventional scientific interpretation of the geologic column is a central concern of this essay.

Selected Responses of Early Christian Geologists and Theologians to the Geologic Column

Some early Christian geologists quickly addressed the issue of how to account for death in the geologic column before the appearance of human beings. However, as Rodney Lee Stiling observes in his recent dissertation, "The Diminishing Deluge: Noah's Flood in Nineteenth-Century American Thought," the "surprising feature of the discussion of the apparent presence of death on the earth before the appearance of humans was the relative silence of theological writers on the subject."[13] Christian geologists struggled with the issue largely by themselves. For example, writing in 1840 about death before the fall, American geologist Edward Hitchcock states: "The general interpretation of the Bible has been, that until the fall of man, death did not exist in the world even among the inferior animals. For the Bible asserts that *by man came death (1 Cor. 15:21) and by one man sin entered into the world and death by sin (Rom. 5:12).* But geology teaches us that myriads of animals lived and died before the creation of man."[14]

Hitchcock harmonizes the creation narrative with geology by endorsing both the gap theory of Genesis 1:2, 3 and the day-age interpretation of the six days of creation, and by interpreting Romans 5 to mean that human sin only introduced human death and not death into the animal kingdom generally.[15] Contemporary mainline theologians have taken Hitchcock's accommodation a step further as we will note later.

Perhaps one of the most influential voices articulating the theological implications of the geologic column is John Hick, who states in his classic treatment of theodicy, entitled *Evil and the God of Love,*[16] that "until comparatively recent times the ancient myth of the origin of evil in the fall of man was quite reasonably assumed to be history."[17] Hick goes on to claim that the historicity of the fall is now utterly unacceptable because it is "open to insuperable scientific . . . objections."[18] What are the fatal objections? "We know today that the conditions that were to cause human . . . mortality [death] . . . were already part of the natural order prior to the emergence of man and prior

111

therefore to any first human sin."[19] This means that human sin, in Hick's view, did not in any sense cause or originate animal death.

In his book entitled *Credo* (1993) Hans Küng implies that the idea of an original sin is now meaningless, because "there never was this human couple who sinned for all humankind."[20] Driving the point home, Küng quotes with approval Karl Schmitz-Moormann: "The notion of [the] traditional view of redemption as reconciliation and ransom from the consequences of Adam's fall is nonsense for anyone who knows about the evolutionary background to human existence in the modern world."[21]

How then should the contemporary Christian characterize redemption? Schmitz-Moormann answers that salvation "cannot mean returning to an original state, but must be conceived as perfecting through the process of evolution."[22] Clearly, the traditional understanding of the shed blood of Christ as the atoning wage (death) for sin gets overturned in this contemporary theological perspective that accepts the conventional method of the formation of the geologic column (see Figure 2). The resultant deconstruction of the traditional understanding of the atonement is clearly the result of rendering death before the fall of Adam a nonissue. However, for theologians who continue to accept the historicity of Genesis 1–11, the problem of death before sin in the geologic column has serious theological implications, hence, the need to reinvestigate not only Paul's teaching on the origin of death but also the method by which the geologic column formed. We turn now to a brief consideration of the most recent biblical scholarship concerning Paul's position on the origin of death (Rom. 5:12; 8:21-23) as found in the writings of Joseph A. Fitzmyer and Norbert F. Lohfink.

Recent New Testament Scholarship Concerning the Origin of the Death of Humans and Animals as Outlined in Romans 5 and 8

Romans 5:12 states that "just as through one man sin entered the world, and death through sin, and thus death spread to all men" (NKJV). Is Paul teaching that Adam's sin brought only human death? Or does Paul mean death in a universal, unqualified sense, the death of all living organisms, including that of subhuman creatures, thus establishing the causal connection between all forms of death and the first human sin? In his 1993 commentary on Romans in the *Anchor Bible* Series Fitzmyer implies that Paul's comments in Romans 8:20-23 resolve the potential ambiguity in Romans 5:12.

The relevant phrases in Romans 8:20 read as follows: "For the creation [*ktisis*] was subjected to futility, not of its own will but by the will of him [God] who subjected it in hope" (RSV). According to the next verse, the biblical phrase "subjected to futility" means that the creation came under, in the words of the Bible, "slavery to corruption," implying disease and death. Fitzmyer concludes that the term creation (*ktisis*) in this context must mean all creation distinct from humanity.[23] Thus according to Fitzmyer, such a conclusion carries the following significance: "Subhuman material creation, as it proceeded from the hand of the Creator God, was not marked with the frustration and futility of which Paul speaks. Its present situation stems not from its own natural inclination or purpose."[24]

Such an interpretation suggests that Paul clearly intends to teach that the subhuman creation became subject to disease and death through Adam's sin. This implies that in Romans 5:12 he is teaching that death of any kind is a consequence of Adam's sin. Therefore, when Paul states in Romans in an unqualified sense that sin entered the world because of one man's sin, he intends us to understand death in a universal sense, including its human, subhuman, physical, and spiritual dimensions, and that all death first entered the world by means of human sin.[25]

Lohfink also links the introduction of human death to human sin. After presenting an exegesis of the fall narrative, he concludes that the text in its original setting actually intends to teach that physical death is "not involved in [human] existence, but comes from [human] freedom."[26] Together, the exegesis of both New Testament scholars implies that if the fossils in the geologic column lived and died for millions of years before the appearance of Adam and his sin, the geologic column destroys the causal relation between sin and human death as well.

The Interconnections Between the Geologic Column and Calvary

If we accept the conventional interpretation of the geologic column, we would have to conclude that animal death and Adam's sin have no causal connection in any sense, a position that clearly contradicts the teaching of Genesis 1–3 if we interpret the passage as a reliable account of historical events. Above all, it calls into question the historicity of the biblical claim of the relationship between Adam's sin and human death by undermining the historicity of the fall itself. In other words, if geology shows that the biblical claim of the causal relationship between Adam's sin and the death of animals is false, we could ask on what grounds would the biblical claim about the historicity of the causal connection between Adam's sin and his death as outlined in the fall narrative be true? The relationship between Adam's sin and all forms of death simply cannot be broken. To sever the connection between subhuman creatures and Adam's sin also destroys the relationship between human sin and human death.

113

Because the conventional interpretation of the geologic column does, in fact, deny any causal relationship between animal death and human sin, it thereby calls into questions the causal connection between human sin and human death, thus undermining the atoning or sin-forgiving power of Jesus' death. His death can then no longer constitute the wage of sin (see Figure 2). This means that the interpretation of the construction of stacked layers of sedimentary rock can potentially undermine the gospel. Surprisingly, only a few evangelical Christian theologians have voiced this implication, but their comments are powerful.

Recent Responses by Some Evangelical Theologians to the Implications of Death in the Geologic Column

In an article entitled "Theological Problems With Theistic Evolution," David H. Lane writes: "If the general theory of evolution and a historical fall of some kind are both historical facts . . . then human death preceded the entrance of sin into the human race, and cannot be its penalty."[27] He, among other thinkers,[28] identifies the ramifications of such a conclusion as follows: "Theistic evolution denies the doctrine of sin as the cause for physical death, which has its basis in the historical truth of the fall. It thereby destroys the basis of the doctrines of Christ's substitutionary atonement and redemption of sinners."[29]

Cameron, who has also explored the problem, argues that were Adam from the beginning under the effects of the curse of physical death as implied in evolutionary theory and in theistic evolution, "this overthrows the sin-death causality, and in so doing pulls the rug from under the feet of the evangelical understanding of the atonement."[30]

Marco Terreros has the distinction of being the first individual to write a Ph.D. dissertation dealing precisely with this topic. His work, entitled "Death Before the Sin of Adam: A Fundamental Concept in Theistic Evolution and Its Implications for Evangelical Theology," thoroughly investigates the problem. He shows that thinkers throughout the intertestamental and Christian eras have pondered the origin of death. Leading evangelical scholars in North America are still wrestling with it. After examining the biblical data and critically analyzing major scholarly affirmations of animal death prior to the fall, Terreros concludes that such a concept undermines evangelical atonement theory, because, as he observes: "The origin of animal death as well as human death is linked exclusively to human sin, which means that human and animal death cannot be separated as consequences of sin. Thus, evangelical scholars who accept animal death as occurring before the sin of our first parents necessarily nullify, from a biblical point of view, the causal link between death and human sin required in historic atonement theology."[31]

Terreros implies here that even the concept of progressive creation, in which God intermittently (during a period of 570 million years) creates creatures who die and then creates Adam without being subject to death until his fall, lacks biblical support and consequently cannot safeguard the atonement.

The work of such scholars shows that the conventional understanding of the geologic column has fatal implications for the gospel. As a result, how we understand the biblical account of the flood can be vital to our theology.

The Geoloaic Column, God's Global Flood, and Calvary

The global deluge geologically establishes the needed causal connection between human sin and all death by burying animals into the geologic column subsequent to Adam's sin, thus confirming the truth of the biblical claim that all death is the wage of sin. In this fashion God's global flood corroborates the fact that the death of Jesus constitutes the wage of sin, one that He bore salvifically for human beings. Considered in this light, the forgiveness of human sin seems to depend in part upon the historicity and universality of the flood. The biblical deluge is thus a crucially important historical event. That is why flood geology remains so important to conservative interpreters of Scripture. On the negative side, this means, theoretically, that if geology could absolutely disprove a global flood, geology would also undermine the atoning power of Calvary. This would mean that without such a global flood human beings would appear to be yet in their sins and without hope (see Figure 2). Too often we have swept the serious theological implications of evolutionary geology under the rug. Instead, we must address them openly and with integrity. Other chapters in this book written by Richard Davidson,[32] Ariel Roth,[33] Randall Younker,[34] and Gerhard Hasel[35] interweave to indicate convincingly that just such a literal, historical interpretation of the biblical creation and flood narratives remains the proper method of interpreting such texts in a post-Darwinian age.

However, in view of the fact that few mainline Christian theologians and Christian geologists[36] have entertained a global flood model after the eighteenth century,[37] the pressing question arises: In a post-Darwinian/postmodern age, and in view of the claims of conventional geology that seriously question the geological existence of a so-called Noachian flood,[38] is a serious reconsideration of a literal, historical, single, global flood a sacrifice of the intellect? In other words, how can the Christian theologian and believing geologist ethically spend time defending biblical claims if science has already falsified these positions? On the one hand, the Christian investigator cannot defend irrationality and remain faithful to a responsible search for truth. But on the other hand, the Christian should embrace scientific information. Thus the urgent need is to reinvestigate faithfully and objectively both the current discoveries and claims of science and the Scriptures. Only then can we discover whether there may, after all, be some fit between the scientific evidence and the traditional understanding of the global flood and the atonement. We must go on exploring. Moreover, in the ongoing scholarly discussion of this and related sensitive issues, all participants in the dialogue need to exercise genuine respect, love, and courtesy to one another, and to demonstrate an openness to new ideas lest we deny both His name and the spirit of true scientific enquiry.

The following material is not intended in any fashion to settle the geological issues and to answer all the questions. It does provide a brief sampling of some of the current field research in progress that touch upon the theme of this chapter, and reminds us that we need to do much more research.

Contemporary Conventional Geological Theory Is Considering Scenarios of Limited Catastrophes

While contemporary geology does not subscribe to a "Noachian" flood model, field evidence has led significant aspects of the cutting edge of geological thinking forcefully away from geologic uniformitarianism[39] and toward various forms of regional catastrophism. We see this illustrated by the title of Darek Ager's 1993 work on geology called *The New Catastrophism: The Importance of the Rare Event in Geological History*.[40] Another example comes from the work of Rhodes Fairbridge, former professor of geology at Columbia University. He finds that one such regional catastrophe best explains the formation of the Silurian shale beds in the central Sahara. Fairbridge notes that these fossil-rich beds rest directly on glacial formations and exist without any sandy layers incorporated into the shale beds, showing that no slow-moving, sand-mixing, and encroaching sea deposited the shale beds. According to him, such facts prove that the transgressing Silurian sea "must have 'drowned' most of North Africa in one tremendous inundation," which, he observes, must have "involved a sudden rise of sea-level of at least 300 meters, possibly as much as 500 meters. . . . Thus some catastrophic event is called for."[41]

While it has not yet been tested, Fairbridge finds himself "attracted by the idea that the ice's eccentric loading of the Earth's crust and its subsequent redistribution as water caused a sudden change in the polar axis [say of 1 percent], which would lead to readjustment in the actual shape of the globe . . .

[causing] an instantaneous rise of sea level . . . by 373 meters which would be just about right for explaining the great postglacial inundation."[42]

Such examples do not prove the biblical flood, but illustrate a new direction in conventional geological theory pointing toward regional catastrophe.

Recent Geological Research of Special Interest

Two field research studies, among others currently in progress, have important possible implications for the topic of this chapter. The first study deals with the Tapeats Sandstone of the Grand Canyon and the second addresses the issue of paleocurrents in the Paleozoic portion of the geologic column of North America.

Reassessment of the Grand Canyon Tapeats Sandstone Depositional Environment

Traditionally, geologists have interpreted the Tapeats Sandstone in the lower middle Cambrian (Paleozoic Era) of the Grand Canyon as having been deposited in a near-shore shallow marine system. However, recent field research based upon a number of criteria suggests that the Tapeats may have formed in water as deep as 840 feet (about 260 meters).[43] Submarine slumps (debris flows) of angular rocks (breccia) underlying the Tapeats Sandstone blanket the slopes of the Precambrian deposits. Trace element studies on the matrix of the breccia flows suggest a low oxygen content in the water at the time of the breccia's deposition. Low oxygen conditions are unlikely in water shallower than effective storm wave base, so the data suggests a minimal depth of 260 feet (approximately 80 meters) at the top of the breccia flows. However, the blanketed slopes exhibit a change in elevation (relief) downward (measured) of 500 feet (about 180 meters), thus increasing the total aquatic depth associated with the lowest breccia deposits to a minimum of about 840 feet. Moreover, the fact that the breccia remains intact means that there is no evidence of erosion or reworking of the breccia during the deposition of the Tapeats Sandstone upon the breccia. Such preservation of the breccia suggests rapid deposition of these sands in a deep-water environment in the region of the Grand Canyon.

The deep-water depositional environment of the Tapeats Sandstone becomes additionally interesting in the light of recent field studies confirming a continent-wide largely unidirectional depositional flow of the Paleozoic sediments across North America.

North American Paleozoic Sediments Moved
Generally Southwest Throughout the Paleozoic

In the 1993 *Society of Economic Paleontologists and Mineralogists Meeting*

Abstracts, Arthur Chadwick describes current research regarding the pale-ocurrents in the Paleozoic portion of the geologic column of North America as follows: "We have verified the stable southwesterly pattern of paleocur-rents across the craton documented by others and have chronicled its persist-ence with some variation throughout the Paleozoic. . . . These patterns and transitions must accompany major changes in global current trends."[44] Expanding upon his research Chadwick states that "during the Paleozoic, in sharp contrast to Mesozoic, Cenozoic, and Precambrian tendencies, clear and persistent continent-wide trends are normative. Sediments moved generally from east and northeast to west and southwest across the North American Continent. This trend persists throughout the Paleozoic and includes all sed-iment types and depositional environments."[45] These discoveries invite fresh evaluation of the conventional basinal interpretation of paleocurrent patterns in the Paleozoic portion of the North American geologic column. A few re-flections appear in the following discussion section.

Discussion

What tentative, preliminary interpretations might one reasonably draw from these geologic data indicated above? First, interpreted conventionally, the paleocurrent data of the paleozoic portion of the column that Chadwick is studying would seem to require that a series of unrelated mega depositional flow events accidentally moved in the same southwesterly direction for a pe-riod of about 300 million years. However, traditional geology expects ran-dom, multidirectional basinal current flows rather than some unidirectional flow pattern during this period of time.[46]

Second, because the data show a unidirectional flow pattern, it seems to call for a new explanation not presently found in the conventional geologic paradigm. Allowing the scientific data to lead and to speak for themselves, it appears to this writer that the data regarding the deep water depositional en-vironment of the Tapeats Sandstone in conjunction with the confirmation of the unidirectional southwesterly movement of the paleozoic sediments throughout the Paleozoic era in North America seem to point naturally and compellingly to an occurrence of some unified, overarching group of related, unidirectional deep-water depositional events responsible for rapidly deposit-ing a formation now called the Tapeats Sandstone and for perhaps depositing some strata of the wider North American paleozoic portion of the geologic column. Does the unidirectional deep-water depositional event associated with the decreating of the Tapeats Sandstone properly suggest the image of some moving sea? While, of course, not proving a biblical flood, the recently discovered geologic data appear to be at least consistent with what one might expect in a global aquatic event. Significantly, the field data are consistent, in the sense just suggested, on a scale of magnitude heretofore unknown. In this instance, the geological data suggesting aquatic catastrophe may now be pointing perhaps for the first time beyond regional, basinal boundaries to continent-wide dimensions.

Because the field geological research projects noted above, and others, are discovering data that seem in many ways to be consistent with what might be expected in an aquatic event on the scale suggested by an historical interpretation of Genesis 6-9, the studies may also lend a degree of possible geological affirmation of the sin-death causality by supporting—in the sense indicated above—the actuality of an event able to generate major portions of the fossiliferous geologic column subsequent to the fall (see figure 3). Assuming this to be the case, perhaps the most important underlying implication of these field studies is that they support the notion that the shed blood of Christ continues to possess atoning, sin-forgiving power. This suggests the importance which aspects of such field studies can carry in relation to theology. It also indicates the theological reason why a local flood concept undermines the atonement. As noted before, a flood of limited geographical area is unable to produce the existing global geologic column. However, as suggested, an event able to produce the basic fossiliferous portion of the global geologic column after the fall is needed in order to maintain the integrity of the sin-death causal connection. We conclude this chapter by reflecting upon a striking biblical image representing God's global flood and its connection to Calvary.

The Rainbow and God's Promise

Standing on the Kaibab layer and looking northward across the wide abyss of the Grand Canyon, one can see more stacked sedimentary layers of the geologic column in this single exposed sequence than are visible anywhere else on earth. The visitor fortunate enough to stand at the rim of the Grand Canyon after a rainstorm and under the right atmospheric conditions will see a rainbow against an ominous dark sky, arching in brilliant colors over the layers of the geologic column revealed in the walls of the Grand Canyon. The sight can bring to mind the following words from the book of Genesis:

"'And I establish My covenant with you; and all flesh shall never again be cut off by the water of the flood, neither shall there again be a flood to destroy the earth.' And God said, 'This is the sign of the covenant which I am making between Me and you and every living creature that is with you, for all successive generations. I set My bow in the cloud, and it shall be for a sign of a covenant between Me and the earth. . . . When the bow is in the cloud, then I will look upon it, to remember the everlasting covenant between God and every living creature of all flesh that is on the earth'"(Gen. 9:11-16, NASB).

The beautiful natural phenomena arching over the Grand Canyon has become beautiful truth in the sky, a "sign" of God's global, geologic column-producing flood, and His covenant. Moreover, the text tells us that God looks at the rainbow sign and does not forget what it now means. What about us—have we forgotten? Do we wince at its biblical message in this post-Darwinian age?

The Rainbow and the Geologic Column

The relevant message of the rainbow for the geologist today is that major portions of the geologic column did not form over billions of years, but came into being rapidly by means of the divinely initiated, unimaginably violent, planet-wide flood described in Genesis 6-9. God selected the rainbow to be the flood's memorial, telling us that such an aquatic planetary disaster will never occur again—a divine blending of justice with mercy (verses 8-17). The rainbow means that the flood is neither a superficial event, as advocated by William Buckland and Edward Hitchcock early in the nineteenth century,[47] nor simply one of many local floods,[48] but a single planetary catastrophe that generated major portions of strata of the geologic column (see Figure 3). From this perspective, we may imagine God saying to the geologist standing on the rim of the Grand Canyon and inquiring in his or her mind about the formation of the geologic column: "Look up when you see a rainbow arching over the Grand Canyon and observe its beauty and believe its message. My answer to your understandable question is written there in the sky. My global flood, which I reluctantly sent in judgment upon human sin, was the ultimate cause of many layers of the Grand Canyon."

The Geologic Column and Calvary: The Rainbow Connection

But even more important, the rainbow carries a profound theological message for the Christian believer. As noted earlier, the deluge preserved in the geologic column the causal connection between sin and death, confirming the need for the atoning power of the blood of Christ (see Figure 4). Here is the greatest message of the rainbow, the one that creates a most important connection between it, the construction of the geologic column, and the saving value of Calvary. Praise the Creator for the deep geological and theological significance of the beautiful rainbow (see Figure 5).

In conclusion, what do sedimentary layers have to do with Calvary?

Depending upon how we interpret their origin, they can either support or demolish the gospel. The good news about the geologic column is that current geological evidence strongly suggests that major portions of the column entombing the fossils formed rapidly by some high-energy aquatic catastrophe consistent with what we might expect in a planet-wide flood. From an evangelical Christian perspective, the geologic column supports the causal connection between sin and death. Thus, above all, a rapidly formed geologic column itself upholds the continuing sin-forgiving power of the blood of Jesus. This is the rainbow connection between the geologic column and Calvary, and helps to show why the biblical account of God's historical, global flood is so important to our salvation.

---

[1] Karl Schmitz-Moormann, ed., *Neue Ansätze zum Dialog zwischen Theologie und Naturwissenschaft* (Düsseldorf, Germany, 1992); quoted in Hans Küng, *Credo* (New York: Doubleday, 1993), p. 22. Schmitz-Moormann is the president of the European Society for the Study of the Relation of Science and Theology and a professor in the Fachhochschule, Dortmund, Germany.

[2] Ellen G. White, "What Was Secured by the Death of Christ," *Signs of the Times,* Dec. 30, 1889.

[3] This question is relevant particularly now that modern science has spoken, as implied by Schmitz-Moormann.

[4] Friedrich D. E. Schleiermacher, "The Second Letter," in *On the Glaubenslehre,* trans. James Duke and Francis Fiorenza (Chico, Calif.: Scholars Press, 1981), p. 64.

[5] Nigel M. de S. Cameron, *Evolution and the Authority of the Bible* (Greenwood, S.Dak.: Attic Press, 1983), p. 52.

[6] *Essays and Reviews* (London: John W. Parker and Son, 1860).

[7] Stephen Jay Gould, *Time's Arrow, Time's Cycle* (Cambridge: Harvard University Press, 1987), p. 2.

[8] Special creationists have not always accepted the reality of the geologic column. For example, in 1923 George McCready Price published his famous work *The New Geology,* in which he attempted to show by reference to selected geological phenomena that the geologic column as conventionally interpreted is an incredible assumption, i.e., there exists no consistent order to the earth's crust.

[9] For a review of this well-known and -documented point see Arthur N. Strahler, *Science and Earth History: The Evolution/Creation Controversy* (Buffalo, N.Y.: Prometheus Books, 1987), pp. 309-325.

[10] Stephen Jay Gould, *Wonderful Life: The Burgess Shale and the Nature of History* (New York: W. W. Norton, 1989), p. 57.

[11] Richard A. Kerr, "Between Extinctions, Evolutionary Stasis," *Science* 226 (Oct. 7, 1994): 29.

[12] Gould, *Wonderful Life,* p. 306.

[13] Rodney Lee Stiling, "The Diminishing Deluge: Noah's Flood in Nineteenth-Century American Thought" (Ph.D. diss., University of Wisconsin at Madison, 1991), p. 218.

[14] Edward Hitchcock, *Elementary Geology* (Amherst, Mass.: J. S. and C. Adams, 1840), pp. 273, 274.

[15] Stiling, pp. 221-223.

[16] John Hick, *Evil and the God of Love* (London: Macmillan, 1966).

[17] *Ibid.,* p. 283.

[18] *Ibid.,* p. 285.

[19] *Ibid.*

[20] Hans Küng, *Credo* (New York: Doubleday, 1993), p. 21.

[21] *Ibid.,* p. 22.

[22] Karl Schmitz-Moormann, "Evolution and Redemption: What Is the Meaning of Christians Proclaiming Salvation in an Evolving World?" *Progress in Theology* 1, No. 2 (June 1993): 7.

[23] Joseph A. Fitzmyer, *Romans, The Anchor Bible* (New York: Doubleday, 1993), p. 506.

[24] *Ibid.,* p. 507.

[25] For additional exegetical reasons leading to a similar conclusion, see John Murry, *The Epistle to the Romans* (Grand Rapids: Eerdmans, 1966), p. 305.

[26] Norbert F. Lohfink, *The Inerrancy of Scripture and Other Essays,* trans. R. A. Wilson (Berkeley, Calif.: BIBAL Press, 1991), p. 56. Originally published in German in 1965.

[27] David H. Lane, "Theological Problems With Theistic Evolution, Part II," *Bibliotheca Sacra* 50 (April-June 1994): 170.

[28] For treatments of the theological implications of death in the geologic column prior to the first human sin, see the following studies: Maria Boccia, "Creation and Evolution: Opposing Worldviews," *Searching Together* 17, No. 1 (Spring 1988): 7-19, particularly p. 9 (Boccia earned her Ph.D. from the University of Massachusetts in Amherst specializing in zoology); L. J. Gibson, "Theistic Evolution: Is It for Adventists?" *Ministry,* January 1992, pp. 22-25 (Gibson is the current director of the Geoscience Research Institute); John T. Baldwin, "Progressive Creationism and Biblical Revelation: Some Theological Implications," *Journal of the Adventist Theological Society* 3, No. 1 (Spring 1992): 105-119 (Baldwin's University of Chicago dissertation focusing on the philosophical relation of science and religion is entitled "The Argument to Design in British Religious Thought: An Investigation of the Status and Cogency of Posthumean Forms of Teleological Argumentation With Reference Principally to Hume and Paley," 1990).

[29] Lane, p. 174.

[30] Cameron, p. 66.

[31] Marco T. Terreros, "Death Before the Sin of Adam: A Fundamental Concept in Theistic Evolution and Its Implications for Evangelical Theology" (Ph.D. diss., Andrews University, Seventh-day Adventist Theological Seminary, 1994), p. 227.

[32] Originally presented before the Evangelical Theological Society, Nov. 18, 1994.

[33] *Ibid.*

[34] *Ibid.*

[35] Originally presented by Michael Hasel before the Evangelical Theological Society, Nov. 18, 1994.

[36] Jedidiah Morse, *The American Geography; or, A View of the Present Situation of the United States of America* (Elizabethtown, N.J.: Shepard Kollock, 1789), quoted in Stiling, p. 26.

[37] Stiling, p. 351.

[38] See Edward Hitchcock, *Religion of Geology and Its Connected Sciences* (Boston: Phillips, Sampson, and Company, 1854), for a discussion that we find no traces in nature of the Noachian deluge. For a helpful analysis of this point see Stiling, p. 157.

[39] See, for example, H. Paul Buchheim, "Paleoenvironments, Lithofacies, and Varves of the Fossil Butte Member of the Eocene Green River Formation, Southwestern Wyoming," *Contributions to Geology* 30, No. 1 (Spring 1994): 3-14. In this study Buchheim presents his field research suggesting an adjusted model to the standard varve hypothesis. ("Varve" implies annual deposition of sedimentary laminae.) Concerning a portion of his research, Buchheim states, "Most of the near-shore Laminae were deposited in response to periodic non-annual processes, and thus are not true varves or annual deposits" (*ibid.,* p. 3).

[40] Derek Victor Ager, *The New Catastrophism: The Importance of the Rare Event in Geological History* (Cambridge: Cambridge University Press, 1993).

[41] Rhodes Fairbridge, "Traces From the Desert: Ordovician," in Brian Stephen John, ed., *The Winters of the World: Earth Under the Ice Ages* (London: David & Charles, 1979), pp. 152, 153.

[42] *Ibid.,* p. 153.

[43] E. G. Kennedy, R. Kablano, and A. V. Chadwick, "A Reassessment of the Shallow Water Depositional Model for the Tapeats Sandstone, Grand Canyon, Arizona: Evidence for Deep Water Deposition," *Geological Society of America Abstracts With Programs* 28, No. 7 (1996): A-407. For some of the details in this section, the author is indebted to personal conversations with Kennedy and Chadwick.

[44] Arthur Chadwick, "Megatrends in North American Paleocurrents," *Society of Economic Paleontologists and Mineralogists Meeting Abstracts* 8 (1993): 58. Chadwick has compiled into a computer database more than half a million measured paleocurrent directions at 15,615 localities on the North American continent. In the process he has verified the megadirectional paleocurrent flow suggested by earlier fieldwork of individuals such as: Paul Edwin Potter, and Wayne Arthur Pyron,

"Dispersal Centers of Paleozoic and Later Clastics of the Upper Mississippi Valley and Adjacent Areas," *Geological Society of America Bulletin* 72:8 (1961): 1195-1259.

[45] A. V. Chadwick, "Megatrends in North American Paleocurrents" (unpublished paper presented at the Society of Economic Paleontologists and Mineralogists Symposium on Paleogeography and Paleoclimatology at Pennsylvania State University, August 1993).

[46] Cf. P. E. Potter, and F. J. Pettijohn, *Paleocurrents and Basin Analysis* (Berlin: Springer-Verlag, 1977). Chadwick observes that Potter and Pettijohn "have suggested paleocurrents on a larger scale be used for studying crustal evolution of a continent including the defining of borderlands and the timing of uplift and tectonics" (*ibid.*).

[47] Stiling, p. 351.

[48] *Ibid.*, pp. 145-157.

CHAPTER 7

EVOLUTION: A THEORY IN CRISIS

Norman R. Gulley
Southern Adventist University

Introduction

Evolution is possibly the most influential worldview ever to affect the human race. It has become all-pervasive in nearly every modern discipline. Darwin believed that "his theories would necessitate a complete redrafting of the problems and scope of several sciences, including psychology, paleontology, and comparative anatomy."[1] Evolution radically altered biology and later became married to Mendelian genetics, producing what historians of science call the neo-Darwinian, or modern synthesis, phase of evolution.

The Origin of Species, published in 1859, "has had a massive influence not only on the sciences, which increasingly are built on evolutionary assumptions, but on the humanities, theology, and government."[2] As Ernst Mayr noted, Darwin's book "brought about a fundamental reorientation in the study of behavior."[3] Darwin's influence is so great that with him came a new paradigm change. Mayr, professor of zoology at Harvard University, says of Darwin's theory, "It was one of the most novel and most daring new conceptualizations in the history of ideas."[4] No wonder many widely consider him the Newton of biology.

Alfred R. Wallace[5] and Charles Darwin independently thought of natural selection as the mechanism for evolution. Both took theology before going on to make contributions to evolutionary studies, and Darwin drifted into agnosticism and atheism through his study into evolutionary theory. He lost his faith during the years 1836-1839, some 20 years before publishing *The Origin of Species.*[6] His loss of faith was one major factor in Darwin's turn to natural selection as the mechanism for his theory.[7] It is also a fact that his evolutionary theory has caused many others to lose their faith. Martin Lings contends that "more cases of loss of religious faith are to be traced to the theory of evolution . . . than to anything else."[8]

Evolution has influenced social theory, with the "survival of the fittest" applied to the extermination of 6 million Jews in the Holocaust under Hitler's

Third Reich. It continues to influence society. Robert Wright wrote a major article (*Time,* Aug. 15, 1994) entitled "Infidelity: It May Be in Our Genes." Viewing male promiscuity as a product of evolution, he says, "According to evolutionary psychology, it is 'natural' for both men and women—at some times, under some circumstances—to commit adultery." Wright claims that nearly 1,000 of the 1,154 past or present societies studied have permitted a man to have more than one wife. Furthermore, the article contends that "it is to a man's evolutionary advantage to sow his seeds far and wide." In America the divorce rate is 50 percent. Wright concludes that "lifelong monogamous devotion just isn't natural, and the modern environment makes it harder than ever."[9] With such widespread belief that humans are mere animals, no wonder we see so much moral disarray that regards life as well as marriage as disposable.

As Henry Morris rightly observes, "untold damage has been wrought, especially during the past century, by this dismal doctrine that man is merely an evolved animal. Racism, economic imperialism, Communism, Nazism, sexual promiscuity and perversions, aggressive militarism, infanticide, genocide, and all sorts of evils have been vigorously promoted by one group or another on the grounds that, since they were based on evolution, they were 'scientific' and, therefore, bound to prove beneficial in the long run. Even cannibalism, of all things, is beginning to receive favorable attention by certain evolutionists."[10] What a tragedy that Darwin was blind to such possibilities, even saying that evolutionary theory ennobles![11]

Influence on Evangelical Theology

Evolution has even made remarkable inroads into evangelical theology by calling into question the historicity of the Genesis account of creation. Paul K. Jewett notes that "few who confess the Christian doctrine of creation would suppose that the world was fashioned in a week of time some six thousand to ten thousand years ago. Drafts of time of a vastly different magnitude are indicated by the findings of the natural sciences."[12] Theology accommodates science by interpreting the Genesis record in the light of the current scientific worldview.[13] Some evangelical theologians believe that death existed in the human race prior to the fall,[14] which raises questions whether death is sin's wages, and hence undermines the atonement. According to evolutionary theory, death is something natural and not a result of human sin. Karl Barth claims that death is a part of being finite. God has no beginning or end, but in contrast, humans have a beginning and an end. Therefore, death is a part of being human.[15]

Theistic evolution attempts to accept evolutionary theory while holding on to the fact that God as Creator launched the process and perhaps even superintended it. Some contemporary theologians "deny any original act of creation, and equate creation with that universal, continuing activity which traditional theology called 'preservation' or 'providence.'"[16] Called "continuing creation," process theologians influenced by Alfred Whitehead especially espouse it,[17] and it appears in the theology of John Macquarrie.[18] Theistic evolutionists look at the Genesis account of creation as either myth, saga, or poetry, in which the only factual information is that God created through natural processes. Many hold that the other creation stories in Mesopotamia, such as the Enumah Elish account, form the basis for the biblical account. All of these ideas question the authority of the biblical record and shove it aside to make room for evolutionary theory.

The root problem of theistic evolution is that it overlooks the worldview of evolution. Darwin did not believe in miracles or in the intervention of God either at the beginning or anywhere else along the evolutionary process. His worldview was a closed system that removed God from the natural laws of cause and effect. It believed that natural selection without God accomplished evolutionary development. Clearly, anyone accepting biblical creationism believes in the supernatural act of God in creating. Theistic evolution is logically a misnomer. It is like saying that God began the process and yet had no part in it. Behind the term *theistic evolution* lie two opposing philosophical views, and hence opposing paradigms: supernaturalism and naturalism. A marrying of the two doesn't explain anything, for one cancels the other.

Although theistic evolution cannot explain the origin of humanity, the Jesuit paleontologist Pierre Teilhard de Chardin espoused it.[19] Augustine of Hippo[20] and Thomas Aquinas[21] believed in progressive creation.[22]

The Second Vatican Council (1962-1965) addressed the relationship between Scripture and science. It speaks of "the rightful independence of science"[23] and of "the legitimate autonomy of human culture and especially of the sciences."[24] This is in keeping with the Catholic division between Scripture and tradition. The "Document on Revelation" places "sacred tradition" before "sacred revelation."[25] In the same way it expects science to take precedence over Scripture in the area of evolution. The current *Catechism of the Catholic Church* (1994) says, "The question about the origins of the world and of man has been the object of many scientific studies which have splendidly enriched our knowledge of the age and dimensions of the cosmos, the development of life-forms and the appearance of man." The document gives thanks to God "for the understanding and wisdom he gives to scholars and researchers."[26]

Evolution of Evolution

Darwin became an evolutionist during March 1837, or certainly by July 1837.[27] Although Darwinian evolution began with *The Origin of Species,* various forms of evolution reach back through Hume to the classical philosophers such as Democritus, Epicurus, Aristotle, and the Ionian nature philosophers such as Empedocles.[28] As Isaac Asimov points out in his *New Guide to Science,* "from Aristotle on, many men speculated on the possibility that organisms had evolved from one another."[29] Evolution as the transmutation of species, though, goes back only to the eighteenth-century Enlightenment,[30] as indicated by Peter J. Bowler,[31] Loren Eiseley,[32] and John C. Greene.[33]

We should keep in mind that evolutionary theory has had its own evolution. We could divide into a number of stages, including classical Darwinism (1858-1890s); the modern synthesis,[34] also called neo-Darwinism (1915-1930s);[35] post-Darwinianism,[36] later questioned by DNA and molecular biology (1950s); and the punctuated equilibria views and cladistic taxonomy (1980-onward).[37] The classical period focused on natural selection as the sole mechanism for evolution until Mendellian genetics forced a synthesis with natural selection to form neo-Darwinism. In the 1950s the discovery of DNA by Watson and Crick in molecular biology caused a reanalysis of evolutionary theory.[38]

Throughout the first two periods of the theory's history scientists considered gradualism, or a series of microevolutionary changes over sufficient time, as the way evolution occurred. Not so today. Punctuated equilibrium (Stephen Jay Gould, Niles Eldredge) suggests that new species appeared abruptly, just as we see demonstrated in the fossil records. Philosophers of science have rightly called this new focus a new paradigm change in evolutionary theory,[39] because, in part, it rejects natural selection as the sole mechanism for change and gradualism as its time frame. The modern form of taxonomy called cladistics (Simpson, Cox, Halstead, Hennig, Greenwood, Forey, Gardiner, Patterson, and Nelson)[40] finds distinct gaps between species, with no ancestral linkage. Paleontologists, geneticists, immunologists, embryologists, and taxonomists are among those whose research supports the post-Darwinian view.

Although evolution has had its own evolution, it is still evolution. Therefore, in the literature, when later evolutionary views criticize former views, it does not mean to say that the exponents of the new concepts have given up evolutionary theory. It simply indicates that both Darwinian evolution as well as neo-Darwinian evolution have been radically called into question by scientists whom I consider as belonging to post-Darwinian evolution.

In this chapter we will consider some evidence that questions the theory of evolution in its various stages. The reader should keep in mind that evolutionists still actively defend the concept. As Peter J. Bowler, historian of science, Queen's University, Belfast, states, "biologists have begun a more active campaign to defend the theory (Eldredge, 1982; Godfrey, 1983; Halstead, 1983; Kitcher, 1982; Montagu, 1982; Newell, 1982; Ruse, 1982; Futuyma, 1982)."[41]

Recent Publications Questioning Evolutionary Theory

We will mention a few of the recent major publications that raise issues about evolutionary theory. Some representative titles include: *The Collapse of Evolution,* by Scott Huse;[42] *Evolution: A Theory in Crisis,* by Michael Denton;[43] *Darwin on Trial,* by Philip Johnson;[44] *The Creation Hypothesis: Scientific Evidence for an Intelligent Designer,* edited by J. P. Moreland;[45] *Of Pandas and People: The Central Question of Biological Origins,* by Percival Davis and Dean H. Kenyon;[46] *The Descent of Darwin: A Handbook of Doubts About Darwinism,* by Brian Leith;[47] and Alvin Platinga's seminal article, "When Faith and Reason Clash: Evolution and the Bible," in *Christian Scholar's Review.*[48] From an earlier time comes Michael Polanyi's insightful article, "Life's Irreducible Structure," in *Science,*[49] and a book by W. R. Bird, *The Origin of Species Revisited: The Theories of Evolution and of Abrupt Appearance.*[50] Together they make a formidable attack on evolutionary theory.

The Parameters of Science

Evolution claims to be a science and therefore able to demonstrate its theory through empirical evidence. By contrast, adherents to evolutionary theory claim that creationism is nonempirical and hence nonscientific. The comparison does have problems, though. It is true that we can demonstrate change in nature, but the evidence limits itself to minor differences (microevolution). Evolution, however, requires macroevolution, or transformation from one species to an entirely different species. Empirical evidence is insufficient to prove the claims made. Extrapolating macroevolutionary change from microevolution is merely an unproven and untestable theory. We cannot, on the basis of known evidence, demonstrate it. Scientists can accept it only by faith. This is no different from accepting by faith that God created the world and all within it. While we do have a few examples of what appear to be major changes, such exceptions still seem to prove the rule of no macroevolutionary change.[51]

Faith in either macroevolution or in creation by God is still only faith. It is not empirical evidence. Because it is faith and not empirical evidence, that

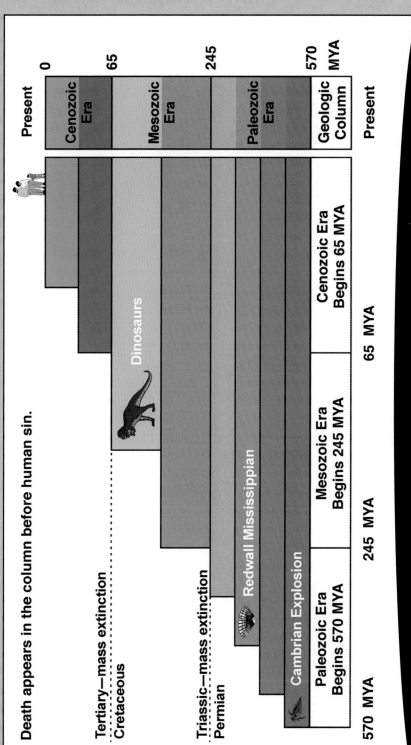

FORMATION OF THE GEOLOGIC COLUMN

FIGURE 2

THE POSTMODERN EVOLUTIONARY WORLDVIEW

Christ's Death Is
Not the Wage
of Our Sins

Atonement Is **Nullified**

=

No Causal
Connection
Between
Sin and Death—
Wages of Sin
Is Not Death

=

Without God's Flood

Death in the Geologic
Column Appears
Before Human Sin

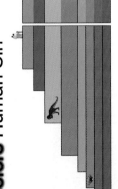

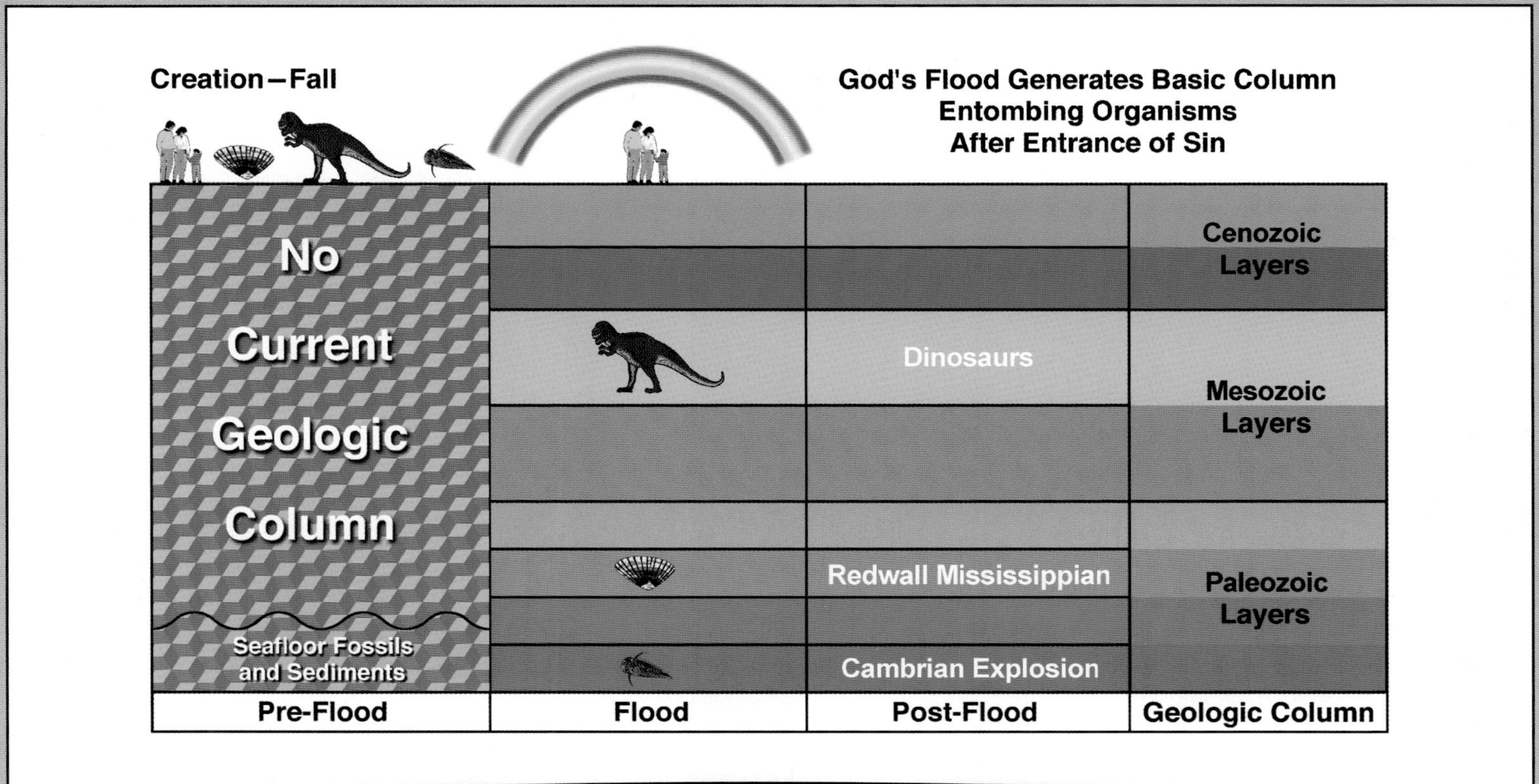

FORMATION OF THE GEOLOGIC COLUMN

RESULTING FROM THE BIBLICAL CREATION, GREAT CONTROVERSY WORLDVIEW

FIGURE 3

FIGURE 4

BIBLICAL CREATION, GREAT CONTROVERSY WORLDVIEW

Christ's Death Is
the Wage
of Our Sins

With God's Flood

Dead Forms Entombed
in the Geologic Column
After Human Sin

=

Causal
Connection
Between
Sin and Death
Is Real

=

Atonement Is Preserved

THE RAINBOW CONNECTION

The Geologic Column

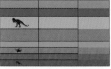

+

Calvary

**With God's Flood Producing
the Geologic Column...**

...the Atonement Is Preserved.

This shows why the global flood is so important to our salvation.

FIGURE 5

is, not something that science can demonstrate in the lab today, the origin of humanity by evolution or God's creation lies beyond the proper domain of science. That which stands beyond the demonstrable is in the realm of philosophy or metaphysics and not that of science. Colin Patterson, senior paleontologist at the British Natural History Museum, characterized evolution and creationism "as scientifically vacuous concepts which are held primarily on the basis of faith." [52]

Is evolution a science? Most people automatically consider that it is. But true science is testable, being either verified or falsified through experimentation. Can evolutionary theory qualify as science on those terms? It has elicited a number of different answers. At one time Karl Popper, a leader in the philosophy of science, questioned whether evolution is scientific because it is not falsifiable. In 1974 he wrote: "I have come to the conclusion that Darwinism is not a testable scientific theory, but a metaphysical research programme." [53] Later he conceded that parts of evolution are testable, and to that extent it is scientific. [54] But even then much of evolutionary theory remains beyond the objectivity of science, such as the origin of life in the beginning and the assumed process of gradualism in which small transitional stages transformed molecules into human beings. The claim that random genetic mutation and natural selection produced increasingly complex forms of life without any evidence of transitionals in the fossil record questions the theory as being scientific. To these matters we will return later.

What about biblical creationism—is it scientific? Gunther S. Stent considers that "the very term 'scientific creationism' is an oxymoron." [55] Judge William Overton, considering the Arkansas law that mandated the teaching of creationism, ruled that creation science does not constitute a genuine science. [56] J. P. Moreland rightly shows that the statements "By its very nature, Natural Science must adopt Methodological Naturalism" (in support of evolution) and "Theistic science is religion and not science" (in opposition to biblical creationism) are not first-order claims of science about some scientific phenomenon. "Rather, they are second-order philosophical claims *about* science. They are metaclaims that take a vantage point outside science and have science itself as their subject of reference. Thus the field of philosophy, especially philosophy of science, will be the proper domain from which to assess these claims, not science. Scientists are not experts in these second-order questions, and when they comment on them, they do so qua philosophers, not qua scientists." [57] The leading philosopher of science, Alvin Plantinga, says, "We need theistic science." [58]

Theistic science takes the position that we need not restrict scientific methodology to methodological naturalism, as in evolutionary theory. Philosopher and historian of science Michael Ruse confines the scope of science to "unbroken, natural regularity."[59] Why should science be confined to the natural realm? Although it is true that empirical evidence lies at the core of scientific enquiry, Paul K. Feyerabend speaks about the various problems in empiricism. Different thinkers have "proceeded in different ways and thereby given rise to different kinds of scientific knowledge." He warns that "the unity of doctrine insinuated by the scientist's appeal to experimentation and by his hostility toward 'hypotheses' must therefore be viewed with extreme caution."[60] So different kinds of scientific knowledge do exist. Why cannot divine action, or the supernatural, be seen as one kind of scientific thinking, as when God is the cause of creation in theistic science? After all, as Charles B. Thaxton notes, "science includes many elements; it includes asking what causes things."[61]

Causation as a Part of Science

Darwin's central thesis was that evolution operated through natural selection. But we cannot, however, cut methodological naturalism loose from causation. Darwin's *Origin of Species* never explains anything about the development of life from some prebiotic soup. *"Origin"* is a misnomer, in that Darwin never tells how that origin was possible. Nevertheless, the fact that he does mention origins means that he assumes some form of causation. It is not good enough to speak about natural laws as if they somehow transcend causation. J. P. Moreland said it well: "It is simply false to assert that scientists explain things merely by using natural laws, say by invoking a covering law model of scientific explanation. Scientists also explain certain aspects of the universe not only by using natural laws but also by citing the big bang as a single causal event."[62]

If evolutionary theory can speak of causation, why cannot theistic science? Henry M. Morris was right when he said that science is assumed to be "rational and causal and unified," and yet "banning by definition even the possibility of a supernatural First Cause of the rationality, causality, and unity of the universe with which science deals." Such an "assumption is purely arbitrary."[63]

Abraham Wolf, one of the greatest philosophers of science and former professor and head of the Department of the History of Method of Science at London University, said every event has a cause. "This assumption is commonly known as the postulate or principle of universal causation." He pointed out that "the principle of conservation of matter or energy would lose all significance without the idea of causal continuity, according to which certain successive events not only *follow,* but *follow from,* one another. In fact, mere laws of sequence are only intelligible in the last resort, when they can be shown to result from direct or indirect causal connections."[64]

Sir Julian Huxley said of Darwin that "he had a passion for natural history, which showed itself from early childhood."[65] The evolutionary view is historical, for it believes that every living animal is related by common ancestry. It is my contention that Darwin, even though focusing on natural selection in evolution, was still enamored with history (ancestral line) when he wrote his *Origin of Species.* Steven C. Meyer points out correctly that Darwin's *Origin of Species* "does not explain by natural law. Common descent explains by postulating a hypothetical pattern of historical events which, if actual, would account for a variety of presently observed data. . . . In Darwin's historical argument for descent, as with historical explanations generally, postulated past causal events (or patterns thereof) do the primary explanatory work. Laws do not."[66] For example, "the law 'Oxygen is necessary to combustion' does not explain why a particular building burned at a particular place and time."[67] Many different factors, such as an arsonist, lack of security, faulty wiring, kerosene stove, cigarette, or lack of a sprinkler system could be possible causes.

So evolutionary theory is premised on causality through the ancestral line. Is it not hypocritical of evolutionary theorists to reject supernatural causation when they believe in natural causation? To restrict causation to the natural realm alone is to restrict the search for evidence. Is such limitation really true to a scientific objectivity that seeks to be open to all evidence? Does not the precluding of the supernatural interpose a subjective assumption before we even consider the facts? Natural theory presupposes descent. Supernatural theory presupposes design. How can a scientist determine whether homology among animals results from descent rather than design? How objective can scientists be when they prescribe the area of search beforehand through biased presuppositions? What would happen if the scientist could really be objective and consider all the options, both supernatural and natural? Does the empirical evidence support descent or design? To this we now turn.

The Origin of Life

The origin of life is unknown to empirical science. Evolutionists have suggested many ideas. One popular thesis assumes that life arose out of a prebiotic soup when molecules crossed the divide from organic chemistry to biology. While at the University of Chicago in 1953, graduate student Stanley Miller, in Harold Urey's lab, experimented with amino acids in a mixture of water, methane, ammonia, and hydrogen—substances assumed present in the primitive earth. He subjected the chemicals to an electrical spark.[68] "Because amino acids are used in building proteins, they are sometimes called the 'building blocks of life.' Subsequent experiments based on the Miller-Urey model produced a variety of amino acids and other complex compounds employed in the genetic process, with the result that the more optimistic researchers concluded that the chemicals needed to construct life could have been present in sufficient abundance on the early earth."[69]

During the 1980s a major skepticism developed toward the Miller-Urey experiments. Atmospheric physicists doubt that the early earth's atmosphere contained significant amounts of ammonia, methane, or hydrogen. Molecular biologists discovered that RNA—a bridge from the chemicals to DNA—is "exceedingly difficult to synthesize under the conditions that likely prevailed when life originated." Moreover, RNA is no longer thought to replicate itself easily as biochemists once believed.[70] "Perhaps the most discouraging criticism has come from chemists, who have spoiled the prebiotic soup by showing that organic compounds produced on the early earth would be subject to chemical reactions making them unsuitable for constructing life. In all probability, the prebiotic soup could never have existed, and without it there is no reason to believe that the production of small amounts of some amino acids by electrical charge in a reducing atmosphere had anything to do with the origin of life."[71]

Thus because we have no empirical evidence for how life began, science has not been able to deny the biblical record of divine creation. Cambridge University astrophysicist Sir Frederick Hoyle, in his book *Evolution From Space* (1981), said: "The likelihood of the spontaneous formation of life from inanimate matter is one to a number of 40,000 naughts after it!" He concludes: "It is big enough to bury Darwin and the whole theory of evolution."[72]

It is incredible that some scholars believe life began many times in the universe (Dawkins, Asimov, Billingham).[73] They teach it even though we have no evidence of life anywhere in the universe outside of the earth. The winner of the Nobel Prize for Physiology or Medicine in 1962 for his work on DNA, Francis Crick, postulates that life began on some other planet some 9 billion years ago.[74] In his view of "Directed Panspermia," Crick believes that bacteria such as *Escherichia coli,* organisms about one micron wide and two microns long, were packaged and put aboard a spaceship and sent to earth. The advantage of such bacteria is they could be frozen alive and most of them will survive. "At a very low temperature, such as that of space, many of them might well survive for well over ten thousand years. They would be almost immune to impact shock and other similar hazards."[75]

However, such scholars do not explain how life began on those other planets. Transporting bacteria on a spaceship from outer space will not solve the failure to give an explanation of how life started on our planet. The question simply shifts to that planet—how did life begin there? Furthermore, we have no empirical evidence that bacteria evolve into more complex organisms. As far as our planet is concerned, science finds no evidence of a prebiotic soup in the earliest rocks.[76] And even if we did have such evidence, Klaus Dose, from the Institute of Biochemistry, Johannes Gutenberg University, Germany, concludes, "It is extremely unlikely that the first forms of life could have evolved spontaneously in a primordial soup."[77]

Descent or Design?

Some biologists have used demarcation arguments to separate the so-called scientific approach to origins (descent) from what they consider the nonscientific (design). Such demarcation arguments come from the influence of a philosophy of science called logical positivism.[78] Logical positivism has its roots in a seminar by Moritz Schlick at the University of Vienna in 1923. Others joining the movement were A. J. Ayer, Rudolf Carnap, Herbert Feigel, and the early Ludwig Wittgenstein. They set up standards for what they considered meaningfulness. Millard Erickson notes:

"According to the view, there are only two types of meaningful language: (1) mathematicological truths, in which the predicate is contained within the subject, such as 'the sum of the angles of a triangle is 180 degrees,' and (2) empirical truths such as 'the book is on the table.' Empirical truths are propositions which are verified by sense data. These are the only meaningful types of language. All other propositions, that is, propositions which are neither mathematical-type nor empirical or scientific-type statements verified by sense data, are literally 'nonsense' or meaningless."[79]

As Erickson rightly concludes, logical positivism consigned the language of metaphysics, ethics, theology, and other disciplines to meaninglessness. The problem with that conclusion is that it can't verify its own theory. So logical positivism fails because it cannot meet its own criteria.

With the collapse of logical positivism, analytical philosophy came to study language in the context of its use, a process known as functional analysis. This meant that we must evaluate the language used in biology and theology from within the quite different contexts of biology and theology. Thus we cannot use the criteria for evaluating the authenticity of the one to determine the authenticity of the other. Ludwig Wittgenstein, in his later thinking, compared the different contexts to different games. No one would apply the rules of baseball to football. Each game plays according to its own rules. Likewise, the language of theology in discussing creation and design must be true to its own context and is as valid within that context as any other use of language in different contexts, including biological views on descent.

Stephen Meyer has written on the methodological equivalence of intelligent design and naturalistic descent. He says: "Design and descent prove equally scientific or equally unscientific depending upon the criteria used to adjudicate their scientific status and provided metaphysically neutral criteria are selected to make such assessments."[80] The fact is that the word "design" has come back into scientific vocabulary because of the work of physicists. They have "unveiled a universe apparently fine-tuned for the possibility of human life."[81]

"Despite this renewal of interest in the [intelligent] design hypothesis among physicists and cosmologists, biologists have remained reluctant to consider such notions. As historian of science Timothy Lenior has observed, 'teleological thinking has been steadfastly resisted by modern biology. And yet in nearly every area of research biologists are hard pressed to find language that does not impute purposeness to living forms.'"[82] Yet as Mae-Wan Ho and Peter T. Saunders have stated, "The all-powerful force of natural selection has come more and more to resemble explanation in terms of the conscious design of the omnipotent Creator."[83]

The Function of DNA

In 1953 Francis Crick and James Watson unraveled the architecture of the double helix DNA molecule.[84] The discovery of DNA has added enormously to our understanding of how living organisms develop. Research has now shown that the idea of natural selection and random genetic mutation, with its emphasis on descent, is too limited a view. DNA is a unique information storage device that speaks far more of design by an intelligent Creator.

Michael Denton, in his seminal book *Evolution: A Theory in Crisis,* describes DNA's amazing ability to contain information. "The capacity of DNA to store information vastly exceeds that of any other known system; it is so efficient that all the information needed to specify an organism as complex as man weighs less than a few thousand millionths of a gram. The information necessary to specify the design of all the species of organisms which have ever existed on the planet, a number according to G. G. Simpson of approximately one thousand million, could be held in a teaspoon and there would still be room left for all the information in every book ever written."[85]

John W. Oller, Jr., and John L. Omdahl compared human language with that of DNA. They noted that "the origin of the human language capacity is not unlike the problem of the origin of life itself."[86] They conclude that "the intricate and articulate structures of language are mirrored in the delicate arrangements of biological representations in correspondence to information coded in DNA. We have shown logically that the language capacity cannot have originated in a purely materialistic manner. The logical gulf that separates mind from matter really is an uncrossable barrier to any materialistic origin. If the definitions of Peirce and Einstein are accepted, the gulf they describe cannot be crossed without the intervention of a truly transcendent Intelligence—a conclusion both of them accepted."[87]

It is not good enough to say, with Oxford University zoologist Richard Dawkins, that God cannot be the origin of DNA. "To explain the origin of the DNA/protein machine by invoking a supernatural Designer is to explain precisely nothing, for it leaves unexplained the origin of the Designer," he wrote. "You have to say something like 'God was always there,' and if you allow yourself that kind of lazy way out, you might as well just say 'DNA was always there,' or 'Life was always there,' and be done with it." What Dawkins completely overlooked was the two-leveled reality at work in the living organism, that is, the DNA at the higher level suggesting design and the physical-chemical development at the lower level that some claim to be illustrative of descent. What Dawkins needs to do is to take seriously the seminal work done by another Oxford University professor, Michael Polanyi.

In an influential article, "Life's Irreducible Structure," Michael Polanyi, former Fellow of Merton College, Oxford University, compared machines with evolutionary theory. Human beings make machines even though such devices operate according to laws of inanimate nature. "So the machine as a whole works under the control of two distinct principles. The higher one is the principle of the machine's design, and this harnesses the lower one, which consists in the physical-chemical processes on which the machine relies."[88]

Polanyi considers living mechanisms and information in DNA as boundary conditions, with a sequence of boundaries above them. He reasons that "a boundary condition is always extraneous to the process which it delimits." For example, when Galileo conducted his experiment of balls running down a slope, the choice of the slope had nothing to do with the laws of mechanics. Furthermore, the shape and manufacture of test tubes have nothing to do with the laws of chemistry. Nor can we define the structure of machines by the laws they harness. He concludes: "Thus the morphology of living things transcends the laws of physics and chemistry."[89]

Because of DNA, Polanyi questions evolutionary theory. "In the light of the current theory of evolution, the codelike structure of DNA must be assumed to have come about by a sequence of chance variations established by natural selection. But this evolutionary aspect is irrelevant here; whatever may be the origin of a DNA configuration, it can function as a code only if its order is not due to the forces of potential energy. It must be as physically indeterminate as the sequence of words is on a printed page. As the arrangement of a printed page is extraneous to the chemistry of the printed page, so is the base sequence in a DNA molecule extraneous to the chemical forces at work in the DNA molecule."[90]

Polanyi asks, "Can the control of morphogenesis by DNA be likened to the designing and shaping of a machine by an engineer?"[91] He answers in the positive. The codelike structure of DNA, with all its information regulating the growth of the organism, acts on the organism like an engineer acts on a machine. The fact that the organism harnesses the physical-chemical substances within it in no way fully defines the organism itself, for it is under dual control—from DNA and the physical-chemical substances, with DNA being the primary level of influence. It would seem to me that this model places design (not descent) from the DNA as the primary influence in morphogenesis.

Scott M. Huse observes that "computer scientists have demonstrated conclusively that information does not and cannot arise spontaneously. Information results only from the expenditure of energy (to arrange the letter and words) and under the all-important direction of intelligence. Therefore, since DNA is information, the only logical and reasonable conclusion that can be drawn is that DNA was formed by intelligence."[92]

On the basis of the work done on DNA, it seems more reasonable to say that it demonstrates an intelligent Creator, and thus speaks eloquently on behalf of design rather than for descent.

Complexity

Evolutionary theory is a paradigm that has not been proved, but is still accepted as a basic presupposition. Within this assumed paradigm the study of nature has become a search to find evidence to support the paradigm itself. Thus the paradigm biases the research. When we come to consider complexities in nature, we find them on every level. We have to ask ourselves the serious question How can such complexity develop from random genetic mutation and natural selection? A comment Michael Denton makes about DNA illustrates the enormity of the problem. "To the skeptic, the proposition that the genetic programmes of higher organisms, consisting of something close to a thousand million bits of information, equivalent to the sequence of letters in a small library of one thousand volumes, containing in encoded form countless thousands of intricate algorithms controlling, specifying, and ordering the growth and development of billions and billions of cells into the form of a complex organism, were composed by a purely random process is simply an affront to reason. But to the Darwinist the idea is accepted without a ripple of doubt—the paradigm takes precedence."[93]

What observed process do we know to be responsible for the development of such complexity at the infinitesimal level? The fact of the matter is that evolutionary theory has not come up with any clue as to how such complexity can exist at the very basic level of living organisms. Brian Leith, in his insightful book *The Descent of Darwin,* comments: "I don't think there is an evolutionist alive who is particularly happy with existing ideas about how complex features arise."[94]

Richard Dawkins, in the *New Scientist,* states he sees only two alternatives to Darwinism to explain "the organized and apparently purposeful complexity of life. These are God and Lamarkism." It is incredible to what lengths the evolutionary paradigm pushes Dawkins as he rejects the idea of God as reasonable origin for complexity in nature. "I am afraid I shall give God rather short shrift. He may have many virtues: no doubt He is invaluable as a pricker of the conscience and a comfort to the dying and the bereaved, but as an explanation of organized complexity He simply will not do. It is organized complexity we are trying to explain, so it is footling to invoke in explanation a being sufficiently organized and complex to create it."[95]

Dawkins at least admits the existence of God, who "pricks" and "comforts" human beings. He accepts, to that degree, the supernatural. Why does he then limit causation to the natural? Is it not his paradigmatic prejudice that refuses to take in all of the possibilities, as we would expect from normal scientific methodology? Stephen C. Meyer was right when he observed: "If competing hypotheses are eliminated before they are evaluated, remaining theories may acquire an undeserved dominance."[96] It has clearly happened in the limited naturalistic paradigm of evolutionary theory. What we need is to allow supernatural causation as a more reasonable cause for complexity than random genetic mutation and natural selection. From the mega universe to the micro universe, complexity appears everywhere. The idea that it is only the result of random and purposeless evolution staggers the mind.

Kurt P. Wise speaks of complexity as evidence that evolution leaves unexplained. "Anyone who has taken college biochemistry has been impressed with the extraordinary complexity of replication, transcription, the Krebs cycle, and other features of living things. For those who did not take such a course, these are a few of the many chemical processes that occur within any one of your trillions of body cells at any given moment. Photosynthesis, as an example on a subcellular process, is thought to involve as many as five hundred chemical steps—of which we 'fully' understand only a few. Yet a number of these kinds of processes occur spontaneously within individual cells."[97] He traces complexity up through different levels from the chemical processes in the cell, to human organs and their interrelationships, to communities of organisms and their network of complex interactions, and finally to the earth and the complex astrophysical arrangements that allow life to exist on earth. He concludes: "Macroevolutionary theory has never successfully explained the acquisition of any level of this complexity, let alone the total complexity."[98] As Michael Denton has said, "In practically every field of fundamental biological research ever-increasing levels of design and complexity are being revealed at an ever-accelerating rate."[99] This effectively calls into question the theory of evolution.

Beyond complexity itself lies the question of integration. "As if the basic complexity of things were not enough, the integration of that complexity is truly astounding. Not only do subcellular chemical processes involve a large number of complex molecules and chemical steps, but those items and events are connected in a well-balanced and well-timed series of items and steps to produce a well-integrated process. Similarly, the workings of subcellular organelles, cells in tissues, tissues in organs, organs in systems, systems in bodies, organisms with other organisms, organisms in communities in the biosphere, all show staggering integration. As with the complexity of these items and events on any given level, such a level of integration has never been observed to arise from nonintelligent natural law and process. Integration seems to argue for intelligent cause."[100]

"The integration that is so striking *within* levels is even more striking *between* levels. Not only do subcellular organelle systems and chemical processes show integration, but the chemical and organelle systems are themselves linked together, and must be for the cell to survive. Even more impressive, a similar integration exists between all levels. Once again, this level of integration is unexplained by evolutionary theory but is addressable by intelligent cause theory."[101]

The Human Eye

In 1861, two years after the publication of his *Origin of Species,* Darwin wrote a letter to biologist Asa Gray, saying that "the eye to this day gives me a cold shudder."[102] "To suppose that the eye, with all its inimitable contrivances for adjusting the focus to different distances, for admitting different amounts of light, and for the correction of spherical and chromatic aberration, could have been formed by natural selection, seems, I freely confess, absurd in the highest possible degree. . . . The belief that an organ as perfect as the eye could have formed by natural selection is more than enough to stagger anyone."[103]

If what Darwin knew then about the eye made him shudder, imagine how he would react when we have discovered so much more about the eye! "Electrophysiological studies have recently revealed very intricate connections among the nerve cells of the retina, which enable the eye to carry out many types of preliminary data processing of visual information before transmitting it in binary form to the brain. The cleverness of these mechanisms has again been underlined by their close analogy to the sorts of image intensification and clarification processes carried out today by computers, such as those used by NASA, on images transmitted from space. Today it would be more accurate to think of a television camera if we are looking for an analogy to the eye."[104]

A look at the human eye had every reason to make Darwin tremble, for how could natural selection produce such ordered and precise design and complexity? Furthermore, how could natural selection, a slow process, have a workable eye at every stage of its development? Richard Dawkins admits that the human eye "could not possibly come into existence through single-step selection."[105] He believes the human eye could have taken several hundred million years to evolve.[106] Yet Dawkins can argue, "The eye is, par excellence, a case where a fraction of an organ is better than no organ at all; an eye without a lens or even a pupil, for instance, could still detect the looming shadow of a predator."[107]

But how can a fraction of an eye really be an eye? How can the alleged slow process to produce the eye really be possible when the eye is only a part of a wider complex network of interdependent parts forming the visual network? "Here is the problem," Alvin Platinga says. "How does the lens, for example, get developed by the proposed means—random genetic variation and natural selection—when at the same time there has to be development of the optic nerve, the relevant muscles, the retina, the rods and cones, and many other delicate and complicated structures, all of which have to be adjusted to each other in such a way that they can work together? Indeed, what is involved isn't, of course, just the eye; it is the whole visual system, including the relevant parts of the brain. Many different organs and suborgans have to be developed together, and it is hard to envisage a series of mutations which is such that each member of the series has adaptive value, is also a step on the way to the eye, and is such that the last member is an animal with such an eye." [108]

The eye is too complex both in itself and in its visual network to just evolve gradually. That is why Dawkins' idea that an eye is an eye even during its hypothetical early stages does not make sense. Harvard scholar Stephen Jay Gould asked what good 5 percent of an eye might be. Realizing that it could not see, he thought it might have some other function than sight. Dawkins disagreed with Gould and argued that the organism used the 5 percent eye "for 5 percent vision." But how can 5 percent of an eye have 5 percent of vision when no vision is possible until the eye is 100 percent an eye, with all its parts in place and fully functioning as noted above by Plantinga? Lawyer Phillip E. Johnson saw the illogic of Dawkins' conclusion, stating that "the fallacy in that argument is that '5 percent of an eye' is not the same thing as '5 percent of normal vision.' " [109]

Dan E. Nilsson and Susanne Nilsson of Lund University suggested that the human eye could have developed in "a few hundred thousand generations" or "1,829 steps," [110] yet they start with a flat, light-sensitive patch of cells. Saying nothing about where those light-sensitive cells came from, they just assume their presence, thus ignoring a fundamental part of what they should be proving. True science will start the process at the beginning, not way down the line.

What we have said about the eye applies to other organs, or body parts, such as the avian lung[111] and bird wings, just to name two. Each of these organs comprises a complex network, so that no one part can evolve without all parts developing at the same time. The problem is, how can an emerging lung be a lung, or an incomplete wing be a wing? How can an avian lung, through which air passes in only one direction, have developed from the two-way passage found in all other vertebrates? Beyond all this is the complexity of the human brain. Caltech neurobiologist Roger Sperry, winner of the 1981 Nobel Prize for study on the two hemispheres of the human brain, argues "that the brain system as a whole somehow controls its parts in ways that supersede the mechanistic physical states of the brain's 10 billion neurons." [112] Although he dismisses the supernatural, Sperry at least apparently realizes that more exists to the brain than the "mechanistic physical" dimensions. The intricacies of the human brain are equivalent to the most complex computer network known to mankind, and speak eloquently for a Creator rather than random chance for its existence.

Michael Denton observes: "If complex computer programs cannot be changed by random mechanisms, then surely the same must apply to the genetic programmes of living organisms."[113] It is not correct to compare the "evolution" of planes from Bleriot's monoplane to Boeing's 747, for that development did not depend upon chance.[114] The sheer perfection throughout the universe, at every level, cannot be explained on the basis of chance and random processes.[115]

Random chance introduces the theory of probability into evolutionary thinking. Enormous amounts of time have been a safe haven for the evolutionary hypothesis. Such theorists believe that, given sufficient time, any evolutionary development is possible. If we considered evolution a steady linear development, then sufficient time made the theory seem possible. Thus in the probability game, as on a roulette wheel, the number 26, for example, could come up exactly when needed along the evolutionary line. But such an approach to probability is no longer possible today, because we better understand the complexities of evolution. Huston Smith says: "We now see that significant organic changes require that innumerable component developments occur *simultaneously* and *independently* in bones, nerves, muscles, arteries, and the like. These requirements escalate the demand on probability theory astronomically. It would be like having 26 come up simultaneously on ten or 15 tables in the same casino, followed by all the tables reporting 27, 28, and 29 in lockstep progression; more time than the earth has existed would be needed to account for the sequences that have occurred."[116]

The Cell

Darwinian evolution believes that we can explain through gradual microevolutionary steps the entire development of life from the prebiotic soup all the way to human beings. (It even posits that life may continue to evolve beyond human beings.)[117] This suggests that evolution is change from the simple to the complex. We have already noted the complexity of human beings. Much could be said about the general complexity of the animal kingdom too. Our point here is that complexity is not the end of some evolutionary process, but appears even in the smallest building block of life, as in DNA and in the single cell.

Molecular biology has opened up a whole new world of complexity that staggers the imagination and exposes how incredulous is the theory of evolution. W. R. Bird, in his book *The Origin of Species Revisited,* speaks of the enormous complexity of a single cell. Quoting Sagan, he concludes that the simple cell has "information . . . comparable to about a hundred million pages of the *Encyclopedia Britannica.*"[118] Richard Dawkins compares it to 30 volumes of the encyclopedia.[119] Whichever analogy one takes, it is a staggering amount of storage in just one tiny cell! *Of Pandas and People* goes so far as to say that "if the amount of information contained in one cell of your body were written out on a typewriter, it would fill as many books as are contained in a large library."[120] The tiny bacterial cells are incredibly small, and "each is in effect a veritable microminiaturized factory containing thousands of exquisitely designed pieces of intricate molecular machinery, made up together of one hundred thousand million atoms, far more complicated than any machine built by man and absolutely without parallel in the nonliving world."[121]

Who can explain how the simplest, tiniest cell became complex? We have no known evolutionary development of such so-called primitive cells. In fact, as Jacques Monad rightly states, "the simplest cells available to us for study have nothing 'primitive' about them."[122]

Natural Selection

After looking at the issue of complexity, we next take up the central mechanism that Darwin believed causes evolutionary development. In *The Origin of Species* he spells out the difficulties to his theory in chapter 6: "Can we believe that natural selection could produce, on the one hand, an organ of trifling importance, such as the tail of a giraffe, which serves as a fly-flapper, and, on the other hand, an organ so wonderful as the eye?"[123]

During the nineteenth century, scientists, while accepting evolution as a fact, increasingly came to question the supposed mechanism of evolution through natural selection.[124] Today we can even say that natural selection has been "relegated to a backseat in terms of its shaping power in the origin of species."[125]

In *The Origin of Species* Darwin speaks of domestic breeding and concludes, "There is no reason why the principles which have acted so efficiently under domestication should not have acted under nature."[126] Darwin did not have any examples of natural selection when he wrote *The Origin of Species*, but he did know how animal breeders selected domesticated animals to improve the stock. Much evidence does exist that selective breeding does aid both animals and plants—at least for human purposes. But this comparison is valid only if the human owners of animals will do the same as the animals would have done if left to themselves.

Paradoxically, Darwin excludes an intelligent God from the process of natural selection, but finds in intelligent humans an empirical evidence for natural selection. Here is a basic logical inconsistency in his claim. He is not comparing apples with apples, even though there is a partial analogy. As Phillip Johnson rightly says, "the analogy to artificial selection is misleading.

Plant and animal breeders employ intelligence and specialized knowledge to select breeding stock and to protect their charges from natural dangers. The point of Darwin's theory, however, was to establish that purposelessness natural processes can substitute for intelligent design."[127]

What Darwin should have learned from domestic breeding is that change has definite boundaries. "Mutations are almost always (99.995) harmful, if not lethal, to the unfortunate organism in which they occur. In other words, mutations produce organisms that are weaker and at a marked disadvantage; they are less able to compete for survival. This fact directly contradicts the assumptions of the modern evolutionary theory."[128] We need to recognize mutations for what they are. It is not a case that they are always beneficial, and also plentiful. In fact, "mutations are quite rare. This is fortunate, for the vast majority are harmful, although some may be neutral. Recall that DNA is a molecular message. A mutation is a random change in the message akin to a typing error. Typing errors rarely improve the quality of a written message; if too many occur, they may even destroy the information contained in it. Likewise, mutations rarely improve the quality of the DNA message, and too many may even be lethal to the organism."[129]

Even if mutations are helpful, how likely is it that they can occur to form even one new structure? Suppose an insect wing requires only five genes, an extremely low estimate, and suppose that the new wing information could come from a single mutation per gene. Next we estimate that a single mutation will occur in only one individual out of 1,000. The probability of two mutations within the same individual is one in 1 million. "The odds of five mutations occurring are one in one thousand million million." The occurrence of this in the life cycle of one organism is not realistic. And this is only one mutation. "Yet, an organism is made of many structures that must appear at the same time and work together in an integrated whole, if they are not to work to its disadvantage."[130]

Most accept the reality of microevolution. The question is whether one can extrapolate macroevolution from that fact. Alvin Plantinga points out that "there is some experiential reason to think not; there seems to be a sort of envelope of limited variability surrounding a species and its near relatives. Artificial selection can produce several different kinds of fruit flies and several different kinds of dogs, but, starting with fruit flies, what it produces is only more fruit flies. As plants or animals are bred in certain directions, a sort of barrier is encountered; further selective breeding brings about sterility or a reversion to earlier forms."[131]

Whereas Darwin looked to natural selection as the central driving force for his theory of evolution, today "a growing number of scientists accepts natural selection as a reasonable explanation for the modification of traits but not for the origins of new structures." Even if natural selection did operate on genetic variability to produce new species, "then the Darwinist is faced with several difficult problems. First of all, if organisms can be modified easily by natural forces to produce all of the variety we see among species today, why does any line exist at all that is stable enough and distinct enough to be called a species? Why is the world not filled with intermediate forms of every conceivable kind? In fact, the world corresponds much more closely to what can be expected from the intelligent design point of view: it is filled with distinct and stable species that retain their identity over long periods of time, and intermediate forms expected by Darwinists are missing."[132] Constancy, rather than change, seems to be the basic pattern found in nature.

We need to take a closer look at natural selection. It doesn't explain the arrival of the fittest,[133] the origin of species,[134] altruism found in nature,[135] or entropy.[136] If natural selection did produce all the species extant today, why do we still find so much stasis?[137] Actually we have no evidence that natural selection has creative power.[138] Natural selection predates Darwin, and Edward Blyth considered it responsible for maintaining the fixity of species, an idea "postulated by virtually all proponents of intelligent design, including the father of taxonomy, Carolus Linnaeus."[139] How do evolutionists validate their choice that natural selection produces species under the descent model when others have also seen it as maintaining the fixity of species under the design model? Particularly when it is unknown if natural selection can produce a new species.[140] We must remember that Darwin's loss of faith was a major contribution to his substituting natural selection in place of the work of God in creation.

Furthermore, for Darwin natural selection explained everything. But if it explains everything, does it really explain anything? As Brian Leith observed, "If the presence of adaptations is evidence for selection, but the absence of adaptations is not evidence *against* selection, then is it possible to deny the existence of selection at all? In other words if selection can explain everything then it really explains nothing. Good scientific theories should be testable and even falsifiable."[141]

The Fossil Record Doesn't Support Darwin

A. Hallam, of the department of geological sciences, University of Birmingham, Great Britain, observes that fossils "are the only direct evidence we have of the history of life on our planet, and in particular of the course of evolution."[142] If that is so, then evolutionary theory rests on an extremely flimsy foundation, as we will see in this section. In fact, a tautological relationship exists between evolution and fossils. "The only justification for assigning fossils to specific time periods in that chronology is the assumed evolutionary progression of life. In turn, the only basis for biological evolution is the fossil record so constructed. In other words, the assumption of evolution is used to arrange the sequence of the fossils, then the resultant sequence is advanced as proof of evolution."[143]

Paleontologists have recorded nearly 100,000 fossil species, and yet "where sequence does exist it is exceptional or relatively trivial."[144] Moreover, 99 percent of the biology of any organism resides in the soft anatomy that doesn't get preserved, so the fossil record is only 1 percent of the organism.[145] At best, researchers estimate that only 87.8 percent of the 329 living families of terrestrial vertebrates were fossilized. Birds especially have left a poor record.[146]

Evolution necessitates a change from one species to another up the increasingly complex progression from the first cell to human beings. If that in fact happened, we would expect to find remains of transitional forms between the evolving species. But we can search the fossil record at every level and find no such evidence. In the first edition of *The Origin of Species* Darwin admits that the fossil record is "the most obvious and gravest objection which can be urged against my theory."[147] Instead of giving up his theory, though, he seems to blame the fossil record for the absence of the transitional forms. "I do not pretend that I should ever have suspected how poor a record of the mutations of life, the best preserved geological section presented, had not the difficulty of our not discovering innumerable transitional links between the species which appeared at the commencement and close of each formation, pressed so hardly on my theory."[148]

Darwin clearly blames the fossil record in a chapter on the imperfection of the geological record. Elsewhere he argues that the reason we do not find innumerable transitions is due to "the record being incomparably less perfect than is generally supposed. The crust of the earth is a vast museum; but the natural collections have been imperfectly made, and only at long intervals of time."[149] As a result "the geological record is far more imperfect than most geologists believe."[150] Darwin concludes that "the noble science of geology loses glory from the extreme imperfection of the record," for fossils are "a poor collection made at hazard and at rare intervals."[151]

Apparently Darwin came to the fossil record with his own preconceived assumption about evolution, then forced that upon the fossil record rather than allowing the absence of transitional forms to call his theory into question. And he did it in the name of science. Such a procedure runs counter to scientific methodology that allows the objective data or experimentation to verify or falsify a theory.

Martin J. S. Rudwick, lecturer in history and philosophy of science, Cambridge University, in his book *The Meaning of Fossils* notes the subjectivity of fossil study. "The 'meaning' of fossils has been seen in many different ways in different periods. Indeed, the same fossil specimens (for example, sharks' teeth) have been reinterpreted several times within different frames of reference—they have, as it were, been seen with different eyes."[152] Moreover, study has shown that "there was no fossil evidence of one species changing gradually into another when traced through successive strata; and—much more seriously—there was no fossil evidence that any of the major groups, with their distinct types of anatomical organization, had had any common ancestors."[153] L. Beverly Halstead in *Nature* agrees, stating "no fossil species can be considered the direct ancestor of any other."[154]

Evolutionary paleontologists attempt to find evidence for evolution in the fossils. "The Darwinist approach has consistently been to find some supporting evidence, claim it as proof for 'evolution,' and then ignore all the difficulties."[155] On the other hand, what is perhaps surprising to many people is the fact that the fossil experts, rather than clergy, have been "Darwin's most formidable opponents."[156]

Punctuated Equilibrium

Despite more than 130 years of study of the fossil record, the lack of evidence for transitional forms is the same today as in Darwin's day.[157] That is why during the 1970s Harvard professor Stephen Jay Gould and paleontologist Niles Eldredge proposed a theory called "punctuated equilibrium." It attempted to explain the absence of transitional forms in the fossil record. Clearly the fossil record gives evidence of stasis (no directional change) as opposed to evolutionary gradualism. Also species appear suddenly in the fossil record, without any sign of transitional forms. Stasis then always follows the sudden introduction. This fact radically questions the evolutionary theory. As Phillip Johnson says, "The fossil problem for Darwinism is getting worse all the time."[158]

Gould and Eldredge were not the first to question gradualism by suggesting an "abrupt evolution." Hugo de Vries "led the Continental 'mutationists' with ideas of large-scale, abrupt evolution."[159] Scientists have modified "Darwin's basic tenet of gradual change to the concept of stasis (no change) alternating with episodes of rapid change," for the "pattern of fossil organism is not, by and large, a graded series, but clusters separated by gaps."[160]

Beyond the idea of "abrupt evolution," "explosive evolution,"[161] "'Instant' speciation,"[162] or "punctuated equilibrium," and yet inextricably linked to them, is the discovery that new species appearing suddenly in the fossil record have no trace of ancestral linkage. "The new data from biochemistry where organismal differences can be measured somewhat more quantitatively, generally confirm this pattern of clustering. By studying sequences of amino acids in proteins, it has been found that organisms cannot be lined up in a series, A-B-C, where A is an ancestor of B and B an ancestor of C, but are instead, approximately equidistant from most other organisms in a different taxon. This feature remains reasonably consistent over a wide range of species."[163] In agreement, Alvin Plantinga notes that "nearly all species appear for the first time in the fossil record fully formed, without the vast chains of intermediary forms evolution would suggest."[164]

Cambrian Explosion

As geologists study the stratified layers in the geological column, they assume that the oldest strata contain primitive fossils, and the later strata contain more complex fossils. Thus they consider the geological column to support the evolutionary development from primitive to more complex as we move through the time layers. However, it is well known that the early strata, known as Cambrian, contain a plethora of organisms. "There is a virtual 'explosion' of life-forms recorded in the rocks at the beginning of the Cambrian. Any theory of the origin and development of life must explain how such a dramatic range of body plans made the early, abrupt appearance they did."[165]

The abrupt arrival of complex animals in the Cambrian strata undermines the idea of continuous ancestry. Whereas Darwin's evolutionary tree has all species linked through one ancestral line, Stephen Jay Gould, with his punctuated equilibria, questions the one ancestral line. Bernhard Rensch, professor of zoology, University of Münster, speaks of "parallel evolution" rather than one ancestral line.[166] Phillip Johnson considers that "one of the most powerful examples" against one ancestral line "is the Cambrian Explosion, in which the complex animal groups appear suddenly, without any evidence of step-by-step descent from single-celled predecessors."[167]

In fact, the geological column presents some more complex animals in lower strata, and some less complex ones in higher levels. The assumption behind the geological column—that it was laid down during a 4 billion-year period—flips upside down if we accept the biblical story of a worldwide flood (Gen. 7; 8). Such a flood would have caused the geological column.

147

Geologists should be studying the geological column as evidence of the demise of the preflood world rather than its evolution.

Cladistics

Whereas Darwin believed in an infinite number of intermediary links,[168] typologists did not believe in the theory of a common ancestor.[169] Typologists and taxonomists had carefully classified the species before Darwin wrote his book in 1859. Actually, classification goes all the way back to Aristotle, and Linnaeus continued it in his *Systema Naturae* during the eighteenth century.[170] The most influential of the new schools of taxonomy is known as cladistics, founded during the early 1960s by German systematist Willi Hennig.[171] Cladistics emphasize the distinctness of biological classes, with no ancestral linkage, thus radically calling into question evolutionary theory.

The British Museum of Natural History decided to exhibit "Man's Place in Evolution" in 1980. The museum's book *A New Look at Dinosaurs* concluded, so Halstead reports, "that no fossil species can be considered the direct ancestor of any other."[172] The statement caused a great stir, as we see exhibited in the pages of the journal *Nature*. Cladistics and evolutionary theory were at loggerheads. Keith Thompson of Yale University commented on the battle: "No one needs reminding that we are well into a revolutionary phase in the study of evolution, systematics, and the interrelationships of organisms . . . to the thesis of Darwinian evolution . . . has been added a *new cladistic antithesis* which says that the search for ancestors is a *fool's errand,* that all we can do is determine sister group relationships based on the analysis of derived characters. . . . It is a change in approach that is not easy to accept for, in a sense, it runs counter to what we have all been taught."[173]

Molecular Biology

Molecular biology has taken the debate between evolutionists and those who question the theory to a more profound level. We have already noted how the complexity of a single cell has raised serious questions about the idea of development from the simple to the complex, for nature at its micro level is already complex. Furthermore, a study of molecules has provided further evidence for stasis. "As more protein sequences began to accumulate during the 1960s, it became increasingly apparent that the molecules were not going to provide any evidence of sequential arrangements in nature, but were rather going to reaffirm the traditional view that the system of nature conforms fundamentally to a highly ordered hierarchic scheme. Moreover, the divisions turned out to be more mathematically perfect than even most die-hard typologists would have predicted."[174]

The Darwinian thesis that life arose through a naturalistic process now faces still more fundamental challenges. Alvin Plantinga observes that "Darwin thought this claim very chancy; discoveries since Darwin and in particular recent discoveries in molecular biology make it much less likely than it was in Darwin's day."[175] On the evolutionary paradigm, how did humans come to talk, to reason, to ask questions, to have a conscience? As we alluded to earlier, microbiologists Michael Denton and Dimitri Kouznetsov find a profound similarity between human language capacity and "the unfolding series of biological language systems including the genetic code. For this reason, it is nearly impossible to address the question of how the human language capacity came to be without coming eventually to consider the closely related mystery of how life itself came to be. Conversely, biologists today are increasingly aware that insights from linguistics are apt to aid our understanding of molecular biology and biophysics (and vice versa)."[176]

Molecular study has shown distance instead of ancestral linkage between species.[177] Also "at the molecular level, the effect of natural selection is therefore mainly to prevent change."[178]

Evolutionary Logic Questioned

Philip E. Johnson, in his book *Darwin on Trial,* uses his lawyer mind to evaluate the claims of Darwinian evolution. After admitting that he is not a defender of creation-science, he states that his purpose "is to examine the scientific evidence on its own terms." He assumes that "creation-scientists are biased by their precommitment to Biblical fundamentalism" and thus investigates "whether Darwinism is based upon a fair assessment of the scientific evidence, or whether it is another kind of fundamentalism."[179] Throughout the book Johnson seeks to separate scientific empirical evidence from metaphysical or philosophical presuppositions. Repeatedly he concludes that evolution rests upon theory and lacks empirical evidence. We will consider only one example of faulty logic that he critiques.

Stephen Jay Gould's article "Evolution as Fact and Theory" included the following comparison: "Facts are the world's data. Theories are structures of ideas that explain and interpret facts. Facts do not go away while scientists debate rival theories for explaining them. Einstein's theory of gravitation replaced Newton's, but apples did not suspend themselves in mid-air pending the outcome. And human beings evolved from ape-like ancestors whether they did so by Darwin's proposed mechanism or by some other, yet to be identified."[180]

Here Gould compares the fall of apples with evolutionary ascent. The problem with such a comparison is that we can demonstrate the plummet of apples, whereas we cannot do so for evolutionary ascent. As Johnson rightly says: "The analogy is spurious. We observe that apples fall when dropped, but we do not observe a common ancestor for modern apes and humans. What we do observe is that apes and humans are physically and biochemically more like each other than they are like rabbits, snakes, or trees. The apelike common ancestor is a hypothesis in a theory, which purports to explain how these greater and lesser similarities came about. The theory is plausible, especially to a philosophical materialist, but it may nonetheless be false. The true explanation for natural relationships may be something much more mysterious."[181]

One of the major weaknesses of every phase of evolutionary theory is the acceptance of evolutionary theory as a fact, and then interpreting empirical data from that perspective. The quest is biased with more basic presuppositions than we would expect in a more objective scientific study. The lack of empirical evidence for the theory, and the faith required to believe in it, makes it more of a philosophy than a science. But it is even more than a philosophy. It is also a religion.

Evolution as a Religion

When we remove God or the supernatural from the realm of causality, something has to fill the vacuum. Not only has naturalism taken the place of God, but evolution has become a religion in place of the biblical religion that worships the Creator. Physicist H. S. Lipson observed that "evolution became in a sense a scientific religion: almost all scientists have accepted it and many are prepared to 'bend' their observations to fit in with it."[182] Alvin Plantinga noted that "evolution has deep religious connections; deep connections with how we understand ourselves at the most fundamental level,"[183] that evolution "is by no means religiously or theologically neutral."[184]

A conflict rages between Scripture and science when it comes to the doctrine of creation. We should remember that it is not just the historicity of Genesis that scientists question, for the doctrine of creation appears in 60 places throughout the New Testament.[185] The doctrine of God as Creator, and not nature, is fundamental to the biblical worldview. Scientists rejecting the Genesis account of creation are really denying the biblical worldview. Thomas Kuhn has persuasively shown that some current teachings of science may not be correct, and that scientific paradigms have changed. Although Kuhn never mentioned the naturalistic evolutionary worldview, his thesis applies to it also.[186]

Plantinga opposed the surrender of science to Scripture or Scripture to science, for how do we know if the position to which we surrender is the right one? "The belief that when there is a conflict, the problem must inevitably lie with our interpretation of Scripture, so that the correct course is always to modify that understanding in such a way as to accommodate current science—is every bit as deplorable as the opposite error. No doubt science can correct our grasp of Scripture; but Scripture can also correct current science."[187] He believes that a battle rages between perennial naturalism, Enlightenment humanism, and Christian theism, all "three basically religious ways of viewing ourselves and the world." He observes that "according to a popular contemporary myth, science is a cool, reasoned, wholly dispassionate attempt to figure out the truth about ourselves and our world, entirely independent of religion, or ideology, or moral convictions, or theological commitments. I believe this is deeply mistaken. Following Augustine (and Abraham Kuyper, Herman Dooyeweerd, Harry Jellema, Henry Stob and other Reformed thinkers), I believe that there is conflict, a battle between the *Civitas Dei*, the City of God, and the City of the World."[188]

The Changing Evolutionary Worldview
and the Challenge to Seventh-day Adventist Mission

Seventh-day Adventists believe that Satan lies behind the various forms of evolutionary theory locked into the confined worldview of naturalism. The apostle Peter predicted the premise of uniformitarianism, so important to evolution, when he said that "in the last days scoffers will come, scoffing and following their own evil desires. They will say, 'Where is this "coming" he promised? Ever since our fathers died, everything goes on as it has since the beginning of creation'" (2 Peter 3:3, 4, NIV). That everything goes on as it has since creation means there was no flood. Such uniformitarianism is a basic part of evolutionary theory, because evolutionary scientists do not regard the geological columns as evidence for the destruction of the world by a global deluge, but as a demonstration that the world has evolved from its beginning. It was in the nineteenth century that catastrophism, or belief in a global flood, collapsed under the new doctrine of uniformitarianism predicted in Scripture.

Sir Julian Huxley speaks about Darwin's reluctance to write out his theory. In 1842 he put his ideas down on paper. Then, "two years later, in 1844, he enlarged this into an 'Essay.' As a matter of fact, this so-called essay was a sizable book of 230 pages, covering almost the same ground as the *Origin,* and more than adequate as an exposition of the whole subject."[189] So Darwin wrote out his theory in full in 1844, or 15 years before its publication as the *The Origin of Species* in 1859. What a significant date—1844, the launching of the Seventh-day Adventist Church in its pioneer stage; 1844—the beginning of the first angel's message to "every nation, tribe, language and people" (Rev. 14:6, NIV), calling them to "worship him who made the heavens, the earth, the sea and the springs of water" (verse 7, NIV).

Think of it—the Seventh-day Adventist Church began at the precise hour that Darwin wrote out his frontal attack on the Creator. The Lord has called us out to lead humanity to worship Christ as Creator. The first angel's message started on time to meet the enormous challenge of the counterfeit creation theory of evolution.

As we move toward the time of Christ's return, we find major new developments in evolutionary thinking. The inclusion of causation in science, the fantastic marvels of DNA, the sheer complexity in nature, the impossibility of the various parts of the visual network developing at the same time to produce an eye (as well as other examples), the enormous complexity of a single cell, the total absence of support for Darwinian evolution in the fossil record on the one hand, and plentiful evidence of abrupt appearance of new species with no intermediaries (punctuated equilibrium) on the other hand, the work of cladistics providing empirical evidence for definite gaps between the species, the revolutionary research in molecular biology that finds complexity at the microsphere without any trace of prior development—all these point to the same conclusion: to design by the Creator instead of descent through natural selection and random genetic mutation. Throughout the many interconnected levels of nature we find evidence of purpose rather than purposelessness. In place of the assumptions of evolutionary theory, which lack empirical support, we find much empirical evidence for an intelligent Designer/Creator behind the complexities of His interdependent universe.

Two worldviews are locked in deadly battle today: naturalism with its evolutionary theory and supernaturalism with its belief in Jesus Christ as the Creator of the heavens and the earth and all within them. It is a major fight in the end-time controversy between Satan and Christ. Satan hates Christ. Evolutionary theory is one of his many schemes to direct attention away from Him. Belief in evolution distances Christ from humanity in its origin, removing the fall of humanity so that the atonement by Christ is not necessary. Many claim that Christ does not need to save human beings. They have evolved through natural means. In fact, humans are still evolving. New Age philosophy, the writing of Catholic paleontologist Teilhard de Chardin, Mormon theology, as well as the reincarnational belief of Eastern religions, to name a few, all speak of humans as developing toward godhood. It is the same lie that Satan gave to Eve in Eden. "'You will not surely die,' the serpent said to the woman. 'For God knows that when you eat of it your eyes will be opened, and you will be like God'" (Gen. 3:4, 5, NIV).

In the light of this ancient battle with its modern form, it is inconsistent for evangelicals to subscribe to theistic evolution. With so many questions being raised today against the various phases of evolution, Seventh-day Adventists have a window of opportunity[190] to proclaim intelligently the first angel's message to a world that needs to know that Christ created human beings (Heb. 1:2), made them in His image (Gen. 1:27), creates within them now (Ps. 51:10; 2 Cor. 3:18), will create again when the redeemed are made immortal (1 Cor. 15:54), and when the dead are resurrected (1 Thess. 4:16), and will create a new heaven and a new earth, then come to dwell with humanity forever (Rev. 21:1-4).

Because Christ is in the business of creating throughout history, from Eden to beyond the millennium, humanity has hope. It is to hide that hope, and thrust the human race back into a jungle of survival of the fittest with all its degrading social results, that Satan has promoted evolutionary theory. It is a counterfeit religion that takes the place of Christ. The challenge to Seventh-day Adventists is to lift up Christ as central in all their beliefs, showing how all their fundamental doctrines find their inner coherence in the message of Christ as Creator/Redeemer.

---

[1] Michael Bartholomew, Bernard Norton, and Robert M. Young, *Block VI, Problems in the Biological and Human Sciences* (London: The Open University, 1981), p. 17.

[2] W. R. Bird, *The Origin of Species Revisited: The Theories of Evolution of Abrupt Appearance,* in *Science* (New York: Philosophical Library), vol. 1, p. 1.

[3] Ernst Mayr, "Behavior Programs and Evolutionary Strategies," *American Scientist* 62 (November-December 1974): 650.

[4] ————, "Darwin and Natural Selection: How Darwin May Have Discovered His Highly Unconventional Theory," *American Scientist,* May-June 1977, p. 321.

[5] Naturalist Alfred R. Wallace wrote a paper on natural selection and sent it to Charles Darwin in 1858. The document shocked Darwin, who had been working on his theory for 20 years, and he feared that his own work on natural selection was now at risk as an original idea, even though both men had done their work independently. Charles Lyell, a friend of Darwin, arranged with the Linnean Society in London that Darwin and Wallace could both present their papers in 1858. From 1869 onward Wallace had an important difference with Darwin. He concluded that natural selection was not responsible for the emergence of human beings. In 1910, at the age of 87, Wallace made a second major step away from Darwin. He wrote, "After 40 years of further reflection, I now uphold the doctrine that not only man but the whole world of life leads us to the same conclusion—that to afford any rational explanation or its phenomena, we require to postulate the continuous action and guidance of a higher intelligence." He thereby broke beyond the naturalist paradigm of Darwin to allow for the supernatural (Paul Kilkdare, "Monkey Business," *Christian Order,* December 1982, p. 592; see also Bartholomew et al., pp. 19, 20.

[6] Henry M. Morris, *The Biblical Basis for Modern Science* (Grand Rapids: Baker, 1990), p. 111.

[7] Mayr, "Darwin and Natural Selection," p. 327.

[8] Martin Lings, quoted in Huston Smith, "Evolution and Evolutionism," *The Christian Century,* July 7-14, 1982, p. 755.

[9] Robert Wright, "Our Cheating Hearts," *Time,* Aug. 15, 1994, pp. 44-52.

[10] Morris, p. 403.

[11] Charles Darwin, *The Origin of Species* (New York: Carlton, 1859), p. 373.

[12] Paul K. Jewett, *God, Creation, and Revelation* (Grand Rapids: Eerdmans, 1991), pp. 479, 480.

[13] Scholars who, in varying degrees, place evolutionary theory as the context in which to interpret the Genesis account of creation include: Augustus Strong, *Systematic Theology* (Philadelphia: Judson, 1907), pp. 465, 466; Bernard Ramm, *The Christian View of Science and Scripture* (Grand Rapids: Eerdmans, 1954), pp. 76-79; Langdon Gilkey, *Maker of Heaven and Earth* (Garden City, N.Y.: Doubleday, 1965); Millard J. Erickson, *Christian Theology* (Grand Rapids: Baker, 1986), pp. 381, 382; Jewett, pp. 478-484.

[14] Marco T. Terreros, "Death Before the Sin of Adam: A Fundamental Concept in Theistic Evolution and Its Implications for Evangelical Theology" (Ph.D. dissertation, Andrews University Theological Seminary, 1994). See *Andrews University Seminary Studies* 32, Nos. 1, 2 (Spring-Summer 1994): 114.

[15] Karl Barth, *Church Dogmatics* (Edinburgh: T & T Clark, 1960), vol. 3, part 2, pp. 511-640; cf. Barth (1964), vol. 2, part 1, pp. 608-677.

[16] Thomas N. Finger, *Christian Theology: An Eschatological Approach* (Scottdale, Pa.: Herald, 1989), vol. 2, p. 413.

[17] Alfred Whitehead, *Process and Reality* (New York: Free, 1929), pp. 25, 26.

[18] John Macquarrie, *Principles of Christian Theology* (New York: Scribner, 1966).

[19] Pierre Teilhard de Chardin, *The Phenomenon of Man,* trans. Bernard Wall (New York: Harper, 1959).

[20] Augustine seems to posit the idea that God implanted seeds in the natural order for an ongoing creation. *On the Holy Trinity* (3.8), in *The Nicene and Post-Nicene Fathers* (Edinburgh: T & T Clark, 1988), First Series, vol. 3, pp. 60, 61.

[21] In his *Summa Theologica* Thomas Aquinas, after considering the procession in the Trinity (Q 27-43), takes up the procession of creatures from God (Q 44-49). He views the two processions in a type/antitype correspondence (45.6). Thus "every being in any way existing is from God" (44.1) in what seems to be progressive creation (*Summa Theologica,* trans. Fathers of the English Dominican Province [Westminster, Md.: Christian Classics, 1981], vol. 1, pp. 229-256).

[22] Theistic evolution is a divine working immanental in nature, whereas progressive creation focuses on the transcendental activity of God. See Bernard Ramm, *The Christian View of Science and Scripture* (Grand Rapids: Eerdmans, 1971), p. 147.

[23] "The Church Today," *The Documents of Vatican II,* ed. Walter M. Abbott, trans. Joseph Gallagher (London: Geoffrey Chapman, 1967), p. 234.

[24] *Ibid.,* p. 265.

[25] *Ibid.,* p. 117.

[26] *Catechism of the Catholic Church* (Liguori, Mo.: Liguori Publications, 1994), p. 74.

[27] Mayr, "Darwin and Natural Selection," p. 321.

[28] Michael Denton, *Evolution: A Theory in Crisis* (Bethesda, Md.: Adler and Adler, 1986), p. 37.

[29] Isaac Asimov, *Asimov's New Guide to Science* (New York: Basic Books, 1972), p. 772.

[30] Marvin L. Lubenow, "Augustine: Evolutionist or Creationist" (unpublished paper presented to the Evangelical Theological Society, Nov. 17-19, 1994, Chicago).

[31] Bowler argues that Aristotle was not the real discoverer of evolution. Rather Darwin's natural selection was a "genuine scientific revolution" (Peter J. Bowler, *Evolution: The History of an Idea* [Berkeley, Calif.: University of California, 1989], pp. 20, 21).

[32] Eiseley argues that eighteenth-century biologists contributed to a new understanding of evolution, such as Buffon's premonition of the Law of Succession, that animals developed in the area in which they are now found, rather than coming from Noah's ark (p. 44). Other ideas include: Erasmus Darwin's (Darwin's grandfather) belief "in the inheritance of acquired characteristics" (p. 48). Jean Baptiste Lamarck held a similar view (p. 49). "Both he and Erasmus Darwin placed . . . an emphasis upon volition, the 'striving' of the organism for survival and adjustment" (p. 51). "Lamarck appears to have been the first to grasp the importance of the concept of use and disuse in their effect upon individual organs. Later on this was to be appropriated by Charles Darwin" (p. 55) (Loren Eiseley, *Darwin's Century* [Garden City, N.Y.: Doubleday, 1958], pp. 44-55).

[33] Green argues that "Buffon was very close to the idea of natural selection" (p. 152). "The mutability of species, a conception toward which Buffon had slowly groped his way, became Lamarck's

starting point" (p. 159). Lamarck's "developmental hypothesis" was fundamental to his view of evolution (p. 161). "Lamarck provided the first systematic elaboration of the evolutionary idea" that goes back to Darwin's grandfather, Erasmus Darwin (p. 166) (John C. Greene, *The Death of Adam: Evolution and Its Impact on Western Thought* [Ames, Iowa: Iowa State University, 1959], pp. 145-169).

[34] In 1942 Sir Julian Huxley coined the term *modern synthesis* (Roger Lewin, "Evolutionary Theory Under Fire: An Historical Conference in Chicago Challenges the Four-Decades-Long Dominance of the Modern Synthesis," *Science* 210 [Nov. 21, 1980]: 883).

[35] Sir Julian Huxley mentions the 1915 date, and Ernst Mayr cites the 1930s date. Perhaps this is the time during which the synthesis of Darwin's natural selection with Mendel's genetic heredity took place (Sir Julian Huxley, in Sol Tax, ed., *The Evolution of Life: Its Origin, History, and Future* [Chicago: University of Chicago Press, 1960], p. 10; Ernst Mayr, *Populations, Species, and Evolution* [Cambridge, Mass.: Harvard, 1970], p. 1). Theodosius Dobzhansky was one of the architects of the neo-Darwinian modern synthesis (Brian Leith, *The Descent of Darwin: A Handbook of Doubts About Darwinism* [London: Collins, 1982], p. 19).

[36] "Post-Darwinianism" is an expression I coined to represent the demise of the strictly Darwinian model. Although the modern synthesis added random genetic mutation to Darwin's sole principle of natural selection, the marriage proved to be only an assumed strengthening of Darwin's basic thesis. With the advent of molecular biology and the study of DNA, there came a persuasive challenge to the central thesis of Darwinian evolutionary theory. This continued in the work of Niles Eldredge and Stephen Jay Gould in their view of "punctuated equilibrium." The sudden appearance of species in the fossil record radically called in question Darwinian gradualism.

[37] In 1980 Stephen Jay Gould and Niles Eldridge proposed a new theory of abrupt, rather than gradual, changes in evolutionary development (Phillip E. Johnson, *Darwin on Trial* [Downers Grove, Ill.: InterVarsity, 1991], pp. 11, 39, 50).

[38] Leith, pp. 13, 14.

[39] Johnson, p. 118.

[40] L. Beverly Halstead, "Halstead's Defence Against Irrelevancy," *Nature* 292 (July 30, 1981): 404.

[41] Peter J. Bowler, *Evolution: The History of an Idea* (Berkeley, Calif.: University of California Press, 1989), p. 356.

[42] Scott M. Huse, *The Collapse of Evolution* (Grand Rapids: Baker, 1983).

[43] Denton.

[44] Johnson.

[45] J. P. Moreland, ed., *The Creation Hypothesis: Scientific Evidence for an Intelligent Designer* (Downers Grove, Ill.: InterVarsity, 1994).

[46] Percival Davis and Dean H. Kenyon, *Of Pandas and People: The Central Question of Biological Origins* (Dallas: Haughton, 1989).

[47] Leith.

[48] Alvin Plantinga, "When Faith and Reason Clash: Evolution and the Bible," *Christian Scholar's Review* 21, No. 1 (1991): 8-32.

[49] Michael Polanyi, "Life's Irreducible Structure," *Science* 160 (June 1968): 1308-1312.

[50] Bird.

[51] In fairness it may be claimed that there are a few transitionals, such as the *Archaeopteryx,* but they seem to prove the rule as exceptions. The *Archaeopteryx* looks like the small dinosaur called *Compsognathus.* It has wings and feathers, but has claws on its wings and teeth in its mouth (see Johnson, p. 78).

[52] Johnson, p. 9.

[53] Karl Popper, quoted in Leith, p. 26.

[54] Leith, p. 28.

[55] Gunther S. Stent, in Ashley Montagu, ed., *Science and Creationism* (Oxford University Press, 1984), p. 137.

[56] Michael Ruse, ed., *But Is It Science?* (Buffalo, N.Y.: Prometheus, 1988), p. 6.

[57] Moreland, p. 43.

[58] Alvin Plantinga, "When Faith and Reason Clash: Evolution and the Bible," *Christian Scholar's Review* 21, No. 1 (1991): 30.

[59] Michael Ruse, "Creation Science Is Not Science," *Science, Technology, and Human Values* 7, No. 40 (Summer 1982): 74.

[60] Paul K. Feyerabend, in Robert G. Colodny, ed., *Beyond the Edge of Certainty: Essays in Contemporary Science and Philosophy* (Englewood Cliffs, N.J.: Prentice-Hall, 1965), p. 146.

[61] Charles B. Thaxton, in Davis and Kenyon, p. viii.

[62] Moreland, p. 55.

[63] Morris, p. 31.

[64] Abraham Wolf, quoted in Morris, p. 35.

[65] Sir Julian Huxley, in Sol Tax, ed., *Evolution After Darwin,* vol. 1 of *The Evolution of Life: Its Origin, History and Future* (Chicago: University of Chicago Press, 1960), p. 2.

[66] Stephen C. Meyer, in Moreland, p. 81.

[67] *Ibid.,* p. 79.

[68] Julius Rebek, Jr., "Synthetic Self-replicating Molecules," *Scientific American,* July 1994, p. 48.

[69] Johnson, p. 102.

[70] Walter L. Bradley and Charles B. Thaxton, in Moreland, p. 175.

[71] Johnson, p. 103.

[72] Sir Frederick Hoyle, quoted by Paul Kildare in "Monkey Business," *Christian Order,* December 1982, p. 589.

[73] Richard Dawkins, in Ruse, *But Is It Science?* p. 202.

[74] Francis Crick, *Life Itself: Its Origin and Nature* (New York: Simon and Schuster, 1981), p. 116.

[75] *Ibid.,* p. 128.

[76] Denton, p. 263.

[77] Klaus Dose, "The Origin of Life: More Questions Than Answers," *Interdisciplinary Science Reviews* 13, No. 4 (1988): 352.

[78] Stephen C. Meyer, in Moreland, p. 72.

[79] Millard J. Erickson, *Christian Theology* (Grand Rapids: Baker, 1986), p. 49.

[80] Stephen C. Meyer, in Moreland, p. 71.

[81] *Ibid.,* p. 67.

[82] *Ibid.,* p. 68.

[83] Mae-Wan Ho and Pewter T. Saunders, eds., *Beyond Neo-Darwinism: An Introduction to the New Evolutionary Paradigm* (London: Academic, 1984), p. x.

[84] Davis and Kenyon, p. 61.

[85] Denton, p. 334.

[86] John W. Oller, Jr., and John L. Omdahl, in Moreland, p. 238.

[87] *Ibid.,* p. 265.

[88] Michael Polanyi, p. 1308.

[89] *Ibid.,* p. 1309.

[90] *Ibid.*

[91] *Ibid.*

[92] Huse, p. 95.

[93] Denton, p. 351.

[94] Leith, p. 36.

[95] Richard Dawkins, "The Necessity of Darwinism," *New Scientist,* Apr. 15, 1982, p. 130.

[96] Stephen C. Meyer, in Moreland, p. 100.

[97] Kurt P. Wise, in Moreland, p. 228.

[98] *Ibid.,* p. 230.

[99] Denton, p. 342.

[100] Kurt P. Wise, in Moreland, p. 230.

[101] *Ibid.*

[102] Charles Darwin, quoted in Denton, p. 326.

[103] ———, quoted in Huse, p. 73.

[104] Denton, p. 333.

[105] Dawkins, *The Blind Watchmaker,* p. 140.

[106] *Ibid.,* p. 40.

[107] Dawkins, in Ruse, p. 210; cf. Dawkins, *The Blind Watchmaker,* p. 41.

[108] Plantinga, p. 25.

[109] Johnson, p. 34.

[110] Dan-E. Nilsson and Susanne Pelger, "A Pessimistic Estimate of the Time Required for an Eye to Evolve," *Nature,* Apr. 21, 1994.

[111] The avian lung has a one-way flow of air through the parabronchi, whereas inhalation and exhalation is a two-way passage of air in all other vertebrates. This speaks eloquently for discontinuity rather than continuity between reptiles and birds (see Denton, pp. 209-213).

[112] John Gliedman's comment, in "Scientists in Search of the Soul," *Science Digest* 90 (July 1982): 78. Roger Sperry dismisses the supernatural and the existence of extraphysical phenomena.

[113] Denton, p. 315.

[114] *Ibid.,* pp. 316, 317.

[115] *Ibid.,* p. 342.

[116] Smith, p. 756. See also Huse, p. 92, where he argues that "the handiwork of time is disassociation and disintegration, not synthesis."

[117] Dawkins suggests that "human vanity cherishes the absurd notion that our species is the final goal of evolution" (*The Blind Watchmaker,* p. 50).

[118] Bird, p. 300.

[119] Dawkins, *The Blind Watchmaker,* p. 18.

[120] Davis and Kenyon, p. 7.

[121] Denton, p. 250.

[122] Jacques Monod, *Chance and Necessity: An Essay on the Natural Philosophy of Modern Biology,* trans. Austryn Wainhouse (London: St. James's Place, 1972), p. 134.

[123] Darwin, *The Origin of Species,* p. 124.

[124] Bartholomew et. al., p. 34. Ronald L. Numbers claims that perhaps most professional naturalists remained skeptical of the primacy of natural selection from the mid-1870s (*The Creationists* [New York: Knoff, 1992], p. 5).

[125] Leith, p. 60.

[126] Darwin, *The Origin of Species,* pp. 358, 359.

[127] Johnson, p. 17.

[128] Huse, p. 90.

[129] Davis and Kenyon, p. 12.

[130] *Ibid.,* pp. 13, 14.

[131] Plantinga, pp. 23, 24.

[132] Davis and Kenyon, p. 88.

[133] Huse, p. 89.

[134] Leith, p. 78.

[135] Leith, p. 56. Richard Dawkins' selfish gene cannot be reconciled with altruism in nature (see Richard Dawkins, *The Selfish Gene* [London: Oxford University Press, 1976]).

[136] Morris, p. 205. Morris claims that "a law of science (entropy) should take precedence over a scientific belief (evolution)."

[137] Davis and Kenyon, p. 88.

[138] Johnson, p. 96.

[139] Davis and Kenyon, p. 67.

[140] Leith, p. 59.

[141] *Ibid.,* p. 21.

[142] A. Hallam, ed., *Patterns of Evolution: As Illustrated by the Fossil Record* (New York: Elsevier Scientific, 1977), preface.

[143] Huse, p. 14.

[144] Denton, p. 185.

[145] *Ibid.,* p. 177.

[146] *Ibid.,* p. 189.

[147] Darwin, *The Origin of Species.*

[148] *Ibid.*

[149] *Ibid.*, p. 125.

[150] *Ibid.*, p. 356.

[151] *Ibid.*, p. 372.

[152] Martin J. S. Rudwick, *The Meaning of Fossils: Episodes in the History of Paleontology* (London: Macdonald, 1972), p. 266.

[153] *Ibid.*, p. 229.

[154] Halstead, p. 403.

[155] Johnson, p. 84.

[156] *Ibid.*, p. 45.

[157] The *Archaeopteryx*, a claimed intermediate between reptiles and birds because it has certain skeletal features similar to both, is only an assumed intermediary in a fossil record that fails to give any certain examples. More recently found "transitional" fossils between reptiles and birds await further study.

[158] Johnson, p. 57.

[159] Leith, p. 65.

[160] Thaxton, p. 39.

[161] Mayr uses the term "explosive evolution" (Mayr, *Populations, Species, and Evolution*, p. 6).

[162] Roger Lewin, "Evolutionary Theory Under Fire: An Historic Conference in Chicago Challenges the Four-Decades-Long Dominance of the Modern Synthesis," *Science*, Nov. 21, 1980, p. 884.

[163] Thaxton, p. 40.

[164] Plantinga, p. 24.

[165] Thaxton, p. 22.

[166] Bernhard Rensch, *Evolution Above the Species Line* (New York: Columbia University Press, 1960), p. 191.

[167] Phillip E. Johnson, "Response to Hasker," *Christian Scholar's Review*, pp. 299, 300.

[168] Denton, p. 69.

[169] *Ibid.*, p. 132.

[170] *Ibid.*, pp. 122, 123.

[171] Leith, *The Descent of Darwin*, pp. 102, 103.

[172] Halstead, p. 403.

[173] Keith Thompson, in Denton, p. 139.

[174] Denton, pp. 277, 278.

[175] Plantinga, p. 20.

[176] Oller and Omdahl, in Moreland, p. 242.

[177] Johnson, pp. 90-93.

[178] *Ibid.*, p. 96.

[179] *Ibid.*, p. 14.

[180] Quoted in Johnson, pp. 66, 67.

[181] *Ibid.*, p. 67.

[182] H. S. Lipson, "A Physicist Looks at Evolution," *Physics Bulletin* 31, No. 138 (1980).

[183] Plantinga, p. 17.

[184] *Ibid.*, p. 15.

[185] Morris, p. 392.

[186] Thomas Kohn, *The Structures of Scientific Revolution* (Chicago: University Press, 1970).

[187] Plantinga, p. 14.

[188] *Ibid.*, p. 16.

[189] It was reprinted, with Darwin's sketch of 1842, in C. Darwin and A. R. Wallace, *Evolution by Natural Selection*, ed. G. R. de Beer (Cambridge: Cambridge University Press, 1958). See Sol Tax, p. 5.

[190] I concur with John T. Baldwin's conclusion in his article "Inspiration, the Natural Sciences, and a Window of Opportunity," *Journal of the Adventist Theological Society* 5, No. 1 (Spring 1994): 131-154.

CHAPTER 8

THEISTIC EVOLUTION: IMPLICATIONS FOR THE ROLE OF CREATION IN SEVENTH-DAY ADVENTIST THEOLOGY

E. Edward Zinke[1]

Introduction

This chapter seeks to answer the question How would the adoption of an evolutionary concept for the origin and creation of our world affect Adventist theology? Evolution has certainly changed the way our society looks at things—not only origins, but many different aspects of contemporary life. Our moral values: did God give them or are they somehow the result of evolution? What about our concept of the nature of the world, the reason for our existence, the future, and God's role in our life today? Evolution affects the answers to these and many more questions.[2]

The mixing of evolution and theology sometimes results in a theory called theistic evolution. While a totally humanistic or completely secularistic concept of evolution declares that matter and life just developed by chance, theistic evolution suggests that God created the initial forms of life millions or billions of years ago. Through the process of evolution, God gradually developed this bit of life until finally it became a human being.

We may briefly summarize the biblical concept of the creation of life which stands in sharp contrast to theistic evolution. God created life on the earth in six literal twenty-four hour consecutive contiguous creative days and then rested on the seventh day, a fact indicated not only in Genesis 1 but also in Exodus 20 and 31. Christ confirmed a literal interpretation of Genesis when He referred to Adam and to the flood.

Even a radical theologian such as R. Bultmann affirms that the biblical writers, whoever they were, had such a literal interpretation in mind in writing about creation.[3] Bultmann did not accept something as prominent in Scripture as the resurrection of Christ, or a literal visible Second Coming, or even the authority of Scripture. Nevertheless, he acknowledged that the writers of the Bible believed in and meant to describe a six-day creation.[4] This does not mean that Bultmann accepted the six-day creation. He argued that we live in a contemporary modern society and therefore we know better than the Bible writers in areas such as science and history and psychology and sociology. However, Bultmann recognized that the Bible writers referred to a six-day creation even though he himself opted for theistic evolution.[5]

How would the acceptance of the theory of theistic evolution affect Adventist theology? Does it matter? Did the creation of life happen millions of years ago or only a few thousand years ago as indicated by the Bible? What's the difference? Is the biblical concept of creation important to Adventist theology?

In this chapter we shall look at some of the doctrines of our church and ask what the implications would be for those doctrines if we put an *X* through the biblical concept of creation. How would the rejection of the biblical doctrine of creation affect the rest of our understanding as a church?[6] This chapter is a theological exploration.

The Impact of Theistic Evolution
The Nature of the Bible

If we accept the theory of theistic evolution instead of the biblical concept of the six-day creation, what effect would that have on our concept of the nature of the Bible? First, it might mean that the Bible has no authority at all.[7] The Bible simply expresses opinions that we must verify or reject by a human discipline such as science, history, sociology, psychology, or by human experience.[8]

Second, it might mean that the Bible is authoritative only in some realm such as the spiritual, but not in areas that have to do with human disciplines.

Third, it might be argued that the Bible has a canon within the canon. Only certain parts of the Bible are authoritative. Genesis 1 and 2 are not part of the authoritative portion of the Bible.[9]

Fourth, closely associated with the question of biblical authority is the question of biblical interpretation.[10] Some theistic evolutionists claim that the writers of Genesis did not intend to convey history. They were speaking poetically or allegorically. Thus they did not expect us to accept such forms of speech literally. Furthermore, they would argue that we should not take seriously, as truth for today, the affirmations of Christ and others in the rest of the Bible to the literalness of Genesis 1 and 2.[11]

The Origin of the Bible

The concept of theistic evolution also alters our concept of how Scripture came to be.[12] The Bible claims to be the Word of God given by Him under the Holy Spirit through prophets, who conveyed that word to the people in their own thought forms and language. The result was not the word of man, but the inspired Word of God.

The concept of theistic evolution also implies an evolutionary origin for the Bible. The Bible is not the Word of God—it is the evolving spiritual literature of certain ancient Near Eastern societies. During many generations and in many different social contexts various editors and schools of thought brought the pieces of literature together in the form that we now find in the Bible.[13] In this view the theologian who discerns and delivers the leading edge of spiritual evolution today carries on the role of the prophet.

Scripture and Nature

The concept of theistic evolution affects our understanding of the relationship between the Bible and the natural world in two possible ways.[14] First, we might make the Bible subservient to the insights we have gained from our study of the natural world. We would then interpret the Bible from the standpoint of contemporary humanistic disciplines.

Second, we might place the Bible, science, history, tradition,[15] church councils, the pope, philosophy,[16] and reason[17] all on the same level. We may regard them all as equally transmitting God's revelation. Therefore, the task of the theologian is to interpret them rightly and synthesize the results into a coherent whole. The second approach has usually resulted in conclusions similar to the first.

In contrast to the previous approaches, the Reformation asserted that the Bible is not subservient to human reason and that Scripture was the sole authority *(sola scriptura)* by which we must measure all other authorities. The Seventh-day Adventist Church has based its beliefs on this perspective. While theistic evolution attempts to find a synthesis between the Bible and science, the principle of *sola scriptura* clearly rules out such an approach.[18]

The Power of the Bible

Theistic evolution transforms our notion of the power of the Word of God. The Bible declares that creation took place by the word of God, and Scripture claims to be the Word of God. Therefore, the Reformers taught that when we read the Bible under the guidance of the Holy Spirit, it makes God's power available to those receptive to it. It is the same creative power that brought the world into existence, that brought healing to the deaf, sight to the blind—the power of conversion, the power of transformation.

But theistic evolution denies such a power. It views the power of creation at best as a guiding spirit gradually manipulating matter and life during a period of millions of years to bring about change. Theistic evolution does not regard Christianity as a divinely revealed religion, because religion itself is considered to be in the process of evolving. Christianity may be the evolutionary peak for the present, but something else will supersede it.

Theistic evolution attempts to ground its theory of origins in the power of science. In contrast, the Bible states that we accept creation by faith (Heb. 11:3), a gift of God (Eph. 2:8) that comes by hearing the Word of God (Rom. 10:17) under the power of God (1 Cor. 1; 2).

The Nature of Matter and Humanity[19]

The Bible asserts that God spoke and worlds came into existence. Questioning this teaching, theistic evolution wonders whether God created matter in the same way that He made humanity—by the process of evolution during millions of years. Is matter self-existent apart from God? If so, do we have a duality in the universe? On the other hand, if God spoke and brought matter into existence, then why did He not do the same for humanity?

Some views of theistic evolution change our concept of the nature of humanity. Seventh-day Adventists believe that human beings are a unity— that God breathed into Adam's nostrils, and he became a living soul. At death the breath or spirit of God returns to God and the soul ceases to exist until the resurrection.

Some versions of theistic evolution do not regard human beings as created living souls. Many hold that at some point in the process of evolution human beings received a soul. The soul is simply a fixture added on to human life. Thus a human being is not a unity, because the soul was originally separate from the body. Since the soul is separate from the rest of the human being, it permits the concept of the natural immortality of the soul and its preexistence.

The concept of humanity in the type of theistic evolution noted above seems to be self-contradictory. First, it questions whether God steps into history[20] and whether miracles actually take place.[21] But is not the infusion of a soul at some point in time a historical and miraculous event? If so, why not simply accept the biblical account? Second, theistic evolution questions the idea of human resurrection. If God either cannot or does not create by fiat creation, why should He do so in a resurrection? And if He does it in the resurrection, why not in the beginning?

More important, this form of theistic evolution contradicts Scripture. If, as the Bible states, God created humanity in His image, at what point, and how, in the evolutionary process did it take place? Further, the Bible states that humanity fell from the image of God at the entrance of sin. Theistic evolution throws doubt about sin by suggesting that humanity is actually in a process of improvement over time.

The Nature of God

Theistic evolution challenges Adventist theology's understanding of the nature of God.[22] First, it questions His intelligence, power, and love. If God is all-knowing and all-powerful,[23] is He truly a God of love? Would a God of love drag His creation through such a long process of evolution—of survival of the fittest finally to bring forth humanity?[24] If God is indeed a God of love, the divine method of creation propounded by theistic evolution would appear to call either God's intelligence or power into question. Either He is intelligent, but not very powerful, or powerful, but not very intelligent—otherwise He would have created in a more loving manner. It does not seem possible to accept theistic evolution and at the same time to also uphold all three of the classic properties of God's nature: God's infinite love, intelligence, and power. Unfortunately, only some combination of two of the three properties can coincide with theistic evolution.

Second, theistic evolution doubts God's personal nature. Is God personal, or is He just a pervasive influence or spirit, or perhaps even an impersonal energy that does not relate to us at all? If indeed, God created us for relationship, at what point did human beings become suited for a relationship with God, and why did it take Him so long to bring it about?[25] By contrast, the Bible asserts that God created us for personal relationship with Him, and that the plan of salvation seeks to restore that original relationship.

Third, theistic evolution questions whether God communicates with us. Theistic evolution asserts that humanity existed for millions or billions of years without any direct contact from God. If the theistic evolutionist then wishes also to accept the Bible as God's communication, it would be necessary to say that after millions and billions of years God suddenly came on the scene to speak to us.

Fourth, theistic evolution downplays the nature of God's action in history. Does God act directly in history or is He simply some kind of backdrop to it, never actually stepping into events Himself?[26] With the latter view of God, it is understandable that the theistic evolutionists reject or reinterpret the biblical concept of creation. God simply doesn't or can't act the way the Bible depicts. We moderns know better.[27]

Fifth, if God does not directly involve Himself in history, then what do we do with Jesus Christ? Is He indeed God come to live incarnate, or was He simply a man in the process of evolution, albeit at its highest peak for His time. Or was He the embodiment of the spirit or force that has been driving creation since the beginning of time?[28]

Sixth, if theistic evolutionists have problems with the miracle of creation, they will likely experience difficulties with other miracles recorded in the Bible: the flood, the crossing of the Red Sea, the resurrections recorded in both testaments, the bodily resurrection of Jesus Christ Himself, and the future miracle of the literal, visible Second Coming and re-creation of the earth.

Seventh, theistic evolution struggles with God's relationship to the laws of the universe. Is God in control of the processes of evolution, or is He Himself subject to them and therefore evolving Himself?[29] Similarly, is God the creator and grantor of freedom, or is He Himself bound by the laws of freedom?[30] If God is controlled by the laws of the universe, so that He must operate in harmony with them, is He still God? Would not the laws that restrict Him then be above Him?

Eighth, theistic evolution questions the Bible as the foundation of knowledge.[31] Theistic evolution derives its knowledge of origins, and possibly of the nature of the universe, by observation, by natural means alone. The biblical viewpoint is that the One who spoke worlds into existence, the One who created the nature of the universe, also revealed Himself and the nature and origin of the universe that He created. Thus we depend upon God's revelation if we are to properly carry out our human intellectual disciplines. In the biblical approach God is the creator and grantor of knowledge, while in the evolutionary approach human beings control knowledge. If human beings are in control of knowledge, do they in their autonomy—independence from God—finally put themselves in the place of God?

Ninth, in the process of evolution, is God Himself simply an entity among countless others and therefore Himself caught in the flow of history? Are human beings themselves creators and, though to a lesser extent, nonetheless similar to God? The biblical doctrine of creation safeguards the distinction between God and humanity. God is the Creator; we are the created. He is the Sustainer, while we are the sustained. Such a distinction helps us avoid the temptation to make ourselves God.

Sin and Salvation[32]

The themes of the great controversy and the plan of salvation are vital to Seventh-day Adventist theology. Theistic evolutionists would reinterpret

164

them drastically. They would see the great controversy played out in the process of evolution rather than between Christ and Satan. The plan of salvation would work itself out as an evolutionary progress rather than as God's communication, presence, incarnation, death, resurrection, ascension, sanctuary ministry, second coming, re-creation of the new earth, and so on.

If theistic evolution accepts the biblical concept of sin, then it seems that it must also assert that the process of evolution created humanity in a sinful condition. What would be the implications for a God who would create sinful human beings?[33]

Theistic evolution threatens the biblical concept of the substitutionary death of Christ. If humanity is in the process of progressive evolution, then there was no sin event, and if there was no event of sin, we do not need a Saviour from sin. Jesus might play the role of visionary leader or moral influence, a catalyst to speed up the process of progressive evolution, but He is not our substitute, for we do not need one.

From the perspective of theistic evolution the church cannot teach an everlasting gospel: fear God and give glory to Him, for the hour of His judgment is come, and worship Him, the Creator.[34] Rather the church must present a social gospel. It would be a moral club, a facilitator of ongoing evolution.

The Law and Creation Institutions

Theistic evolution undermines the concept of God's law. If God either cannot or will not enter our history in creation, etc., then surely He made no divine proclamation from Sinai. He did not divinely reveal the ten-commandment law. Law itself is in evolutionary development. Human beings determine their own laws by externally observing the laws of nature, and by internally observing the laws of human personality. There exists no divine absolute.[35]

The absence of divine absolutes will affect other doctrines related to the law of God, such as marriage and the Sabbath. Both institutions, authorized in the divine law, originated at creation. However, theistic evolution would deny that marriage is a divine institution. Marriage would be binding only to the extent that culture made it so. It would be the result of evolutionary social customs rather than the creation and gift of God. Similarly, the Sabbath would not be a divine institution and a mark of distinction of God's people but merely the evolutionary development of folk religion, and therefore classed along with other religious responses to the divine.

Christ's Ministry

Theistic evolution nullifies Christ's ministry in the heavenly sanctuary, in

His church, and in the new earth. First, if God does not create by fiat creation, if He does not communicate directly to humanity, if He does not become incarnate, if there is no fall from the image of God and therefore no need for a substitute to bring about reconciliation, then surely God does not do such things as minister on our behalf in a heavenly sanctuary.

Second, theistic evolution would undermine the spiritual gifts that Christ sends to His church from heaven. Consider, for example, the role of the gift of prophecy. Ellen White stood strongly behind the biblical concept of a six-day creation by the word of the Lord. If her strong emphasis was misguided at this point, in what else can we accept her authority?[36]

Third, theistic evolution would find it necessary to reinterpret Seventh-day Adventist eschatology. If God does not break into history in creation, then surely He will not do so in a literal, visible Second Coming. Since He does not create by the word of His mouth, will He re-create in the resurrection? And if He did not originally create the Garden of Eden, will He re-create the new earth? Eschatology is not the decisive entrance of God into history. It is the continuing process of evolution for a better life, something that humanity accelerates by bringing about a moral and just society through revolt, rebellion, redistribution of wealth, education, and other means.[37]

Conclusion

The Adventist faith will not be itself if it accepts theistic evolution. The active God who created by the word of His mouth, who communicated through the prophets, who lived among us, died in our place, was resurrected and ascended to minister for us, who will return the second time to gather us to Himself, who will resurrect the dead and re-create the new earth, and who will finally destroy sin, cannot be worshiped if He does not exist. We do not worship a god who dragged us through a long process of evolution. Rather, we worship the God of creation, a personal God who desires to fellowship with us and to dwell among us. God is to be worshiped because He is the Creator. That is what distinguishes Him from other gods.[38]

---

[1] Martin Hanna assisted the author in providing endnote sources.

[2] Alvin Plantinga, "When Faith and Reason Clash: Evolution and the Bible," in Matthew H. Nitecki and Doris V. Nitecki, eds., *History and Evolution* (New York: State University of New York Press, 1992), pp. 25-29.

[3] Norbert Max Samuelson, *The First Seven Days: A Philosophical Commentary on the Creation of Genesis* (Atlanta: Scholars Press, 1992); Giovanni Pico della Mirandola, *Heptaplus: Discourse on the Seven Days of Creation* (New York: Philosophical Library, 1977); James Dwight Dana, *Science and the Bible: A Review of "The Six Days of Creation" of Prof. Tayler Lewis* (Andover, Mass.: W. F. Draper, 1856); Leonard Everett Fisher, *The Seven Days of Creation* (New York: Holiday House, 1981); Tayler Lewis, *The Six Days of Creation, or, the Scriptural Cosmology* (Schenectady, N.Y.: G. Y. van

Debogert, 1855); Herbert William Morris, *Work-days of God, or, Science and the Bible* (Philadelphia: J. C. McCurdy, 1877); P. J. Wiseman, ed., *Creation Revealed in Six Days: The Evidence of Scripture Confirmed by Archaeology* (London: Marshall, Morgan & Scott, 1958).

[4] *Science and Creationism: A View From the National Academy of Sciences* (Washington, D.C.: National Academy Press, 1984); Langdon Gilkey, *Religion and the Scientific Future* (Macon, Ga.: Mercer University Press, 1981), p. 123; Langdon Gilkey, *Maker of Heaven and Earth: A Study of the Christian Doctrine of Creation* (New York: Doubleday, 1959); Langdon Gilkey, "Cosmology, Ontology, and the Travail of Biblical Language," *The Journal of Religion* 41, No. 3 (July 1961): 194-205. On science, cosmology, and the Pauline writings, see Bruce Norman, "Pauline Cosmology: Relic or Relevant?" *Journal of the Adventist Theological Society* 3, No. 2 (Autumn 1992): 131, 132; Thomas Luther Marberry, "The Place of the Natural World in the Theology of the Apostle Paul" (Ph.D. diss., Baylor University, 1982); Lewis O. Anderson, "A Study of the Pauline Theology of Creation and Its Relation to the Old Testament Creation Accounts" (M.A. thesis, Andrews University, 1970); Peter Stuhlmacher, *Paul's Letter to the Romans* (Louisville: Westminster: John Knox Press, 1994); Werner G. Kümmel, *The Theology of the New Testament According to Its Major Witnesses: Jesus—Paul—John* (Nashville: Abingdon Press, 1973); F. F. Bruce, *Paul: Apostle of the Heart Set Free* (Grand Rapids: Eerdmans, 1977); Willem Van Gemeren, *The Progress of Redemption: The Story of Salvation From Creation to the New Jerusalem* (Grand Rapids: Zondervan, 1988). On the controversy between evolution and the biblical perspective, see Norman L. Geisler and J. Kerby Anderson, *Origin Science: A Proposal for the Creation-Evolution Controversy* (Grand Rapids: Baker, 1987); J. P. Moreland, *The Creation Hypothesis: Scientific Evidence for an Intelligent Designer* (Downers Grove, Ill.: InterVarsity, 1994); Henry M. Morris, *Studies in the Bible and Science* (Grand Rapids: Baker, 1966); H. M. Morris, ed., *Scientific Creationism* (San Diego: Creation Life Publishers, 1974). For an SDA perspective see also Martin Hanna, "Contemporary Tensions Within Adventism Concerning the Relations of Science to the Doctrine of Creation" (unpublished research paper, Andrews University, 1992); Molleurus Couperus, "Tensions Between Religion and Science," *Spectrum* 10, No. 4 (1978): 74-88; Richard Rice, "Dominant Themes in Adventist Theology," *Spectrum* 20, No. 1 (1989): 58. One who is not a defender of SDA "creation science" documents the fact that in the postmodern period SDAs provided the initial critique of methodological naturalism. See Ronald L. Numbers, *The Creationists: The Evolution of Scientific Creationism* (New York: Alfred A. Knopf, 1992), pp. 72-101. Numbers provides useful reference lists. See also the bibliographies of Harold W. Clark, "Traditional Adventist Creationism: Its Origin, Development, and Current Problems," *Spectrum* 3, No. 1 (Winter 1971): 7-18; and Molleurus Couperus, "Tensions Between Religion and Science," *Spectrum* 10, No. 4 (1978): 74-88. On the idea that the biblical perspective influenced the rise of science, see Henry M. Morris, *The Biblical Basis for Modern Science* (Grand Rapids: Baker, 1984); R. Hooykaas, *Religion and the Rise of Modern Science* (Grand Rapids: Eerdmans, 1972); Eugene M. Klaaren, *The Religious Origins of Modern Science* (Grand Rapids: Eerdmans, 1977); M. B. Foster, "The Christian Doctrine of Creation and the Rise of Modern Science," *Mind* 43 (1934): 446-468; Edwin Burtt, *The Metaphysical Foundations of Modern Science* (Garden City, N.Y.: Doubleday, 1954); Langdon Gilkey, *Naming the Whirlwind* (Indianapolis: Bobbs-Merrill, 1969), p. 35; *Society and the Sacred* (New York: Crossroad, 1981), p. 103; J. P. Moreland, *Christianity and the Nature of Science* (Grand Rapids: Baker, 1989); Christopher B. Kaiser, *Creation and the History of Science* (Grand Rapids: Eerdmans, 1991).

[5] Rudolf Karl Bultmann, *Essays, Philosophical and Theological,* translation of J.C.G. Greig, *Glauben und Verstehen; gesammelte Aufsatze II* (New York: Macmillan, 1955); *Existence and Faith; Shorter Writings of Rudolf Bultmann,* selected, translated, and introduced by Schubert M. Ogden (New York: Meridian Books, 1960); Rudolf Bultmann and Artur Weiser, *Faith* (London: A. and C. Black, 1961); Rudolf Bultmann, *Faith and Understanding,* ed. Robert W. Funk, trans. Louise Pettibone Smith (New York: Harper and Row, 1969); *History and Eschatology* (Edinburgh: University Press, 1957); *The Presence of Eternity: History and Eschatology* (New York: Harper, 1957); *Jesus Christ and Mythology* (New York: Scribner, 1958); Karl Jaspers and Rudolf Bultmann, *Myth and Christianity: An Inquiry Into the Possibility of Religion Without Myth,* translation of *Die Frage der Entmythologisierung* (New York: Noonday Press, 1958); Rudolf Bultmann, *The New Testament and Mythology and Other Basic Writings,* selected, ed., and trans. Schubert M. Ogden (Philadelphia: Fortress, 1984).

⁶ *Seventh-day Adventists Believe . . . A Biblical Exposition of 27 Fundamental Beliefs,* Ministerial Association, General Conference of SDAs (Hagerstown, Md.: Review and Herald, 1988); Martin Hanna, *Seventh-day Adventist Theological Bibliography (1851-1994)* (Berrien Springs, Mich.: SDA Theological Seminary, 1995). On the history of the development of SDA theology see P. Gerard Damsteegt, *Foundations of the Seventh-day Adventist Message and Mission* (Grand Rapids: Eerdmans, 1977); George R. Knight, *Anticipating the Advent: A Brief History of Seventh-day Adventists* (Boise, Idaho: Pacific Press, 1993); Edwin S. Gaustad, ed., *The Rise of Adventism: Religion and Society in Mid-Nineteenth-Century America* (New York: Harper and Row, 1974); John N. Loughborough, *The Great Second Advent Movement: Its Rise and Progress* (Nashville: Southern Pub. Assn., 1905); M. Ellsworth Olsen, *A History of the Origins and Progress of Seventh-day Adventists* (Washington, D.C.: Review and Herald, 1925); Arthur W. Spalding, *Origin and History of Seventh-day Adventists,* 4 vols. (Washington, D.C.: Review and Herald, 1961-1962); Malcolm Bull and Keith Lockhart, *Seeking a Sanctuary: Seventh-day Adventism and the American Dream* (San Francisco: Harper and Row, 1989); LeRoy Edwin Froom, *Movement of Destiny* (Washington, D.C.: Review and Herald, 1971); Gary Land, *Adventism in America* (Grand Rapids: Eerdmans, 1986); C. Mervyn Maxwell, *Tell It to the World* (Mountain View, Calif.: Pacific Press, 1976).

⁷ For an Adventist perspective see Gerhard Hasel, "Scripture and Theology," *Journal of the Seventh-day Adventist Theological Society* 4, No. 2 (Autumn 1992): 47; "The Crisis of the Authority of the Bible as the Word of God," *Journal of the Seventh-day Adventist Theological Society* 1, No. 1 (Spring 1990): 16-38; Richard M. Davidson, "The Authority of Scripture: A Personal Pilgrimage," *Journal of the Seventh-day Adventist Theological Society* 1, No. 1 (Spring 1990): 39-56; Raoul Dederen, "On Inspiration and Biblical Authority," in *Issues in Revelation and Inspiration,* Frank Holbrook and Leo Van Dolson, eds. (Berrien Springs, Mich.: Adventist Theological Society Publications, 1992), pp. 91-103. The question of authority is central to all types of theology. See Carl F. H. Henry, *God, Revelation, Authority: God Who Speaks and Shows* (Waco, Tex.: Word, 1979); Alexander Thompson, *Tradition and Authority in Science and Theology With Reference to the Thought of Michael Polanyi* (Edinburgh: Scottish Academic Press, 1987); Philip Hefner, "Theology in the Context of Science, Liberation, and Christian Tradition," in *Worldviews and Warrants: Plurality and Authority in Theology* (Lanham, Md.: University Press of America, 1987).

⁸ On experience and theology see Henry Wieman, *Religious Experience and Scientific Method* (New York: Macmillan, 1926); William James, *Varieties of Religious Experience* (New York: Longmans, 1902); William Ernest Hocking, *The Meaning of God in Human Experience* (New Haven, Conn.: Yale University Press, 1912); John B. Cobb, Jr., *The Structure of Christian Existence* (Philadelphia: Westminster, 1967).

⁹ Donn F. Morgan, *Between Text and Community: The "Writings" in Canonical Interpretation* (Minneapolis: Fortress, 1990); Jacob Neusner, *Canon and Connection: Intertextuality in Judaism* (Lanham, Md.: University Press of America, 1987); Paul Lauter, *Canons and Contexts* (New York: Oxford University Press, 1991); F. F. Bruce, *The Canon of Scripture* (Downers Grove, Ill.: Inter-Varsity, 1988); Lee Martin McDonald, *The Formation of the Christian Biblical Canon* (Nashville: Abingdon, 1988); James A. Sanders, *From Sacred Story to Sacred Text: Canon as Paradigm* (Philadelphia: Fortress, 1987); Thomas B. Dozeman, *God on the Mountain: A Study of Redaction, Theology, and Canon in Exodus 19-24* (Atlanta: Scholars Press, 1989); Rolf Rendtorff, *Canon and Theology: Overtures to an Old Testament Theology* (Minneapolis: Fortress, 1993); Robert W. Wall, *The New Testament as Canon: A Reader in Canonical Criticism* (Sheffield, Eng.: JSOT, 1992); K. Lawson Younger, Jr., William W. Hallo, Bernard F. Batto, eds., *The Biblical Canon in Comparative Perspective* (Lewiston, N.Y.: Mellen Press, 1991); Gene M. Tucker, David L. Petersen, and Robert R. Wilson, eds., *Canon, Theology, and Old Testament Interpretation: Essays in Honor of Brevard S. Childs* (Philadelphia: Fortress, 1988); D. A. Carson and John D. Woodbridge, eds., *Hermeneutics, Authority, and Canon: Essays on Scripture and Truth* (Grand Rapids: Academie Books, 1986).

¹⁰ See also Paul J. Achtemeier, *The Interpretation of Scripture: Problems and Proposals* (Philadelphia: Westminster, 1980); Joseph A. Mazzeo, *Varieties of Interpretation* (Notre Dame, Ind.: University of Notre Dame Press, 1978); Roger Lundin, *The Culture of Interpretation: Christian Faith and the Postmodern World* (Grand Rapids: Eerdmans, 1993).

¹¹ Sallie McFague, *Metaphorical Theology: Models of God in Religious Language* (Philadelphia:

Fortress Press, 1982); Janet Soskice, *Metaphor and Religious Language* (Oxford: Clarendon Press, 1985); Mary Gerhart and Allan Russell, *Metaphorical Process: The Creation of Scientific and Religious Understanding* (Fort Worth, Tex.: Texas Christian University Press, 1984); Peter W. Macky, *The Centrality of Metaphors to Biblical Thought: A Method for Interpreting the Bible* (Lewiston, N.Y.: Mellen Press, 1990).

[12] John W. Miller, *The Origins of the Bible: Rethinking Canon History* (New York: Paulist Press, 1994).

[13] Sarah Coakley and David A. Pailin, eds., *The Making and Remaking of Christian Doctrine: Essays in Honour of Maurice Wiles* (New York: Oxford University Press, 1993); Mary Potter Engel and Walter E. Wyman, Jr., eds., *Revisioning the Past: Prospects in Historical Theology* (Minneapolis: Fortress, 1992).

[14] Stanley Grenz and Roger Olsen, *20th Century Theology: God and the World in a Transitional Age* (Downers Grove, Ill.: InterVarsity, 1992); Peter M. Hess, *"Nature" and the Existence of God in English Natural Theology From Hooker to Paley* (Ph.D. thesis, Graduate Theological Union, 1993); Stanley L. Jaki, *Universe and Creed* (Milwaukee, Wis.: Marquette University Press, 1992).

[15] On tradition and theology see Delwin Brown, *Boundaries of Our Habitations: Tradition and Theological Construction* (New York: State University of New York Press, 1994); W. Gasque and William Stanfor LaSor, eds., *Scripture, Tradition and Interpretation* (Grand Rapids: Eerdmans, 1978); Gerhard Ebeling, *The Word of God and Tradition: Historical Studies Interpreting the Divisions of Christianity* (Philadelphia: Fortress, 1968).

[16] On theoretical frameworks for interpretation, see Royce Gordon Gruenler, *Meaning and Understanding: The Philosophical Framework for Biblical Interpretation* (Grand Rapids: Zondervan, 1991); Reynold Borzaga, *In Pursuit of Religion: A Framework for Understanding Today's Theology* (Palm Springs, Fla.: Sunday Publications, 1977); Terry F. Godlove, *Religion, Interpretation, and Diversity of Belief: The Framework Model From Kant to Durkheim to Davidson* (New York: Cambridge University Press, 1989).

[17] On reason and theology, see Fritz Marti, *Religion, Reason and Man* (Saint Louis, MO: Warren H. Green, 1974); Gordon H. Clark, *Religion, Reason and Revelation* (Philadelphia: Presbyterian and Reformed Publishing Co., 1961); Carl Michalson, *The Rationality of Faith: An Historical Critique of Theological Reason* (New York: Scribner, 1963); Anton Vogel, *Reality, Reason and Religion* (New York: Morehouse-Gorham Co., 1957); E. L. Miller, *God and Reason: A Historical Approach to Philosophical Theology* (New York: Macmillan, 1972); Immanuel Kant, *Reason Within the Limits of Reason Alone* (New York: Harper and Brothers, 1960); Frank T. Birtel, ed., *Reasoned Faith: Essays on the Interplay of Faith and Reason* (New York: Crossroad, 1993).

[18] Ted Peters, *"Sola Scriptura* and the Second Naivete," in *Dialogue* 16 (Fall 1977): 268-280; Clark H. Pinnock, *The Scripture Principle* (San Francisco: Harper and Row, 1984); Antonius H. J. Gunneweg, *Sola Scriptura: Beitrage zu Exegese und Hermeneutik des Alten Testaments* (Gottingen: Vandenhoeck and Ruprecht, 1983); Sidney Greidanus, *Sola Scriptura: Problems and Principles in Preaching Historical Texts* (Toronto: Wedge Pub. Foundation, 1970).

[19] J. P. Moreland, and David M. Ciocchi, eds., *Christian Perspectives on Being Human: A Multidisciplinary Approach to Integration* (Grand Rapids: Baker, 1993); Edward Farley, *Good and Evil: Interpreting a Human Condition* (Minneapolis: Fortress, 1990).

[20] Jürgen Moltmann, *History and the Triune God: Contributions to Trinitarian Theology* (London: SCM, 1991); Frank G. Kirkpatrick, *Together Bound: God, History, and the Religious Community* (New York: Oxford University Press, 1994); Joseph M. Hallman, *The Descent of God: Divine Suffering in History and Theology* (Minneapolis: Fortress, 1991).

[21] Richard Swineburne, *The Concept of Miracle* (New York: St. Martin's Press, 1970); Yair Zakovitch, *The Concept of the Miracle in the Bible* (Tel-Aviv: MOD Books, 1991); W. Norman Pittenger, *God's Way With Men: A Study of the Relationship Between God and Man in Providence, "Miracle," and Prayer* (London: Hodder and Stoughton, 1969); Og Mandino, *The Greatest Miracle in the World* (New York: F. Fell, 1975); Michael Arthur Hugh Melinsky, *Healing Miracles: An Examination From History and Experience of the Place of Miracle in Christian Thought and Medical Practice* (London: A. R. Mowbray, 1968); Howard Clark Kee, *Miracle in the Early Christian World: A Study in Sociohistorical Method* (New Haven: Yale University Press, 1983); Gerd Theissen, *The Miracle*

Stories of the Early Christian Tradition (Philadelphia: Fortress Press, 1983); Werner Kahl, *New Testament Miracle Stories in Their Religious-Historical Setting: A Religionsgeschichtliche Comparison From a Structural Perspective* (Gottingen: Vandenhoeck & Ruprecht, 1994); David Basinger and Randall Basinger, *Philosophy and Miracle: The Contemporary Debate* (Lewiston, N.Y.: Mellen Press, 1986); Anton Fridrichsen, *The Problem of Miracle in Primitive Christianity* (Minneapolis: Augsburg, 1972); Robert A. H. Larmer, *Water Into Wine? An Investigation of the Concept of Miracle* (Kingston, Ont.: McGill-Queen's University Press, 1988).

[22] Dorothee Sölle, *Thinking About God: An Introduction to Theology* (Philadelphia: Trinity Press International, 1990); John Baillie, *Our Knowledge of God* (New York: Charles Scribner's Sons, 1959); Klaus Blockmuehl, *The Unreal God of Modern Theology* (Colorado Springs, Colo.: Helmers and Howard, 1988); Earl E. Cairns, *God, Man and Time* (Grand Rapids: Baker, 1979); Marchette Chute, *The Search for God* (New York: E. P. Dutton and Co., 1961); Robert Allen Evans, *Intelligible and Responsible Talk About God* (Leiden: E. J. Brill, 1973); John M. Frame, *The Doctrine of the Knowledge of God* (New Jersey: Presbyterian and Reformed Pub. Co., 1987).

[23] Gijsbert van den Brink, *Almighty God: A Study of the Doctrine of Divine Omnipotence* (Kampen, Netherlands: Kok Pharos Pub. House, 1993).

[24] Clark H. Pinnock, and Robert C. Brow, *Unbounded Love: A Good News Theology for the Twenty-first Century* (Downers Grove, Ill.: InterVarsity, 1994).

[25] Joseph Haroutunian, *God With Us: A Theology of Transpersonal Life* (Allison Park, Pa.: Pickwick Publications, 1991); Vincent Brummer, *Speaking of a Personal God: An Essay in Philosophical Theology* (New York: Cambridge University Press, 1992).

[26] Christoph Schwobel, *God: Action and Revelation* (Kampen, Netherlands: Kok Pharos Pub. House, 1992).

[27] Roger A. Johnson, *Rudolf Bultmann: Interpreting Faith for the Modern Era* (San Francisco: Collins, 1987); Carl Ferdinand Howard Henry, *Gods of This Age or—God of the Ages?* (Nashville: Broadman and Holman Publishers, 1994).

[28] William C. Placher, *Narratives of a Vulnerable God: Christ, Theology, and Scripture* (Louisville: Westminster/John Knox, 1994).

[29] Ted Peters, *God—The World's Future: Systematic Theology for a Postmodern Era* (Minneapolis: Fortress Press, 1992); Thomas J. J. Altizer, *The Genesis of God: A Theological Genealogy* (Louisville: Westminster/John Knox, 1993).

[30] Allen C. Guelzo, *Edwards on the Will: A Century of American Theological Debate* (Middletown, Conn.: Wesleyan University Press, 1989); David B. Burrell, *Freedom and Creation in Three Traditions* (Notre Dame, Ind.: University of Notre Dame Press, 1993); Ivor H. Jones and Kenneth B. Wilson, eds., *Freedom and Grace* (Westminster, Eng.: Epworth, 1988); Peter Crafts Hodgson, *God in History: Shapes of Freedom* (Nashville: Abingdon Press, 1989); Leroy S. Rouner, ed., *On Freedom* (Notre Dame, Ind.: University of Notre Dame Press, 1989); William Lane Craig, *The Only Wise God: The Compatibility of Divine Foreknowledge and Human Freedom* (Grand Rapids: Baker, 1987); John Feinberg et al., *Predestination and Free Will: Four Views of Divine Sovereignty and Human Freedom* (Downers Grove, Ill.: InterVarsity, 1986); David B. Burrell, *Freedom and Creation in Three Traditions* (Notre Dame, Ind.: University of Notre Dame Press, 1993).

[31] W. Andrew Hoffecker, ed., *Building a Christian World View: God, Man and Knowledge* (Phillipsburg, N.J.: Presbyterian and Reformed Pub. Co., 1986), vol. 1.

[32] Romanus Cessario, *The Godly Image: Christ and Salvation in Catholic Thought From St. Anselm to Aquinas* (Petersham, Mass.: St. Bede's Publications, 1990); W. Stanley Johnson, *H. Richard Niebuhr's Concepts of Sin and Grace: A Study of Human Redemption* (Ph.D. thesis, Saint Louis University, 1982); Lesslie Newbigin, *Sin and Salvation* (Philadelphia: Westminster, 1956); Duncan Elliot Littlefair, *Sin Comes of Age* (Philadelphia: Westminster, 1975); T. V. Farris, *Mighty to Save: A Study in Old Testament Soteriology* (Nashville: Broadman, 1993); Paul McGlasson, *God the Redeemer: A Theology of the Gospel* (Louisville: Westminster/J. Knox Press, 1993); C. Norman Kraus, *God Our Savior: Theology in a Christological Mode* (Scottdale, Pa.: Herald Press, 1991).

[33] David Ray Griffin, *God, Power, and Evil: A Process Theodicy* (Lanham, Md.: University Press of America, 1991); R. Douglas Geivett, *Evil and the Evidence for God: The Challenge of John Hick's Theodicy* (Philadelphia: Temple University Press, 1993).

[34] Richard Ruhling, *Fear God and Give Glory to Him, for the Hour of His Judgment Is Come: Revelation 14:7* (Camden, Tenn.: Total Health, 1993).

[35] Michael Winger, *By What Law? The Meaning of Nomos in the Letters of Paul* (Atlanta: Scholars

Press, 1992); I. John Hesselink, *Calvin's Concept of the Law* (Allison Park, Pa.: Pickwick Publications, 1992); N. T. Wright, *The Climax of the Covenant: Christ and the Law in Pauline Theology* (Minneapolis: Fortress, 1992).

[36] W. H. Littlejohn, "Seventh-day Adventists and the Testimony of Jesus Christ," *Review and Herald Extra,* Aug. 14, 1883, pp. 13-16; Dudley M. Canright, *Adventism Refuted in a Nutshell* (New York: Fleming H. Revell, 1889); Robert L. Shull, "Ellen G. White in Adventist Theology," *Spectrum* 6, No. 3-4 (1974): 78-85; Stephen T. Hand, "The Conditionality of Ellen White's Writings," *Spectrum* 6, No. 3-4 (1974): 88-90; W. Paul Bradley, "Ellen G. White and Her Writings," *Spectrum* 3, No. 2 (Spring 1971): 43-65; Joseph J. Battistone, "Ellen White's Authority as Bible Commentator," *Spectrum* 8, No. 2 (January 1977): 37-40.

[37] David Novak and Norbert Samuelson, eds., *Creation and the End of Days: Judaism and Scientific Cosmology: Proceedings of the 1984 Meeting of the Academy for Jewish Philosophy* (Lanham, Md.: University Press of America, 1986).

[38] Don E. Saliers, *Worship as Theology: Foretaste of Glory Divine* (Nashville: Abingdon, 1994); David Peterson, *Engaging With God: A Biblical Theology of Worship* (Grand Rapids: Eerdmans, 1993).

CHAPTER 9

SCIENCE AND THEOLOGY: FOCUSING THE COMPLEMENTARY LIGHTS OF JESUS, SCRIPTURE, AND NATURE

Martin F. Hanna

Ph.D. candidate, Seventh-day Adventist Theological Seminary
Andrews University

Introduction

The purpose of this study is to explore the complex relations between science and theology and to suggest a viable solution to this group of problems. It is not possible here to give an exhaustive treatment of all the issues involved in the solution of the science-theology problem. Limited space permits me to include only a few quotations from the many scientists and theologians who recognize the significance of these issues. However, the references provide some indication of the extent of the contemporary discussion both within and outside of Adventist theology.

The essay divides into the following three sections: (1) the problems involved in the interface between science and theology, (2) the relation of science and theology in historical perspective, and (3) a proposed solution to the problem of the relation between science and theology utilizing Adventist perspectives.[1]

The Problems of Science-Theology Relations
The Problem of Definitions

The fact that we have no universally accepted definitions for the terms *science* and *theology* complicates the relationship between the two fields. Bengt Gustafsson comments that the various sciences seem to constitute a turmoil of different and often contradictory assumptions, methods, and results. While specific sciences have attained a limited coherence, the system of the sciences as a whole has not yet produced a completely ordered theoretical worldview.[2] Similarly, Robert King observes an apparent disarray in theology. Theological pluralism is overwhelming even individual communities of faith. Today we find no commanding theologians, no systems of theology that elicit wide support, and no general agreement even as to what theology is.[3]

On the one hand, people have used the terms *science* and *theology* to distinguish the study of nature from the study of God.[4] According to the naturalistic view of science, nature is a closed system in which God does not act. Some scientists go so far as to assume that nature is the ultimate reality and that no God exists beyond nature. From this perspective, theology is unscientific because its methods and objectives differ from those of other sciences. Methodological naturalism dominates these sciences.[5] However, even naturalistic science seems to have theological implications. To view nature as ultimate is to put it in the place of God, making it divine. As Roy Clouser points out, a hidden role for religious belief (or unbelief) may lurk even in naturalistic theories of science.[6]

On the other hand, the term *science* may denote any disciplined methodological search for knowledge in which the method of study suits its objective. From this perspective, we may regard theology as a theistic science, and may view nature as a system open to divine revelation. Therefore, knowledge about God and nature are not independent of each other. As Herman Bavinck expressed it, "natural science is not the only science, and cannot be."[7] Actually, the element of *scientia* in the theological tradition has kept it viable for a long time. Only with German Pietism did a theology understood as devoid of science acquire any notable authority.[8]

The Problem of Multiple Models

The various conceptions of science and theology result in a large number of conflicting theoretical frameworks or models for relations between science and theology. William Austin categorizes the various models in terms of direct relationships—in which science and theology compete with, confirm, and/or contradict each other; and indirect relationships—in which they provide insights, metaphysics, and/or methodology for each other. Some models may also be categorized as complex—they have direct as well as indirect science-theology relationships.[9]

The search for a viable model takes on great importance because we may regard science-theology relationships either as harmful or helpful. For example, in rejecting one model, Carl Raschke writes that "perhaps the most formidable obstacle for theological thinking is the epistemological challenge posed by modern science." However, in support of another model, he suggests that it is "the neglect of theological thinking [that] has led not only to the demise of what was once the premier 'science' [theology], but to the slow deterioration of the various habits on intellectual probing [in other sciences]."[10]

The National Academy of Sciences manifests a similar ambivalence about the relationship of science and theology. The academy denies that there is "an irreconcilable conflict between religion and science." Yet it claims that scientific and theological thinking are "separate and mutually exclusive realms of human thought whose presentation in the same context leads to misunderstanding of both." The academy regards some models for science-theology relationships as a "challenge to the integrity and effectiveness of our national education system and the hard-won evidence-based foundations of science, . . . [to] academic and intellectual freedom and to the fundamental principles of scientific thought."[11]

The Problem of Scripture

Can Scripture provide a basis to evaluate the various models for science-theology relationships? Yes, it can. Dale Moody reports that in the dialogue among theologians it is increasingly evident that the only sufficient ground of Christian unity is the common Christian regard for Scripture.[12] Dorothee Sölle—a radical theologian—suggests that all Christians view Scripture not only as a source but also as the binding, limiting, norm-making *(norma normans)* standard that sets the rules for the use of other normed standards for theology *(normae normatae)*.[13] Similarly, Richard Davidson, a Seventh-day Adventist theologian, suggests that all Christians must come to Scripture acknowledging our biases and preunderstandings, claiming the divine promise to bring us into harmony with normative biblical presuppositions.[14]

Nevertheless, radical theology is very different from and incompatible with Adventist theology. The role of Scripture in contemporary Christian theology is in itself problematic. Even among those who agree that Scripture sets the rules for theology we may find much disagreement as to what those rules are. A focal point of this debate is the *sola scriptura* principle. Lack of agreement on this issue contributes to the largest division in Christianity. Catholics and Protestants all regard experience, reason, and tradition (ERT) as a proper context for the interpretation of Scripture.[15] However, Protestants use the slogan *sola scriptura* to identify Scripture as *the* standard for *their* evaluation of ERT. Catholics also claim to be faithful to Scripture, but they evaluate ERT differently.[16]

The issue of the *sola scriptura* principle also contributes to division among Christians concerning how to relate the study of Jesus, Scripture, and nature. (Notice that human nature, which includes ERT, is the context for the incarnation of Jesus and the inspiration of Scripture.) This provokes a number of difficult questions. Are Jesus, Scripture, and nature revelations of God, and therefore, sources and standards for theology? What are the relationships between God and revelation, between the divine and the human in revelation, and among God's different revelations? Do Jesus, Scripture, and nature shed light on each other?

The Problem of Science-Theology Relations in Historical Perspective
The Premodern Period

We may divide the 2,000-year history of the science-theology problem into three periods: premodern, modern, and postmodern. For 16 centuries before the Protestant Reformation two theologians above all others influenced premodern theology. First, Augustine (d. A.D. 430) promoted Plato's (d. 347 B.C.) idea that wisdom is superior to knowledge. As a result, the intellectual world regarded theology as above science. Later, Thomas Aquinas (d. A.D. 1274) stressed Aristotle's (d. 322 B.C.) concept that science derives from first principles. Thus scholars came to consider theology as the highest derived science.[17]

Nevertheless, premodern theology contained the seeds of the idea of God-world separation that would produce a harvest of science-theology conflict in the modern period. The Eastern strand of premodern theology modeled the relations of God and nature as organic through the mediation of a cosmic Christ.[18] In contrast, Western theology viewed the transcendent world of God *(neotos)* as separated from the immanent human world *(aisthetos)* by a chasm *(chorismos)*. A combination of rational natural theology grounded in nature and revealed theology received by faith bridged this gap.[19] However, many scholars viewed God's word in Christ and in the language of Scripture[20] as primarily a source of timeless doctrine about the transcendent divine order and only secondarily a support for ideas about the immanent natural order.[21]

The Modern Period

From the sixteenth to the nineteenth centuries traditional natural theology declined and methodological naturalism in modern science replaced it. Consequently, scholars regarded nature as a machine separated from God. Two philosopher-theologians especially represent this development. René Descartes (d. 1650) divided reality into matter and mind or spirit. Immanuel Kant (d. 1804) separated knowledge into that which we may come to know and that which we must believe because of practical necessity.[22]

Jerrey Hopper comments that in the premodern period, for the most part, theology set the rules for science. "Now this situation was reversed, and the findings of science were setting the problems for philosophy which in turn was beginning to define new rules for theology."[23] This led to increasing conflict between modern science and traditional theology. On the one hand, modern science has undermined premodern views of the factual relevance of Scripture. On the other hand, modern *critical* hermeneutics views language as essentially descriptive of an immanent natural reality rather than a transcendent supernatural reality.[24]

Modern theologians have responded in different ways. On the one hand, Friedrich Schleiermacher (d. 1834), the father of Protestant liberalism, sought a truce in the science-theology conflict by describing theology as a positive and practical science rather than as a pure science. He viewed Scripture as essentially a record of religious experience. On the other hand, Benjamin B. Warfield (d. 1921) was a foremost proponent of the view that Scripture records factual propositions. His view has come to be associated with fundamentalist and conservative theology.[25]

The Postmodern Period

A growing number of scientists and theologians regard twentieth-century science as radically different than premodern derived science and modern methodological naturalism. However, others emphasize the continuity of the history of science. What is clear is that scientific models have undergone significant change. They now view nature as a history in which the core of reality is mysterious. Theology has also changed. *Postcritical* theologians usually use modern critical methods, but they recognize the limited theological usefulness of the historical-critical paradigm with its emphasis on the human context of the formation of Scripture. Much of postmodern thought tends toward irrationalism and nihilism. However, many contemporary theologians seek to overcome the imbalance of the premodern and modern emphasis on transcendence and immanence by recognizing Jesus, Scripture, and nature as in some sense revelations of a mediated divine transcendence.[26]

Unfortunately, because of the tensions within postmodern thought, no new theological unity has emerged. The tendencies toward division in the premodern and modern periods have developed into a radical pluralism of views about Jesus, Scripture, and nature. The scholastic, liberal, and Fundamentalist influences continue. In addition, other types of theology view Scripture in different ways, including: witness to revelation (neo-orthodox), symbolization of divine-human encounter (existentialist), salvation message (neo-evangelical), source of metaphors (narrative), source of models (feminist), foundation for freedom (liberation), and as an unfolding of divine action (process). Such approaches to theology view the text of Scripture either as a revelation, as a witness to a historical revelation "behind" the text, or as a catalyst for contemporary revelation "in front of" the text. Presently the cutting edge of Christian theology involves the search for a viable model that deals with the manifold revelation of God in Jesus, Scripture, and nature.[27]

Influence of Two Postliberal Theologians

We may gain further perspective on science-theology relations in the postmodern period by tracing the influence of two *postliberal* theologians. On the right of liberal theology, Karl Barth (d. 1968)—the father of neo-orthodoxy—aimed to restate orthodoxy independently of science. On the left of liberal theology, Paul Tillich (d. 1965) developed the idea that Bible symbols provide answers to the ultimate symbolic questions of science. According to John Dillenberger, these two theologians "represent the theological revolution in our time." They are key reference points on the theological landscape.[28]

Langdon Gilkey (1919-   ), on the right of Tillich, practices a *scientific-existentialist theology* and assumes a divine realm beyond science and the complementarity of God and nature. According to Gilkey, some constitutive elements of the Bible have lost their legitimacy in a scientific culture. Science is the normative mode for knowing the space-time world and confines itself to explanation by finite or empirical secular causes. In contrast, theology is unrelated to facts and unable to establish anything relevant to science. Therefore, we need to interpret Scripture in light of the factual conclusions of a science characterized by methodological naturalism. As a result, Gilkey concludes that while the early Christians were certain that God had raised Jesus from the dead, contemporary Christians can speak of the resurrection only in symbolic language. It is impossible to say what happened in literal terms such as "empty tomb" and "bodily ascension," because it was the work of God and not a natural event.[29]

Thomas Torrance (1913-   ), on the left of Barth, practices a *trans-scientific theology* that balances scientific relevance with theological independence and goes beyond the other sciences in theological explanation. Unlike Gilkey, Torrance rejects the idea that we are limited to a knowledge of what early Christians appeared to make of Jesus as they clothed Him with meanings and created "historical events" to suit their needs. He also discards the idea that we must seek by symbolic reinterpretation to let what they did become a focus of meaning for ourselves. Theology must do its work within the

177

context of the revolutionary changes in the scientific foundations of knowledge, but it should never build upon the foundations of any other science. Thus theology must be faithful both to its own scientific objective and to the material content of God's self-revelation. Concerning the resurrection, Torrance concludes: "Everything depends on the resurrection of the body, otherwise all we have is a ghost of a Saviour."[30]

Summary

The complex problem of science-theology relationships developed in the aftermath of a series of dominant models for Christian theology, namely: precritical orthodoxy—in which Scripture refers primarily to timeless reality; critical liberalism—in which Scripture speaks primarily to temporal reality; and postcritical-postliberal theology—in which Scripture involves primarily a mediated transcendence. Postcritical thought is open to irrationalism and nihilism as well as to the idea that Jesus, Scripture, and nature are in some sense revelations of God and are therefore sources and standards for theology. However, no theological consensus has emerged concerning the nature of divine-human communication or science-theology relationships. The difficulties involved in the search for a viable model have contributed to a crisis in contemporary theology, as we see in the tension between the approaches of Barth, Tillich, Gilkey, and Torrance. The inclusive model for Seventh-day Adventist theology that we introduced earlier we will more fully describe in the remainder of this chapter.

A Proposed Solution to the Problem
of Science-Theology Relations: Postmodern Adventism
Introduction to an Inclusive Adventist Model

A biblical and inclusive model for Christian theology proposes a viable solution to the complex problem of science-theology relations. In this model, theology *(theologia)* is the study of God as He is revealed to humanity in His word *(logos theou)*. The word of God in the entire Judeo-Christian Scripture *(tota scriptura)* is a unique *(sola scriptura)* and primary *(prima scriptura)* standard for theology. According to Scripture itself, there is a sense in which Scripture is the source, standard, and context for theology. Scripture interprets Scripture. However, also according to Scripture, Jesus and nature are in a sense unique and primary as source and context for theology. Jesus, the supreme revelation of God, is the source of the special revelation in Scripture and the general revelation in nature. Nature, including human nature, is the context for the incarnation of Jesus and for the inspiration and the interpretation of Scripture.[31]

178

This biblical model implies that there exists a legitimate place for a theological interpretation of the methods and results of other sciences. As the *Seventh-day Adventist Encyclopedia* suggests, "the revelation contained in the Word of God is necessary for meaning and perspective in science" and the "revelation in the world of science gives added meaning to religion."[32] This does not mean that theology establishes the methods and results of other sciences, or that they set the methods and results of theology. In this model, the authority of one divine-human revelation does not compromise the authority of another. According to the book *Seventh-day Adventists Believe,* when rightly understood, the divine-human revelations in Jesus, Scripture, and nature are in perfect harmony. Any apparent conflict results from our imperfect comprehension.[33]

"Sin limits God's self-revelation through creation [nature] by obscuring our ability to interpret God's testimony. [However,] in love God gave a special revelation of Himself [in Scripture]. . . . The Bible both contains propositions that declare the truth about God, and reveals Him as a person. Both areas of revelation are necessary: We need to know God through Jesus Christ . . . as well as 'the truth that is in Jesus.'"[34]

Adventist Crisis

Gerhard Hasel reminds us that Seventh-day Adventists are not immune to the postmodern crisis in Christian theology.[35] In fact, many Adventists are passing through what Fritz Guy refers to as a crisis of belief—a critical moment when a change of belief is possible.[36] As Raoul Dederen writes in a different, but related context: "The issue at stake is essentially one of authority, namely, how SDAs are going to *do* theology while holding to biblical authority. Can we agree on exactly what the Bible means for us and how it is to be heard and interpreted? Can we maintain our claim to biblical authority as a distinctive hallmark if we cannot find a way to move effectively toward theological consensus?"[37]

According to Edward Lugenbeal, this crisis includes "a deep and continuing debate among Adventist scientists and theologians."[38] Some Adventists conceive of science-theology relations in terms of changes in our view of science prompted by the study of Scripture. Others advocate changes in our view of theology derived through the study of nature. Still others suggest a two-way interaction between the study of nature and Scripture that may change our view of both science and of theology. If such discussion proceeds with an openness to the Spirit of Jesus and to His revelation in Scripture and nature, it can only result in a continuing clarification of the Adventist model for theology and for science-theology relationships.[39]

Historic Adventist Theology

John Baldwin suggests that the "principles of historic Adventist theological method need not be abandoned, but that the approach represents a viable and convincing postmodern theological method."[40] Adventist theology is postmodern in that it developed toward the end of the modern period and offers a solution to the contemporary science-theology problem. However, the place of Scripture in Adventist theology distinguishes it from other theological trends. As Fernando Canale comments, authentic Adventist theology does not "utilize humanly originated philosophy at the detriment or plain rejection of the *sola scriptura* principle [by] following the classical, modern, and[/or] postmodern trends in Christian theology."[41]

The Adventist understanding of the *sola scriptura* principle deserves special attention. Gerhard Hasel classifies Adventist theology as "postmodern" and "postcritical" because of its view of Scripture.[42] Allowing for secondary norms, he points out that the "highest and most authoritative norm" for Adventist theology is the revelation that is "most uniquely and directly incarnated in Scripture." This uniquely direct "incarnation" of special revelation in normative Scripture stands in contrast with the normed standards of general revelation in human nature such as experience, reason, and tradition. However, it does not compromise the uniqueness of the revelation incarnate in Jesus or the revelation given in nature.[43]

Evidence From Scripture

Seventh-day Adventists often receive criticism for regarding Ellen White as a resource for theology. Some question how a theology she illuminates may at the same time be faithful to the *sola scriptura* principle. However, an a priori rejection of her ministry is at the same time a denial of the biblical teaching on spiritual gifts.[44] Further, we can evaluate Ellen White's model for theology in terms of its faithfulness to Scripture.

Complementary Lights

Scripture depicts the revelation of God's word in terms of the metaphor of light (Ps. 119:105). First, the revelation of God—who is light (1 John 1:5)—is His Word Jesus, who is the light of the world (John 1:1-14). Second, the light of God's word shines in Scripture (2 Peter 1:19-21; Rom. 3:1, 2). Third, it also shines in nature (Ps. 19:1-6; Isa. 6:3; Rom. 1:20)—including human nature (John 1:9; Rom. 2:14-16).[45] Jesus is supreme as the unique (*monogenous*, John 1:14) and primary (*prototokon,* Heb. 1:6) Son of God. However, He brings many sons to glory (Heb. 2:10). Similarly Scripture is a unique and primary revelation. However, it points to Jesus as the foundation of our faith (John 5:39) and includes nature in its scope (Col. 1:15-20).

There is a sense in which nature is the widest context for theology. Nature travails for the revelation of the sons of God (Rom. 8:18-26). However, sin has darkened human minds so that they do not perceive either the light of general revelation in nature or the light of special revelation revealed in Scripture (Rom. 1-3; 2 Peter 3:16). Therefore, Scripture is "a light shining in a dark place, until the day dawns and the morning star [Jesus] rises in your hearts" (2 Peter 1:19-21, NIV). Indeed, the path of the just is like a light that shines more and more [clearly] until the perfect day (Prov. 4:18). This light of the glory of God in Jesus manifests itself in the unity of the church (John 16:14; 17:21, 22; Eph. 4:4-6, 8, 13). According to Scripture (Rom. 16:26), the Holy Spirit puts this light in the hearts of believers (2 Cor. 4:3-6) and it is a foretaste of the full revelation of God's glory in nature (Rom. 8:18ff).[46]

Science in the Bible

The English word "science" appears only a few times in the King James Version of Scripture. It describes Daniel and his associates as understanding "science" and "all wisdom." The same Hebrew words identify God's gift of the knowledge of wisdom (Dan. 1:4, 17), which is related to salvation (Dan. 12:3, 4, 10). This wisdom includes a knowledge of God's revelation in nature. The heroes of the book of Daniel were wise teachers *(maskilim)* skilled in the science of the Babylonians. Further, the book depicts the structure of history.

The wider context of the Old Testament also contains much that is relevant to science-theology relationships. For example, we find a balancing of the divine transcendence that should not be imaged in worship (Ex. 20:4, 5) with the immanence of divine interaction in all aspects of the lives of His people (Isa. 63:9). The Old Testament presents divine redemption as a matter of empirical fact in the context of a cosmology of creation and fall (Gen. 1-3) that we may compare and contrast with other cosmologies. Scripture depicts wisdom as prior to and as active in the creation of the world (Prov. 8). Clearly the Old Testament encourages the theological interpretation of nature.[47]

The English word "science" appears in the King James Version of the New Testament in warning about pseudoscience *(gnosis)*. The New Testament employs the same Greek word to refer to Christians as filled with "all knowledge" (1 Tim. 6:20). The immediate context of this epistle suggests that Christians are qualified to avoid a false theology of God (verse 21). A closely related epistle teaches that Scripture makes us wise unto salvation and every good work (2 Tim. 3:15-17).[48] In addition, the wider theological context of the New Testament, especially the Pauline epistles, suggests that Christians are also qualified to avoid a false theology of nature.

The Greek natural philosophy that shaped the culture to which Paul ministered also raised the issues of premodern science. Apparently Paul was trained in both the Gentile and the Jewish schools (Acts 17:16-32; Titus 1:12; Acts 22:3). As a result, we find a "thought world" connection between the terms *science* and *theology* and the Pauline terms: *wisdom, philosophy, knowledge,* and *mind.* Paul uses the terms in different ways in his complex and subtle rhetoric. Because of this, others often interpret him contrary to his intended meaning (2 Peter 3:15, 16), that is, as one who rejected science. However, a careful contextual reading of Paul's writings provides much insight on science-theology relationships.[49]

Sources of Revelation

In spite of the distortion caused by sin, Paul regards nature as a divine revelation. God's wrath responds to the suppression of the truth (Rom. 1:18) that He gives of Himself in the world (verses 19-21) and in human nature (Rom. 2:14, 15). Such suppression of truth results from a futile reasoning and pretended wisdom that is actually foolishness. It cannot comprehend God because it misunderstands His glory in the world (Rom. 1:22, 23). The solution to such foolishness is the righteousness of God, which is by faith alone (verses 16-18).

Does Paul's emphasis on "faith alone" mean "faith without reason"? Hardly! Faith is the antidote to the foolishness of sinners and is reasonable in the light of Christ.[50] For Paul, Christian knowledge is different than natural knowledge both in its origin and content. But revelation does use natural channels. Faith, like intuition, is the conviction of things not seen (Heb. 11:1). The gospel is pragmatic: since you desire proof, Christ is powerful in you (2 Cor. 13:2). A place also exists for the rational mind: let all be fully assured in their own minds (Rom. 14:5).[51]

The Mind of Christ

Paul's discussion of the mind is highly relevant to the issue of science-theology relationships. Translators have rendered six Greek words from the Pauline epistles into English as "mind." Five of them refer to factors common to all human beings: soul *(psuche),* opinion *(gnome),* thoughts *(noema),* dispositions *(phronema),* and intellect *(dianoia).*[52] The sixth word *(nous)* often indicates the seat of understanding and conviction: I will pray, sing, and speak with my mind and understanding rather than in an unknown tongue (1 Cor. 14:14-19). Let each one be fully assured in his own mind (Rom. 14:5).

Nous also indicates the content of understanding and conviction: Don't be quickly shaken from your mind (2 Thess. 2:2). According to Paul, lusts, desires, appetites, and ambitions on the one hand or divine revelation on the other may shape what is in the mind. As a result, wisdom and spiritual perception, or their absence, focus into a worldview called a "mind." Fallen human beings possess a worldview that is vain, reprobate, and fleshly: they walk in the vanity of their minds because of the hardness of their hearts (Eph. 4:17); God gave them over to a reprobate mind (Rom. 1:28); the fleshly mind is vainly puffed up (Col. 2:18). However, worldviews may be changed and renewed: Paul's admonition is that we should not be fashioned by the world, but be transformed by the radical metamorphosis *(anakainoo)* of your mind (Rom. 12:2); be made young *(ananeoo)* in your mind (Eph. 4:23). Those who experience such a miracle may say: "We have the mind *[nous]* of Christ" (1 Cor. 2:16).[53]

The Natural and the Spiritual

How is the mind, or worldview, of Christ relevant to the issue of science-theology relationships? Paul uses the term *soulical (pseuhikos)* to identify the person with a natural mind. The term *spiritual (pneumatikos)* identifies one who judges everything, but who is not subject to the judgment of persons lacking the mind of Christ (1 Cor. 2:10-16). Some assume that the spiritual mind judges theology and the natural mind judges science. However, Paul does not separate the natural from the spiritual in terms of a dichotomy between special revelation in Scripture and general revelation in nature. Rather, he employs the terms *natural* and *spiritual* to distinguish pseudoscience from true science.

Philosophy: Love of Wisdom

Paul regards so-called "natural knowledge" as being in opposition to the gospel of Christ. Hence his only use of the word "philosophy" consists of a warning: "Beware lest any man spoil you with philosophy" (Col. 2:8). The apostle is concerned about opposition to the claims of Jesus by some who advocate practices and teachings contrary to the truth of the gospel. In response to false philosophies of beguiling speech (verse 4), empty deceit, false tradition, elemental spirits of the universe (verse 8), false abasement, angel worship, visions (verse 18), and self-made religion (verse 23), Paul presents the antidote of the wisdom, knowledge, and science of Christ.

The apostle is not against true philosophy *(philosophia)*—a search motivated by love *(philia)*. Neither is he against the wisdom *(sophia)* that is the goal of that search. However, he rejects false philosophies (such as Greco-Roman philosophy, Hellenistic Judaism, and Protognosticism) that contradict the gospel. Paul's attitude to knowledge becomes evident in many Bible translations and paraphrases of verse 8; he rejects "hollow and delusive speculations, based on traditions of man-made teaching" (NEB); "intellectualism or high sounding nonsense" (Phillips); "philosophy and empty deception (NASB); and "secondhand, empty, rational philosophy" (Jerusalem).

Similarly, Paul's rejection of worldly wisdom in his preaching to the Corinthians (1 Cor. 2) does not imply that he repudiated true science. The letter to the Corinthians is one of the best examples of the complexity of Pauline rhetoric. The congregation had divided into factions on the basis of a so-called superior wisdom that Paul said was actually foolishness. The apostle spurned such pseudowisdom. In this letter the meaning of knowledge or wisdom changes from one chapter to another. Mixing his categories, Paul refers to the Corinthians as filled with knowledge of Jesus (chapter 1), then as potentially subject to worldly wisdom (chapter 3), and finally, as full of the conceit, bragging, fleshliness, and immaturity that are part of worldly wisdom and are morally and epistemologically undesirable (chapter 4). Paul is not denying the epistemological status of the knowledge of Jesus or its relevance to science. Rather he is contrasting it with pseudoknowledge.[54]

In-Part Knowledge

Some are tempted to depreciate science because of 1 Corinthians 13: when the perfect *(to teleion)* comes, the "in-part" *(to ek merous)* will be abolished (verse 10). According to Paul, the in-part will be "abolished" in the same way that the childish is outgrown (verse 11), the indirect is replaced by the direct, and the puzzle or riddle *(ainigmati)* is solved (verse 12). Paul does not mean that we should despise partial knowledge. In-part knowledge is real knowledge *(ibid.)*. It seems that while we wait for the more perfect day, we should combine our in-part knowledge of nature and our in-part knowledge of Scripture so that we may more clearly see the light of Jesus.[55]

Cosmic Christ

The Gospels link Jesus and nature in the message of the Word of wisdom who created and enlightens everyone and became flesh revealing His glory (John 1:1-14). They also present the signs of nature associated with the return of Jesus (Matt. 24). Similarly, Paul depicts Jesus as the image of God who created, sustains, and reconciles all things (Col. 1:15-20). This is the gospel of God concerning Jesus Christ that leads to a knowledge of God's plan *(oikonomia tou theou)* for the world. The Creator chose Israel and proclaimed through prophets the coming of His Son who suffered, was resurrected and anointed with power, and who reigns until His enemies are all overcome and all Israel (Jew and Gentile) has been saved. Then Jesus will return to consummate the freedom of the children of God in the midst of a world freed from vanity (Col. 1:25; Eph. 1:10; 3:2, 9; Gal. 4:4; 1 Cor. 15:20-28; Rom. 1:1-6; 9:5; 11:25-31; 15:8, 9).[56]

Summary

While Scripture rarely uses the English term *science,* the Bible worldview is relevant to the issue of the relationship of science and theology. God's supreme revelation is Jesus, who is the light of the world. Scripture is the special revelation of light that leads to Jesus. Nature is a general revelation that provides the context for Jesus and Scripture. While sin has obscured the light of God's revelation in nature, Jesus unveils that light. He is the light of both Scripture and the light of nature (John 1:9).

While Scripture focuses on Jesus, it also includes nature in its scope. Emerson Shideler remarks that "the biblical account is as insistently empirical as any scientific record."[57] Rolf P. Knierim concurs that the scientific aspect is as much a part of the Bible as the religious aspect is inevitable in science. The Bible speaks neither about God in isolation from the world nor about the world in isolation from God.[58]

"There is massive evidence that the biblical writers were not only concerned with the knowledge of God but also with the knowledge of the world. Their knowledge of God's presence in the world became transparent through their knowledge of the world. That is the point where 'science' became inevitable."[59]

Stuhlmacher documents how Paul's presentation of the gospel rests on the Old Testament eschatological creation tradition with its concept of a cosmic lawsuit. The benefit of the gift of justification through the righteousness of God is not only individual but cosmological. It is the fulfillment of God's justice toward the world—a gift of presence and power toward the entire creation. In righteousness, God creates well-being and salvation in history and in nature.[60] Paul's distinction between the natural and the spiritual refers to the false and the true rather than to science and theology. He is against pseudophilosophy and worldly wisdom that contradict the gospel, not the exploration of nature. The study of Jesus, Scripture, and nature is in-part, but in-part knowledge is still real knowledge.

Divine revelation is the source of knowledge mediated through Jesus, Scripture, and nature. In fact, the mind of Christ is a unique worldview relevant to the study of nature. According to Abraham Kuyper, while naturalistic and theistic science derive from two different minds, the history of their development has been intertwined from premodern times.[61] Bruce Norman concludes: "Paul used some of the common cosmological terminology of the day to reach both Jew and Gentile. But he used the language with a different meaning. For him, Christ became the beginning and end of cosmology. . . . Herein lies Paul's contribution to ancient and modern cosmology."[62]

Ellen G. White's Contribution

The writings of Ellen G. White—a leading founder of the Adventist Church—continue to be relevant to the postmodern crisis. Adventists regard her ministry as a lesser light under the authority of the greater light of Scripture and the supreme light of Jesus. Her views, which are representative of Adventist theology, are outlined below. Thereafter, we present some of the evidence for the compatibility of this model with Scripture.[63]

Divine-Human Revelations

God's revelations have both divine and human dimensions. First, it is impossible to gain a perfect knowledge of God from nature because sin has obscured God's revelation in the physical world.[64] But despite the distortion caused by sin, nature is "an open book which reveals God,"[65] who works in nature.[66] God's character, thoughts, glory, wisdom, power, and law demonstrate themselves in the physical world.[67] Actually, "the whole natural world is designed to be an interpreter of the things of God."[68] This revelation includes human nature. God's "law is written by His own finger upon every nerve, every muscle, every fiber of our being, upon every faculty which has been intrusted to man."[69] "The brain nerves . . . are the medium through which heaven communicates with man."[70] The mind purified by grace is an intellect in close communion with the divine mind, and God will manifest Himself to it.[71]

Second, Scripture is also an imperfect representation of God due both to its humanity and to the process of its preservation, transmission, and translation.[72] In addition, "the Bible, perfect in its simplicity, does not answer to the great ideas of God; for infinite ideas cannot be perfectly embodied in finite vehicles of thought."[73] However, the divine and human dimensions of Scripture are wonderfully united.[74] "Every chapter and every verse of the Bible is a communication from God to men."[75] Scripture has been preserved through "the unerring pen of inspiration"[76] in its present form as a guidebook for humanity. God, who cannot lie, qualified the human communicators of His word.

He guided the selection of what to speak and write. Thus Scripture is a perfect chain with one portion explaining another. It reliably reveals the knowledge necessary for salvation, God's will, the standard of character, doctrines, historical facts, various other types of knowledge, and the highest science.[77]

Last, but not least, the divine-human communion provided in nature and Scripture points to the divine-human union "in the nature of Christ, who was the Son of God and the Son of man."[78] In Jesus, *the divine and human natures united in one person.* Yet the human was not made divine and the divine was not made human.[79] "The work of God's dear Son in undertaking to link the created with the Uncreated, the finite with the Infinite, in His own divine person, is a subject that may well employ our thoughts for a lifetime."[80]

"The story of Bethlehem is an exhaustless theme. . . . We marvel at the Saviour's sacrifice in exchanging the throne of heaven for the manger, and the companionship of adoring angels for the beasts of the stall. . . . Yet this was but the beginning of His wonderful *condescension.* It would have been an almost infinite humiliation for the Son of God to take man's nature, even when Adam stood in his innocence in Eden. But Jesus accepted *humanity* when the race had been *weakened* by four thousand years of sin. Like every child of Adam He accepted the results of the working of the great law of heredity. . . . He came with such a heredity to share our sorrows and temptations, and to give us the example of a sinless life."[81]

Harmonious Revelations

Harmony alone is not a sufficient evidence of correct interpretations. Not just any agreement will do, because it is possible to correlate incorrect interpretations of nature and Scripture. "Inferences erroneously drawn from facts observed in nature have, however, led to *supposed conflict* between science and revelation; and in the effort to restore harmony, interpretations of Scripture have been adopted that undermine and destroy the force of the word of God."[82] "In order to account for His works [in nature], must we do violence to His word [in Scripture]?"[83]

"Rightly understood, both the revelations of science and the experiences of life are in harmony with the testimony of Scripture."[84] *"The book of nature and the written word do not disagree; each sheds light on the other. Rightly understood* (my emphasis), *they make us acquainted with God and His character by teaching us something of the wise and beneficent laws through which He works. We are thus led to adore His holy name, and to have an intelligent trust* (my emphasis) *in His word."*[85]

"When the Bible makes statements of facts in nature, science may be compared with the written word, and *a correct understanding of both will always prove them to be in harmony* (my emphasis). One does not contradict the other."[86]

"By different methods, and in different languages, they [nature and Scripture] witness to the same great truths. Science is ever discovering new wonders; *but* she brings from her research nothing that, rightly understood, conflicts with divine revelation."[87]

The Hierarchy of Revelation

Correct interpretations depend on the recognition of the hierarchy of Jesus, Scripture, and nature. First, the supreme revelation of God in Jesus is unique and primary as source and subject of every divine revelation. "No other light ever has shone or ever will shine so clearly upon fallen man as that which emanated from the teaching and example of Jesus."[88] Jesus is the key to the correct interpretation of Scripture. "Christ makes no apology when He declares, 'I am the light of the world.' He was, in life and teaching, the gospel, *the foundation of all pure doctrine* (my emphasis). Just as the sun compares with the lesser lights in the heavens, so did Christ, the Source of light, compare with the teachers of His day. He was before them all, and shining with the brightness of the sun, He diffused His penetrating, gladdening rays throughout the world."[89]

"In Christ is gathered all the glory of the Father. In Him is all the fullness of the Godhead bodily. He is the brightness of the Father's glory, and the express image of His person. The glory of the attributes of God are expressed in His character. *The gospel* is glorious because it is *made up of His righteousness. It is Christ enfolded, and Christ is the gospel embodied.* . . . Every text [of Scripture] is a diamond, touched and irradiated by the divine rays (my emphasis).

"We are not to praise the gospel, but [to] praise Christ. We are not to worship the gospel, but the Lord of the gospel."[90]

Jesus also illuminates the study of nature. "Only under the direction of the Omniscient One shall we, in the study of His works, be enabled to think His thoughts after Him."[91] Scientific research that does not acknowledge God is dangerous.[92] "Knowledge and science must be vitalized by the Spirit of God in order to serve the noblest purposes. The Christian alone can make the right use of knowledge."[93] "With the first advent of Christ there was ushered in an era of greater light and glory; but it would indeed be sinful ingratitude to despise and ridicule the lesser light because a fuller and more glorious light had dawned."[94]

Second, the special revelation of God in Scripture is the standard for the theological interpretation of Jesus and nature. The Bible "contains the science of sciences, the science of salvation." It "is the mine of the unsearchable riches of Christ."[95] "Above all other people on earth the man whose mind is enlightened by the word of God will feel that he must give himself to greater diligence in the perusal of the Bible and a diligent study of the sciences."[96]

The theme of the Bible is Jesus. Therefore, "the foundation of all true science is contained in the Bible."[97] It is "necessary that the study of the Bible should have a prominent place among the various branches of scientific education."[98] "The deepest students of science are constrained to recognize in nature the working of an infinite power. But to man's unaided reason, nature's teaching cannot but be contradictory and disappointing. Only in the light of revelation [Scripture] can it be read aright."[99] "The greatest minds, if not guided by the word of God in their research, become bewildered in their attempts to trace the relations of science and revelation."[100] We must not test Scripture by our ideas of nature or of Christ. Instead, we are to test our ideas by Scripture.[101]

Third, the general revelation of God is the widest context for the theological interpretation of Jesus and Scripture. We must not regard Scripture as a textbook for *all* facts about nature or God. The study of nature itself is indispensable and leads to a knowledge of God.[102] Adventist schools are "established for the purpose of teaching the sciences, and at the same time leading the students to the Saviour, whence all true knowledge flows."[103]

"In the study of the sciences also we are to obtain a knowledge of the Creator. All true science is but an interpretation of the handwriting of God in the material world. Science brings from her research only fresh evidences of the wisdom and power of God."[104]

Research in nature also illuminates our study of Scripture. "As we observe the things of the natural world, we shall be enabled, under the guiding of the Holy Spirit, more fully to understand the lessons of God's word."[105] "Scientific research will open vast fields of thought and information." Contemplation of "the things of nature" provides "a new perception of truth."[106]

False Science and Theology

Neglect of the light of God in Jesus, Scripture, or nature results in both a science and a theology that lack a Christ-centeredness.[107] On the one hand, false science manifests a "show of plausibility" and places Satanic "ideas of science and nature" above the word of God as a test.[108] A disguised infidelity that does not recognize the limits of science and misinterprets the facts of nature that actually support faith in Scripture, it explains the world by natural law alone and wrongly attributes infinite power to nature. False science does not distinguish philosophy, theory, and speculation from fact.[109] On the other hand, false theology ignores the "connected chain of truth" in the Bible and manifests "a disjointed medley of ideas" supported by a passage of Scripture here and there "woven together in a tissue of falsehood."[110] The ignorance and folly of such "disconnected theories [are] arrayed in new and fantastic dress—theories that it will be all the more difficult to meet because there is no reason in them."[111]

Reason and Faith

Reason is one of the "great masterly talents" that "will be taken to heaven."[112] God desires that we be "intellectual Christians."[113] He expects us to use our brains. The Lord does not want human beings to be less acute, less inquiring, less intelligent. However, it is a sin of the mind to extol and deify reason to the neglect of Scripture. To exalt reason unduly is to abase it. And to place the human in rivalry with the divine is to make it contemptible. Reason can never explain creation. It is limited and in need of faith, because God alone is supreme.[114]

God does not promise to remove every doubt, but He gives sufficient evidence as a basis for faith. The Bible strengthens the intellect[115] and is the norming source and standard for the reasons for our faith in Jesus. "We should know for ourselves what constitutes Christianity, what is truth, what is the faith that we have received, what are the Bible rules—the rules given us from the highest authority. There are many who believe, without a reason on which to base their faith, without sufficient evidence as to the truth of the matter. . . . They do not reason from cause to effect. Their faith has no genuine foundation, and in the time of trial they will find that they have built upon the sand."[116]

Summary

For Ellen White, correct interpretations of Jesus, Scripture, and nature never conflict. "God is one. His truth, all truth, forms a unity. . . . God is the source of all knowledge and all truth is a revelation of Him."[117] However, not every theological approach is adequate, because we can inadvertently harmonize incorrect interpretations. Correct interpretations must deal with both the divine and the human dimensions of God's revelations. Because the special revelation of Scripture is divine, it is more accurate, authentic, attractive, true, inspired, ancient, comprehensive, wonderful, instructive, and interesting than any other book.[118] And because Scripture is also human, we should study the context, human authorship, literary form, and translation and textual variations of Scripture.[119] Similarly, we find divine and human dimensions in the revelation made through Jesus. Also the divine revelation in nature includes human nature.

Correct and harmonious interpretations must also respect the hierarchy of Jesus, Scripture, and nature. We cannot correctly evaluate divine revelation by human ideas of science and theology. First, we need direct divine aid from Jesus in order to understand science-theology relationships. He is the Word in which we must anchor our faith.[120] Second, Jesus has given Scripture as the standard for theological interpretations of Himself and nature. Our faith has its anchor in the Jesus of Scripture. Third, Scripture recognizes nature as the widest context for theology. False science, however, excludes any explanation other than by natural law. Also, false theology rejects insight from the light of nature. True science and theology involve a reasonable faith and a faithful reason based on the sufficient evidence that Jesus gives in Scripture and nature.

Conclusion

The inclusive Adventist model manifest in the writings of Ellen White defines theology as the study of God as revealed in His word. Jesus, Scripture, and nature are words of God and, therefore, are sources and standards for theology. Authentic theology recognizes the divine and human dimensions of, and the hierarchy among, God's revelations. The divine/human incarnation of Jesus is the supreme revelation. The divine/human inspiration of Scripture is a special revelation. Nature, including human nature, is a general revelation.

The Adventist model for theology is faithful to Scripture. *Sola scriptura* means that Scripture has a unique authority as source and standard for theology. However, according to Scripture, its authority comes from Jesus, who also works in nature. A theology of Jesus other than the Jesus of Scripture leads to the worship of antichrist. But to put Scripture in the place of Jesus (bibliolatry) is as much a false worship as the worship of nature. We do not undermine God's revelation when we interpret Jesus, Scripture, and nature in the light of each other. To do otherwise is to reject the plain teaching of Scripture itself.

We must not subject revelation to human standards. Rather, theology must be subject to revelation. It is important to distinguish between God's word and any human interpretation that can never be absolutely perfect. Only after the return of Christ will the full harmony between Jesus, Scripture, and nature reveal itself. Then the glory of God will cover the earth as the waters cover the sea. Until then, even Adventist experience, reason, and tradi-

191

tion must remain open to revision based on continuing study of the entire Word of God.[121]

Any effort to separate the issues of science and theology seems to involve intellectual suicide and obscurantism. Since one word of God does not contradict another, we should seek for coherence among our interpretations of Jesus, Scripture, and nature. A lack of coherence signals that we have an imperfect comprehension of God's revelation. The words of Clyde Webster apply to both science and theology. "[In the] conquest for knowledge and truth, [do] not force all answers to come from a single source. Where multiple sources exist, examine the differences and then strive to find the harmony between them. Truth has many faces, comes from many places, and will withstand the tests of time."[122]

While real answers to questions about truth do come from nature, it is not the basis of faith. It is futile to build a rational natural theology as a foundation for faith in Jesus.[123] Instead, the interpretation of nature should be an integral part of a theology grounded in the revelation of Jesus in Scripture. Carl Raschke correctly comments that "we do not need a new natural theology, but we are obliged to bring the study of 'nature' once more back into the arena of theological investigation."[124] Theology built on reason will fall because reason apart from God has limited usefulness. However, reason is a useful resource that we should not separate from faith. Rather, we should exercise a reasonable faith and a faithful reason. Reason can be a work of faith that is faithful to God's Word. Faith is not a leap into the dark—it is a leap into the light of God![125]

The gospel of Jesus—which is communicated in Scripture, and which we are called to preach—is a cosmic gospel. In the words of Ellen White: "A knowledge of science of all kinds is power, and it is in the purpose of God that advanced science shall be taught in our schools as a preparation for the work that is to precede the closing scenes of earth's history."[126] "There are many . . . [like Cornelius. They] are not fully informed in regard to the truth for this time; and yet . . . they fear God. . . . In every sphere of action they work on principles that God accepts. . . . Not all men forget God in their investigation of true science.

"God . . . works for these. . . . He prepares the way for them to take the place of those who have been given a knowledge of Bible truth, but who have disappointed the Lord our Saviour. These men will be true to pure, holy principles in their investigation of the laws which rule our world. . . . That they may obtain advanced light, God places them in connection with men [and women] of superior knowledge regarding His Word."[127]

Such words are not only relevant when witnessing to those who are specialists. As Philip Hefner points out, the content of science increasingly becomes a part of the understanding of all people. In fact, contemporary science is well on the way to producing a global village.[128] This is the context of the Seventh-day Adventist global mission. Adventists must no longer allow others to mistake them for "provincial globalists" handicapped by a local worldview.[129]

George Reid has issued a double challenge to Seventh-day Adventists. First, we must continue to do theology in light of the fact that God is the central fact of the universe and that theology is in a sense a monitor for all knowledge. Second, we must continue to develop approaches responsive to contemporary values, including those of science. He warns that if we fail, our unique worldview, otherwise so relevant to the contemporary scientific culture, will be written off by others as irrelevant.[130]

The task of witnessing to the harmony of science and theology is great. However, Jesus is the creator of nature and the author of Scripture. He is the source and standard for authentic Adventist theology. Let us accept *His* challenge to continue to develop Adventist theology on the sure foundation of Jesus and in harmony with the norming standard of Scripture and the normed standard of nature. All His biddings are enablings. In the light of Jesus, the light of Scripture and nature may be properly focused so that we can lighten the whole earth with the glory of God.

---

[1] For SDA theological publications, see Martin Hanna, *Seventh-day Adventist Theological Bibliography (1851-1994)* (Berrien Springs, Mich.: SDA Theological Seminary, 1995).

[2] Bengt Gustafsson, "The Current Scientific World View," in *The New Faith-Science Debate: Probing Cosmology, Technology and Theology,* ed. John M. Mangum (Minneapolis: Fortress, 1989), p. 1; Paul Tillich, *The System of the Sciences According to Objects and Methods* (London and Toronto: Associated University Presses, 1981). Some of these views are a part of the accepted history of science. Others are even now competing in the marketplace of ideas. Even within a single science such as physics, our present understanding of the laws of nature are not harmonized. In response to this fact, some scientists are searching for a grand unified theory (GUT) of physics that will unify the presently contradictory laws of the four fundamental forces—electromagnetism, the weak and the strong nuclear force, and gravity. See Stephen Hawking, *A Brief History of Time: From the Big Bang to Black Holes* (New York: Bantam, 1988); John Polkinghorne, *The Faith of a Physicist* (Princeton University Press, 1994); David Lindley, *The End of Physics: The Myth of a Unified Theory* (Basic Books, 1993).

[3] Robert H. King, "Introduction: The Task of Theology," in *Christian Theology: An Introduction to Its Traditions and Tasks,* Peter C. Hodgson and Robert H. King, eds. (Philadelphia: Fortress, 1985), p. 1; Maurice Wiles, *What Is Theology?* (New York: Oxford University Press, 1976); John P. Newport and William Cannon, *Why Christians Fight Over the Bible* (Nashville: Thomas Nelson, 1974); Richard J. Coleman, *Issues of Theological Warfare: Evangelicals and Liberals* (Grand Rapids: Eerdmans, 1980).

[4] Because of the semantic complexity involved, some theologians such as Eta Linnemann prefer not to use the term *science* to denote "competent intellectual work in theology." See Eta Linnemann, *Historical Criticism of the Bible: Methodology or Ideology?* (Grand Rapids: Baker, 1990), p. 140. Like the word "science," the word "nature" is ambiguous. On the one hand, it may be used

to refer to inanimate, animal, human, and/or superhuman natures (*i.e.,* angelic and divine nature). On the other hand we may use it to distinguish that which is determined by law and that which is free to determine itself and is therefore supernatural or above nature. See Horace Bushnell, *Nature and the Supernatural* (New York: Scribner, Armstrong & Co., 1877); Alvin Plantinga, *Does God Have a Nature?* (Milwaukee: Marquette University Press, 1980); William Alston, *Divine Nature and Human Language* (Ithaca, N.Y.: Cornell University Press, 1989); R. G. Collingwood, *The Idea of Nature* (Oxford: Clarendon Press, 1945); Gordon Kaufmann, "Nature, History and God: Toward an Integrated Conceptualization," *Zygon: Journal of Religion and Science* 27 (December 1992): 379-401; William Temple, *Nature, Man and God* (New York: Macmillan, 1956); E. O. Wilson, *On Human Nature* (Cambridge, Mass.: Harvard University Press, 1978).

[5] According to the generally accepted definitions, "a natural science is a theoretical explanatory discipline which objectively addresses natural phenomena within the general constraints that (1) its theories must be rationally connectable to generally specifiable empirical phenomena and that (2) it normally does not leave the natural realm for the concepts employed in its explanations." See Del Ratasch, *Philosophy of Science* (Downers Grove, Ill.: InterVarsity, 1986), p. 13; Norman Campbell, *What Is Science?* (New York: Dover Publications, 1953); E. Nagel, *The Structure of Science* (New York: Harcourt, Brace and World, 1961); R. Giere, *Understanding Scientific Reasoning* (New York: Holt, Reinhart and Winston, 1979); N. Rescher, *Scientific Explanation* (New York: Free Press, 1970); M. Wartofski, *Conceptual Foundations of Scientific Thought* (London: Macmillan, 1968); G. Gale, *Theory of Science* (New York: McGraw-Hill, 1979); Karin Knorr-Cetina, *The Manufacture of Knowledge: An Essay on the Constructivist and Contextual Nature of Science* (New York: Pergamon Press, 1981); Imre Lakatos, *The Methodology of Scientific Research Programes* (Cambridge: Cambridge University Press, 1978); Karl Popper, *The Logic of Scientific Discovery* (London: Hutchinson, 1972); Tito Arecchi, "Why Science Is an Open System Implying a Meta-Science," in *The Science and Theology of Information* (Geneva: Labor et Fides, 1992). On methodological naturalism see Phillip E. Johnson, *Reason in the Balance: The Case Against Naturalism in Science, Law and Education* (Downers Grove, Ill.: InterVarsity, 1995); Stephen Jay Gould, "Impeaching a Self-Appointed Judge," review of Johnson's *Darwin on Trial* in *Scientific American* (July 1992): 118-120; Nancey Murphy, "Phillip Johnson on Trial: A Critique of His Critique of Darwin," in *Perspectives on Science and Christian Faith* 45 (March 1993): 26-36; Alvin Plantinga, "When Faith and Reason Clash: Evolution and the Bible," *Christian Scholar's Review* 21, No. 1 (1991): 25-29; Norman L. Geisler and J. Kerby Anderson, *Origin Science: A Proposal for the Creation-Evolution Controversy* (Grand Rapids: Baker, 1987); J. P. Moreland, *The Creation Hypothesis: Scientific Evidence for an Intelligent Designer* (Downers Grove, Ill.: InterVarsity, 1994); Henry M. Morris, *Studies in the Bible and Science* (Grand Rapids: Baker, 1966); Henry M. Morris, ed., *Scientific Creationism* (San Diego: Creation Life Publishers, 1974); Nancy R. Pearcey and Charles B. Thaxton, *The Soul of Science: Christian Faith and Natural Philosophy* (Wheaton, Ill.: Crossway, 1994). One who is not a defender of SDA "creation science" documents the fact that in the postmodern period SDAs provided one of the early critiques of methodological naturalism. See Ronald L. Numbers, *The Creationists: The Evolution of Scientific Creationism* (New York: Alfred A. Knopf, 1992), pp. 72-101. Numbers provides useful reference lists. See also the bibliographies of Harold W. Clark, "Traditional Adventist Creationism: Its Origin, Development, and Current Problems" *Spectrum* 3, No. 1 (Winter 1971): 7-18; and Molleurus Couperus, "Tensions Between Religion and Science," *Spectrum* 10, No. 4 (1978): 74-88.

[6] Roy A. Clouser, *The Myth of Religious Neutrality: An Essay on the Hidden Role of Religious Beliefs in Theories* (Notre Dame, Ind.: University of Notre Dame Press, 1991); reviewed by Martin Hanna in *Andrews University Seminary Studies* 32, No. 1-2 (Spring-Summer 1994): 121-123; Wolfgang Smith, "The Idea of the Physical Universe," in his *Cosmos and Transcendence: Breaking Through the Barrier of Scientistic Belief* (Illinois: Sherwood Sugden, 1984), pp. 13-25; Beverly J. Stratton, "Is Science Scientific? Affinities Between Theologians and Scientists as Interpreters in the Search for Truth," *Word & World* 13, No. 3 (Summer 1993): 269-276; Anders Nygren, *Meaning and Method: Prolegomena to a Scientific Philosophy of Religion and a Scientific Theology* (Philadelphia: Fortress Press, 1972); H. Vander Goot, ed., *Life Is Religion* (St. Catharines, Ont.: Paiseia Press, 1981); Paul Nelson, "The Role of Theology in Current Evolutionary Reasoning," in *Facets of Faith and Science,* ed. J. M. van der Meer (University Press of America, 1995, vol. 3); Mary Midgley,

Science as Salvation: A Modern Myth and Its Meaning (New York: Routledge, 1992); Robert John Russell, Nancey Murphy, and C. J. Isham, eds., *Quantum Cosmology and the Laws of Nature: Scientific Perspectives on Divine Action* (Vatican City State: Vatican Observatory Publications, 1993); John C. Polkinghorne, *God in a Scientific World* (West Watson Lectures, 1990); Joseph Sittler, "Nature and Grace: Reflections on an Old Rubric"; James H. Burtness, "All the Fullness"; Harold H. Ditmanson, "The Call for a Theology of Creation"; and Ragnar Bring, "The Gospel of the New Creation," *Dialogue* 3, No. 4 (Fall 1964): 25. Actually there is a distinction but no real separation between naturalism and materialism—in which nature is all there is—and pantheism—in which God is all there is and is identified with nature. Both oppose theism—in which a supernatural God created the natural world with a purpose. See Phillip E. Johnson, *Reason in the Balance,* p. 38; John Hunt, *Pantheism and Christianity* (New York: Kennikat Press, 1970), pp. 2-282.

[7] Herman Bavinck, *The Philosophy of Revelation* (Grand Rapids: Eerdmans, 1953), pp. 84, 85. Thomas Torrance agrees that "there is no secret way of knowing . . . [but] only one basic way of knowing." See Thomas Torrance, *The Ground and Grammar of Theology* (Charlottesville, Va.: University Press of Virginia, 1980), p. 9; Jerry H. Gil, *The Possibility of Religious Knowledge* (Grand Rapids: Eerdmans, 1971). In English, "science" often denotes natural science. On the contrary, "Wissenschaft" in German denotes a "rational, academic discipline" or "field of knowledge." This corresponds with the use of *scientia* in Latin: "disciplined methodological knowledge in any realm of human inquiry." See Peter C. Hodgson, review of *Theology and the Philosophy of Science* in *Religious Studies Review* 3 (1977): 216. Thomas Torrance argues that "natural science and theological science are not opponents but partners before God, in a service of God in which they may learn from each other how better to peruse its own distinctive function, how better to be natural science or how better to be theological science. This is a relationship that is not one-sided but mutual, for natural science has actually learned far more from theological science than is generally realized." See Torrance, *The Ground and Grammar of Theology,* p. 7; *Theological Science* (New York: Oxford University Press, 1969); "The Scientific Character of Theological Statements," *Dialogue* 4, No. 2 (Spring 1965): 112-117. On theological science or scientific theology see Roy D. Morrison II, *Science, Theology and the Transcendental Horizon: Einstein, Kant and Tillich* (Atlanta: Scholars Press, 1994); Langdon Gilkey, "New Modes of Empirical Theology," in *The Future of Empirical Theology* (Chicago: University of Chicago Press, 1969); Harold Nebelsick, *Theology and Science in Mutual Modification* (New York: Oxford University Press, 1981); Stanley L. Jaki, "Religion and Science: The Cosmic Connection," in *Belief, Faith and Reason* (Ottawa: Christian Journals Limited, 1981), pp. 11-28; Murray Rae, Hilary Regan, and John Stenhouse, eds., *Science and Theology: Questions at the Interface* (Grand Rapids: Eerdmans, 1994); Louis Berkhof, "Theology as a Science," in his *Introduction to Systematic Theology* (Grand Rapids: Baker, 1979), pp. 44-48; Ralph Burhoe, *Toward a Scientific Theology* (Belfast: Christian Journals Limited, 1981); Philip Hefner, "Theology in the Context of Science, Liberation, and Christian Tradition," in *Worldviews and Warrents,* ed. William Schweiker and Per Anderson (Lanham, Md.: University Press of America, 1987), pp. 33-49; "Theology's Truth and Scientific Formulation," *Zygon: Journal of Religion and Science* 23 (September 1988): 263-280; Arthur Peacocke, *Theology for a Scientific Age: Being and Becoming—Natural and Divine* (Oxford: Basil Blackwell, 1990); William Carl Placher, "Revealed to Reason: Theology as 'Normal Science,'" *The Christian Century* 109, No. 6 (1992): 192-195; Bernard E. Meland, ed., *The Future of Empirical Theology* (Chicago: University of Chicago Press, 1969); M. D. Chenu, *Is Theology a Science?* (New York: Hawthorn, 1959); John Polkinghorne, *Science and Creation: The Search for Understanding* (London: SPCK, 1988); *Science and Providence: God's Interaction With the World* (Boston: Shambhala, 1989); M. Wiles, *God's Action in the World* (London: SCM, 1986); Stanley Jaki, *The Road of Science and the Ways to God* (Edinburgh: Scottish Academic Press, 1978).

[8] Carl Raschke, *Theological Thinking: An Inquiry* (Atlanta: Scholars Press, 1988), p. 19; *Seventh-day Adventists Believe . . . A Biblical Exposition of 27 Fundamental Beliefs,* Ministerial Association, General Conference of SDAs (Hagerstown, Md.: Review and Herald, 1988), pp. 4-15; Olaf Pederson, *The Book of Nature* (Notre Dame, Ind.: University of Notre Dame Press, 1992).

[9] William H. Austin, *The Relevance of Natural Science to Theology* (New York: Macmillan Press, 1976); Martin Hanna, "Toward a Biblical Understanding of the Relations of Religion, Philosophy, and Science" (unpublished research paper, Andrews University, July 1993). A model is a theoret-

ical framework that guides interpretation. For information on philosophical frameworks that theologians have used, see Royce Gordon Gruenler, *Meaning and Understanding: The Philosophical Framework for Biblical Interpretation* (Grand Rapids: Zondervan, 1991); Reynold Borzaga, *In Pursuit of Religion: A Framework for Understanding Today's Theology* (Palm Springs, Fla.: Sunday Publications, 1977); Terry F. Godlove, *Religion, Interpretation, and Diversity of Belief: The Framework Model From Kant to Durkheim to Davidson* (New York: Cambridge University Press, 1989). For an important series of articles that analyze the various philosophical models and propose the use of a biblical theoretical framework, see Fernando Luis Canale, "Revelation and Inspiration: Method for a New Approach," *Andrews University Seminary Studies [AUSS]*, 31, No. 3 (Autumn 1993): 171-194; F. L. Canale, "Revelation and Inspiration: The Classical Model," *AUSS*, 32, No. 1-2 (Spring-Summer 1994) 8, 9; F. L. Canale, "Revelation and Inspiration: The Liberal Model," *AUSS*, 32, No. 3 (Autumn 1994) 169-195; F. L. Canale, "Revelation and Inspiration: The Historical-Cognitive Model," *AUSS*, 33, No. 1-2 (Spring 1995) 5-38. See also Arthur L. White, "Toward an Adventist Concept of Inspiration," *Adventist Review*, Jan. 12, 1978, pp. 4-6; Jan. 19, 1978, pp. 7-9; Jan. 26, 1978, pp. 6-8; Feb. 2, 1978, pp. 6-8; Alden Thompson, "Adventists and Inspiration," *Adventist Review*, Sept. 5, 1985, pp. 5-7; Sept. 12, 1985, pp. 13-15; Sept. 19, 1985, pp. 7-9; Sept. 26, 1985, pp. 12-15; *Inspiration: Hard Questions, Honest Answers* (Hagerstown, Md.: Review and Herald, 1991). On the various models for science-theology relations, see Vern Poythress, *Science and Hermeneutics* (Grand Rapids: Academie Books, 1988); Richard J. Bernstein, *Beyond Objectivism and Relativism: Science, Hermeneutics and Praxis* (Philadelphia: University of Pennsylvania, 1988); Nancey Murphy, *Theology in the Age of Scientific Reasoning* (Ithaca: Cornell University Press, 1990); Ian Barbour, "Surveying the Possibilities: Ways of Relating Science and Religion," in *Religion and the Natural Sciences: The Range of Engagement*, James E. Huchingson, ed. (Fort Worth: Harcourt Brace Jovanovich, 1993), pp. 6-34; Stephen B. Bevans, *Models of Contextual Theology* (Maryknoll, N.Y.: Orbis Books, 1993); Frederick Ferré, "Mapping the Logic of Models in Science and Theology," in *New Essays in Religious Language*, ed. Dallas High (New York: Oxford University Press, 1969); Joseph A. Mazzeo, *Varieties of Interpretation* (Notre Dame, Ind.: University of Notre Dame Press, 1978); Raymond F. Collins, *Models of Theological Reflection* (New York: University of America Press, 1984); John Polkinghorne, "Contemporary Interactions Between Science and Theology," *Modern Believing* 36:4 (1995): 33-38; James Orr, "Science and Christian Faith," in *The Fundamentals: A Testimony to the Truth*, ed. George M. Marsden (New York: Garland Pub., 1988), vol. 4, pp. 91-104.

[10] Carl Raschke, *Theological Thinking*, pp. 29, 30 (bracketed words mine). Chris McGowan regards science-theology relations as a potential challenge to modern science and a threat of reversion to the dark ages of science. See Chris McGowan, *In the Beginning* (Toronto, Ont.: Macmillan, 1983), pp. xi, 188.

[11] *Science and Creationism: A View From the National Academy of Sciences* (Washington, D.C.: National Academy Press, 1984), pp. 6, 7; William T. Keeton, "A Scientist's Question: Is Theology Based on Evidence?" *Dialogue* 4, No. 2 (Spring 1965): 98-103; Philip Hefner, "In Reply to Mr. Keeton: Theology and the Question of Truth," *Dialogue* 4, No. 2 (Spring 1965): 104-111; "Can a Theology of Nature Be Coherent With Scientific Cosmology?" *Dialogue* 30, No. 4 (Autumn 1991): 267-272; Michael Bauman, "Between Jerusalem and the Laboratory: A Theologian Looks at Science," in *Man and Creation: Perspectives on Science and Theology*, ed. Michael Bauman, Lissa Roche, and Jon Corombos (Hillsdale, Mich.: Hillsdale College Press, 1993), pp. 247-267.

[12] Dale Moody, *The Word of Truth: A Summary of Christian Doctrine Based on Biblical Revelation* (Grand Rapids: Eerdmans, 1981), pp. 1, 2. All references to Scripture indicate the Judeo-Christian Scriptures. However, we should note that religions other than Judaism and Christianity (such as Islam) also possess Scriptures. On Scripture as revelation, see Avery Robert Dulles, *Models of Revelation* (New York: Orbis Books, 1992); John Goldingay, *Models for Scripture* (Grand Rapids: Eerdmans, 1994); Bernard Ramm, *The Christian View of Science and Scripture* (Grand Rapids: Eerdmans, 1954); Bastiaan van Iersel, "Is Scripture Becoming Less Important?" in *Scripture: The Presence of God*, ed. Pierre Benoit, Ronald Murphy, and Bastiaan van Iersel (New York: Paulist Press, 1969), pp. 157-175; Robert Ware, "The Use of Scripture in Current Theology," in *Theology, Exegesis and Proclamation*, ed. Roland Murphy (New York: Herder and Herder, 1971),

pp. 115-128; Joseph A. Fitzmyer, *Scripture, the Soul of Theology* (New York: Paulist Press, 1994); Alan Richardson, *The Bible in the Age of Science* (Philadelphia: Westminster, 1961); Wilfred Cantwell Smith, *What Is Scripture: A Comparative Approach* (Minneapolis: Fortress, 1993); Bernard Ramm, *The Christian View of Science and Scripture* (Grand Rapids: Eerdmans, 1954); David Kelsey, *The Uses of Scripture in Recent Theology* (Philadelphia: Fortress, 1975); Paul J. Achtemeier, *The Interpretation of Scripture: Problems and Proposals* (Philadelphia: Westminster, 1980); John Baillie, *The Idea of Revelation in Recent Thought* (New York: Columbia University Press, 1956); Paul Helm, *The Divine Revelation: The Basic Issues* (Westchester, Ill.: Crossway, 1982); Carl F. H. Henry, *God, Revelation, Authority: God Who Speaks and Shows* (Waco: Word, 1979); William Hordern, "The Nature of Revelation," *Readings in Christian Theology,* ed. Millard J. Erickson (Grand Rapids: Baker, 1973), vol. 1, pp. 177-196; Clark H. Pinnock, *Biblical Revelation: The Foundation of Christian Theology* (Chicago: Moody Press, 1971); Christopher Knight, "A New Deism? Science, Religion and Revelation," *Modern Believing* 36, No. 4 (1995): 38-45; Kevin Vanhoozer, "God's Mighty Speech-Acts: The Doctrine of Scripture Today," in *A Pathway Into the Holy Scripture,* ed. P. E. Satterthwaite and D. F. Wright (Grand Rapids: Eerdmans, 1994), pp. 143-182; Ronald Thiemann, *Revelation and Theology* (Notre Dame, Ind.: University of Notre Dame Press, 1985); William J. Martin, "Special Revelation as Objective," in *Revelation and the Bible: Contemporary Evangelical Thought,* ed. Carl F. H. Henry (Grand Rapids: Baker, 1958), pp. 61-72.

[13] For Sölle, radical theology is akin to what we shall describe as postmodern theology later in this chapter. See Dorothee Sölle, *Thinking About God: An Introduction to Theology* (Philadelphia: Trinity Press International, 1990), p. 22. For more on norms, see Frederick Ferré, "Cosmos: Child of Science? Theoretical Intelligence and Epistemic Norms," *Philosophy of Religion* 31 (1992): 149-163; 165-176; Jean Ladrière, "On the Notion of Criterion," in *Is Being Human a Criterion of Being Christian?* ed. Jean-Pierre Jossua and Claude Geffré (New York: Seabury Press, 1982), pp. 10-15.

[14] Richard M. Davidson, "Interpreting Scripture: An Hermeneutical 'Decalogue,'" in *Journal of the Adventist Theological Society* 4, No. 2 (1993): 96. For SDA perspectives on theological presuppositions, see Bruce Norman, "Presuppositions: The Key to the Formulation of Biblical Doctrine," *Journal of the Adventist Theological Society* 4, No. 1 (1993): 47-64; Fernando Luis Canale, *Towards a Criticism of Theological Reason: Time and Timelessness as Theological Presuppositions* (Berrien Springs, Mich.: Andrews University Press, 1987). Other perspectives on presuppositions are provided by Clyde L. Manschreck, "Presuppositional Directions for the Problem of Authority," *Review and Expositor* 75 (1978): 181-193; E. R. Geehan, "The 'Presuppositional Apologetic' of Francis Schaeffer," *Themelios* 8 (1972): 10-18.

[15] On God's preparation of Judeo-Christian experience, reason, and tradition for inspiration and Incarnation, see Thomas Torrance, *The Mediation of Christ* (Grand Rapids: Eerdmans, 1983). As Fernando Canale puts it, "The nature of the cognition involved in revelation is temporal and historical" ("Revelation and Inspiration: The Historical Cognitive Model," p. 23). Thus it "is not restrictive but rather inclusive of all human experiences. . . . Interpretation includes experience, understanding, deliberation, judgment, decision, and action" (*ibid.,* p. 23, n. 48). See David Tracy, *Plurality and Ambiguity: Hermeneutics, Religion, Hope* (San Francisco: Harper and Row, 1987), p. 9; Alexander Thompson, *Tradition and Authority in Science and Theology With Reference to the Thought of Michael Polanyi* (Edinburgh: Scottish Academic Press, 1987). On experience and theology, see Henry Wieman, *Religious Experience and Scientific Method* (New York: Macmillan, 1926); William James, *Varieties of Religious Experience* (New York: Longmans, 1902); William Ernest Hocking, *The Meaning of God in Human Experience* (New Haven, Conn.: Yale University Press, 1912); John B. Cobb, Jr., *The Structure of Christian Existence* (Philadelphia: Westminster, 1967); Thomas A. Noble, "Scripture and Experience," in *A Pathway Into the Holy Scripture,* ed. P. E. Satterthwaite and D. F. Wright (Grand Rapids: Eerdmans, 1994), pp. 277-296; Edward Schillebeeckx, Bas van Iersel, *Revelation and Experience* (New York: Seabury Press, 1979). On reason and theology, see Fritz Marti, *Religion, Reason and Man* (St. Louis: Warren H. Green, 1974); Gordon H. Clarke, *Religion, Reason and Revelation* (Philadelphia: Presbyterian and Reformed Pub. Co., 1961); Carl Michalson, *The Rationality of Faith: An Historical Critique of Theological Reason* (New York: Charles Scribner's Sons, 1963); Anton Vogel, *Reality, Reason and Religion* (New York: Morehouse-Gorham Co., 1957); E. L. Miller, *God and Reason: A Historical Approach to Philosophical Theology* (New York:

Macmillan, 1972); Immanual Kant, *Reason Within the Limits of Reason Alone* (New York: Harper and Brothers, 1960); John A. Howard, ed., *Belief, Faith and Reason* (Ottawa: Christian Journals Limited, 1981); Thomas Torrance, *God and Rationality* (London: Oxford University Press, 1971). On tradition and theology, see Delwin Brown, *Boundaries of Our Habitations: Tradition and Theological Construction* (New York: State University of New York Press, 1994); W. Gasque and William Stanfor LaSor, eds., *Scripture, Tradition and Interpretation* (Grand Rapids: Eerdmans, 1978); Gerhard Ebeling, *The Word of God and Tradition: Historical Studies Interpreting the Divisions of Christianity* (Philadelphia: Fortress, 1968).

[16] Gerhard Hasel, "The Totality of Scripture Versus Modernistic Limitations," *Journal of the Adventist Theological Society* 2, No. 1 (Spring 1991): 30-52; Ted Peters, "*Sola Scriptura* and the Second Naivete," in *Dialogue* 16 (Fall 1977): 268-280; Wolfhart Pannenberg, "The Crisis of the Scripture-Principle in Protestant Theology," *Dialogue* 2 (1963): 307-313; Robert C. Sproul, "*Sola Scriptura*: Crucial to Evangelicalism," in *The Foundation of Biblical Authority,* ed. James Montgomery Boice (Grand Rapids: Zondervan, 1978), pp. 103-119; Bernard Ramm, "Is 'Scripture Alone' the Essence of Christianity?" in *Biblical Authority,* ed. Jack Rogers (Waco, Tex.: Word Books, 1977), pp. 107-123; Harry William Eberts, Jr., " *'Sola Scriptura':* Then and Now," *Reformed Liturgy and Music* 18 (1984): 64-69; Gerhard Ebeling, "'*Sola Scriptura*' and Tradition," in *The Word of God and Tradition: Historical Studies Interpreting the Divisions of Christianity,* trans. S. H. Hooke (London: Collins, 1968), pp. 102-147; Anthony N. S. Lane, "*Sola Scriptura?* Making Sense of a Post-Reformation Slogan," in *A Pathway Into the Holy Scripture,* ed. P. E. Satterthwaite and D. F. Wright (Grand Rapids: Eerdmans, 1994), pp. 297-327; David W. Lotz, "*Sola Scriptura:* Luther on Biblical Authority," *Interpretation* 35 (1981): 258-273; Klass Runia, "The Hermeneutics of the Reformers," *Calvin Theological Journal* 19 (1984): 121-152; John Kelman Sutherland Reid, *The Authority of Scripture: A Study of the Reformation and Post-Reformation Understanding of the Bible* (London: Methuen and Co., 1957); Alister E. McGrath, *Reformation Thought: An Introduction* (Oxford: Basil Blackwell, 1988); Paul Lehmann, "The Reformers' Use of the Bible," *Theology Today* 3 (1946): 328-344.

[17] Augustine, *The Trinity,* trans. Stephen McKanna (Washington, D.C.: Catholic University of America Press, 1963); Plato, *The Dialogues of Plato,* ed. and trans. B. Jowett (New York: Random House, 1937), vols. 1, 2; Aristotle, *Metaphysics,* in *The Basic Works of Aristotle,* ed. Richard McKeon, trans. W. D. Ross (New York: Random House, 1941), pp. 681-926; Thomas Aquinas, *The Summa Theologica,* vol. 2 of *The Basic Writings of St. Thomas Aquinas,* trans. Anton C. Pegis (New York: Random House, 1945), pp. 225-1121. On the history of science-theology relations, see Wolfhart Pannenberg, *Theology and the Philosophy of Science* (Philadelphia: Westminster, 1976), pp. 228-296; John Dillenberger, *Protestant Thought and Natural Science* (New York: Doubleday, 1960); J. Harvey Brooke, *Science and Religion: Some Historical Perspectives* (Cambridge University Press, 1991); James B. Miller, "From Organism to Mechanism to History," in *The Church and Contemporary Theology: Proceedings of a Consultation of the Presbyterian Church (U.S.A.),* ed. James B. Miller and Kenneth E. McCall (Pittsburgh: Carnegie Mellon University Press, 1990); Crawford Knox, *Changing Christian Paradigms and Their Implications for Modern Thought* (New York: E. J. Brill, 1993); Max Wildiers, *The Theologian and His Universe: Theology and Cosmology From the Middle Ages to the Present* (New York: Seabury Press, 1982); Eugene G. Bewkes et al., *The Western Heritage of Faith and Reason* (New York: Harper and Row, 1963); Justo L. González, *A History of Christian Thought* (Nashville: Abingdon, 1970-1976).

[18] During the Patristic period (100-451) Greek theologians in the Eastern Church linked biblical theism with the Platonic divine transcendence-immanence. The idea of a divinized soul-body complex and a suprarational divine image made humanity a microcosm of theos-cosmos relations and a macrocosm of Christ. This ontological linkage of things with eternal archetypes still appears in Eastern Orthodoxy. Maximus the Confessor (c. 580-662) followed the Capodocian Fathers (fourth century) and the writings attributed to Dionysios the Areopagite (fifth century). His Orthodox successors include Symeon the New Theologian (949-1022) and Gregory Palamas (c. 1296-1359). See Philip Sherrard, *The Eclipse of Man and Nature: An Enquiry Into the Origins and Consequences of Modern Science* (West Stockbridge, Mass.: Lindisfarne Press, 1987), pp. 17-43; Lars Thunberg, *Microcosm and Mediator: The Theological Anthropology of Maximus the Confessor* (London:

1965); V. Lossky, *The Mystical Tradition of the Eastern Church* (London: 1957); Rudolf Allers, "Microsmos From Anaximandros to Parcelsus," *Traditio* 2 (1944): 319-407; James B. Miller, "From Organism to Mechanism to History."

[19] Norman R. Gulley, "The Influence of Philosophical and Scientific World Views on the Development of Theology," *Journal of the Adventist Theological Society* 4, No. 2 (Autumn 1993): 137-160. Between the extremes of reason dominated by faith and faith dominated by reason was the classical approach of faith seeking understanding. See Philip Clayton, *Explanation From Physics to Theology: An Essay in Rationality and Religion* (London: Yale University Press, 1989), pp. 9, 10, 131, 140; "Clayton Response to Robbins: Religion/Science Without God?" *Zygon: Journal of Religion and Science* 27 (December 1992): 457-459; Ian Barbour, "Surveying the Possibilities," p. 10. According to Emerson Shideler, knowledge in science and theology is experience structured by faith. "All knowing is an act of faith by which the person meets his world, and reflects the quest of faith." See Emerson W. Shideler, *Believing and Knowing* (Ames, Iowa: Iowa State University Press, 1966), pp. 150, 153; "A Theological Study of Science," *Dialogue* 4, No. 2 (Spring 1965): 90-97. Concerning reason and faith Richard Rice writes: "No topic in the area of theology or philosophy has attracted more attention, for a longer period of time, from a greater variety of sources, or with more diverse results." See Richard Rice, *Reason and the Contours of Faith* (Riverside, Calif.: La Sierra University Press, 1991), pp. 2, 3. Rice wrote his book after an interesting interchange sparked by his article "The Knowledge of Faith," *Spectrum* 5, No. 2 (Spring 1973): 19-32; Larry M. Lewis, "Perspective and Tension With Faith and Reason," *Spectrum* 1, No. 2 (Summer 1974): 77-79; Dalton D. Baldwin, "Reason and Will in the Experience of Faith," *Spectrum* 1, No. 2 (Summer 1974): 80-83; Eric D. Syme, "The Gift of Reason and the Aid of Revelation," *Spectrum* 1, No. 2 (Summer 1974): 84-86.

[20] David C. Steinmetz, "The Superiority of Pre-Critical Exegesis," *Theology Today* 37 (1980): 27-38. On the different types of biblical interpretation, see Steven L. McKenzie and Stephen R. Haynes, eds., *To Each Its Own Meaning: An Introduction to Biblical Criticisms and Their Application* (Louisville: John Knox, 1993); Mark A. Noll, *Between Faith and Criticism: Evangelicals, Scholarship and the Bible in America* (San Francisco: Harper and Row, 1986). On religious language, see Raoul Mortley, *From Word to Silence I: The Rise and Fall of Logos* (Bonn: Hanstein, 1986); Douglas Farrow, *The Word of Truth and Disputes About Words* (Winona Lake, Ind.: Carpenter Books, 1987); Neil Richardson, *Paul's Language About God* (Sheffield, Eng.: Sheffield Academic Press, 1994), pp. 9, 10; Martin Hanna, "The Language of Reasonable Faith: A Comparative Analysis of the Theologies of Richard Rice and Ellen G. White" (unpublished research paper, Andrews University, 1992); Frederick Ferré, *Language, Logic and God* (New York: Harper, 1961); Langdon Gilkey, "Cosmology, Ontology, and Biblical Language," *The Journal of Religion* 41, No. 3 (July 1961): 194-205; *Naming the Whirlwind: The Renewal of God-Language* (Indianapolis: Bobbs-Merrill, 1969); Frank B. Dilley, *Metaphysics and Religious Language* (New York: Columbia University Press, 1964); G. Stanley Kane, "God-Language and Secular Experience," *International Journal for Philosophy of Religion* 2 (Spring 1971): 78-98; Robert Allen Evans, *Intelligible and Responsible Talk About God* (Leiden: E. J. Brill, 1973); John Macquarrie, *God-Talk: An Examination of the Language and Logic of Theology* (New York: Harper and Row, 1967); James Barr, *The Semantics of Biblical Language* (Oxford: Oxford University Press, 1966); Urban T. Holmes III, *To Speak of God: Theology for Beginners* (New York: Seabury Press, 1974). We should give special attention to the use of metaphor in theology. See Peter W. Macky, *The Centrality of Metaphors to Biblical Thought: A Method for Interpreting the Bible* (Lewiston, N.Y.: Mellen Press, 1990); Sallie McFague, *Metaphorical Theology: Models of God in Religious Language* (Philadelphia: Fortress, 1982); Janet Soskice, *Metaphor and Religious Language* (Oxford: Clarendon Press, 1985); Mary Gerhart and Allan Russell, *Metaphorical Process: The Creation of Scientific and Religious Understanding* (Fort Worth: Texas Christian University Press, 1984).

[21] John Dillenberger, *Protestant Theology and Natural Science*, p. 23. On timelessness, see Fernando Luis Canale, *Towards a Criticism of Theological Reason;* Oscar Cullmann, *Christ and Time* (London: SCM, 1962); Simon de Vries, "Time in the Bible," in *The Times of Celebration,* ed. David Power (New York: Seabury Press, 1981), pp. 3-13; Arthur C. Custance, *Time and Eternity* (Grand Rapids: Zondervan, 1977); Calvin Luther Martin, *In the Spirit of the Earth: Rethinking History and*

Time (Baltimore: Johns Hopkins University Press, 1992); Gerardus van der Leeuw, "Primordial Time and Final Time," in *Man and Time,* ed. J. Campbell (New York: Pantheon Books, 1957).

[22] René Descartes' *Discourse on Method and Other Writings,* trans. A. Wollaston (Baltimore: Penguin, 1960) and Immanuel Kant's *Critique of Pure Reason,* trans. N. K. Smith (London: Macmillan, 1968); Hans Blumenberg, *The Legitimacy of the Modern Age,* trans. Robert M. Wallace (Cambridge, Mass.: MIT Press, 1983); E. J. Dijksterhuis, *The Mechanization of the World Picture,* trans. C. Dikshoorn (Oxford: Oxford University Press, 1961); Edgar V. McKnight, *Postmodern Use of the Bible: The Emergence of Reader-oriented Criticism* (Nashville: Abingdon, 1988); Fernando Canale, "Revelation and Inspiration: The Liberal Model"; D. E. Nineham, "The Use of the Bible in Modern Theology," *Bulletin of the John Rylands Library* 52 (1969-1970): 178-199. The premodern roots of the conflict model for science-theology relations may be seen in Tertulian: "What indeed has Athens [philosophy] to do with Jerusalem [Christianity]?" Quoted in Étienne Gilson, *Reason and Revelation in the Middle Ages* (New York: Charles Scribner's Sons, 1938), p. 9f. For more on the conflict model, see John W. Draper, *History of the Conflict Between Religion and Science* (New York: D. Appleton and Co., 1897); Andrew Dickenson White, *A History of the Warfare of Science and Theology* (New York: D. Appleton and Co., 1922), vol. 1; Colin A. Russell, "The Conflict Metaphor and Its Social Origins," *Science and Christian Belief* 1 (1989): 3-26.

[23] Jerrey Hopper, *Understanding Modern Theology: Cultural Revolutions and New Worlds* (Philadelphia: Fortress, 1987), vol. 1, p. 36; quoted in N. Gulley, "The Influence of Philosophical and Scientific World Views on the Development of Theology," p. 146.

[24] John Dillenberger, *Protestant Theology and Natural Science;* Langdon Gilkey, *Religion and the Scientific Future: Reflections on Myth, Science, and Theology* (New York: Harper and Row, 1970).

[25] As early as the thirteenth century, some Catholic and later some Protestant theologians viewed theology as practical rather than as pure science. See Pannenberg, *Theology and the Philosophy of Science,* pp. 228-296; Donald K. McKim, *What Christians Believe About the Bible* (Nashville, Thomas Nelson, 1985). On liberal theology, see Friedrich Schleiermacher, *On Religion: Speeches to Its Cultures Despisers,* trans. John Oman (New York: Harper Torchbooks, 1958); *The Christian Faith,* ed. H. R. Mackintosh and J. S. Stewart (New York: Harper Torchbooks, 1963); Dillenberger, *Protestant Theology and Natural Science,* pp. 21-23; Daniel D. Williams, "Liberalism," in *A Handbook of Christian Theology* (New York: Word, 1958), pp. 207-210; L. Harold De Wolf, *The Case for Theology in Liberal Perspective* (Philadelphia: Westminster, 1959). On Fundamentalism, see Martin E. Marty and R. Scott Appleby, *Fundamentalisms Observed* (Chicago: University of Chicago Press, 1991); "Religious Fundamentalism and the Sciences," in *Fundamentalisms and Society* (Chicago: University of Chicago Press, 1993).

[26] On the postmodern period, see Jean-François Lyotard, *The Postmodern Condition: A Report on Knowledge* (Minneapolis: University of Minnesota Press, 1979); Paul R. Hinlicky, "The Human Predicament in Post-modernity," *Dialogue* 23, No. 3: 167-173; Matthew H. Nitecki and Doris V. Nitecki, eds., *History and Evolution* (New York: State University of New York Press, 1992). On postmodern theology, see Stanley J. Grenz and Roger E. Olson, *20th Century Theology: God and the World in a Transitional Age* (Downers Grove, Ill.: InterVarsity, 1992); Charles J. Scalise, "Canonical Hermeneutics: Postcritical Theological Prolegomena," in his *Hermeneutics as Theological Prolegomena: A Canonical Approach* (Macon, Ga.: Mercer University Press, 1994), pp. 75-98; Jerry H. Gill, *Mediated Transcendence: A Postmodern Reflection* (Macon, Ga.: Mercer University Press, 1989); Edgar V. McKnight, *Postmodern Use of the Bible* (Nashville: Abingdon, 1988); James B. Miller, "The Emerging Postmodern World," in *Postmodern Theology: Christian Faith in a Pluralist World* (New York: Harper and Row, 1989), pp. 1-19; David Ray Griffin, *God, Religion in the Postmodern World: Essays in Postmodern Theology* (Albany, N.Y.: State University of New York Press, 1989); David Ray Griffin, ed., *The Reenchantment of Science: Postmodern Proposals* (Albany, N.Y.: State University of New York Press, 1988); Roger Lundin, *The Culture of Interpretation: Christian Faith and the Postmodern World* (Grand Rapids: Eerdmans, 1993); Ernest Gellner, *Postmodernism, Reason and Religion* (London: Routledge, 1992); Diogenes Allen, *Christian Belief in a Postmodern World* (Louisville: Westminster, 1989); Harold K. Schilling, *The New Consciousness in Science and Religion* (Philadelphia: United Church Press, 1973); Stephen Toulmin, "The Historicization of Natural Science: Its Implications for Theology," in *Paradigm Change in Theology:*

A Symposium for the Future, ed. Hans Küng and David Tracy, trans. Margaret Köhl (New York: Crossroad, 1991), pp. 233-241; Thomas C. Oden, *Agenda for Theology: After Modernity . . . What?* (Grand Rapids: Zondervan, 1990); *Two Worlds: Notes on the Death of Modernity in America and Russia* (Downers Grove, Ill.: InterVarsity, 1992); Donald Brophy, ed., *Science and Faith in the 21st Century* (New York: Paulist Press, 1967); Timothy R. Phillips and Dennis L. Okholm, eds., *Christian Apologetics in the Postmodern World* (Downers Grove, Ill.: InterVarsity, 1995); J. Richard Middleton and Brian J. Walsh, *Truth Is Stranger Than It Used to Be: Biblical Faith in a Postmodern Age* (Downers Grove, Ill.: InterVarsity, 1995); Gordon Kaufman, *Theology for a Nuclear Age* (Philadelphia: Westminster, 1985); "Forward," in *Theology at the End of Modernity: Essays in Honor of Gordon Kaufman,* ed. Sheila Greeve Davaney (Philadelphia: Trinity International Press, 1991), pp. ix-xii; George Lindbeck, *The Nature of Doctrine: Religion and Theology in a Postliberal Age* (Philadelphia: Westminster, 1984); William Placher, *Unapologetic Theology: A Christian Voice in a Pluralistic Conversation* (Louisville: John Knox, 1989); David Tracy and John B. Cobb, Jr., *Talking About God: Doing Theology in the Context of Modern Pluralism* (New York: Seabury Press, 1983); Lucas Grollenberg, *Bible Study for the 21st Century* (Consortium Books, 1976). On the limits of historical-criticism, see Gerhard Hasel, "The Origin of the Biblical Sabbath and the Historical-Critical Method: A Methodological Test Case," *Journal of the Adventist Theological Society* 4, No. 1 (Spring 1993): 17-46; Larry Herr, "Genesis One in Historical-Critical Perspective," *Spectrum* 13, No. 2 (December 1982): 51-62; Jerry Gladson, "Taming Historical Criticism: Adventist Biblical Scholarship in the Land of the Giants" *Spectrum* 18, No. 4 (April 1988): 19-34; Eta Linnemann, *Historical Criticism of the Bible: Methodology or Ideology?;* "Historical-Critical and Evangelical Theology," *Journal of the Adventist Theological Society* 5, No. 2 (Autumn 1994): 19-36; Peter Stuhlmacher, *How to Do Biblical Theology* (Allison Park, Pa.: Pickwick Publications, 1995); Gerhard Maier, *Biblical Hermeneutics* (Wheaton, Ill.: Crossway Books, 1994).

[27] Donald K. McKim, *What Christians Believe;* David Tracy, *Blessed Rage for Order: The New Pluralism in Theology* (San Francisco: Harper and Row, 1988); *Plurality and Ambiguity* (San Francisco: Harper and Row, 1987); A.K.M. Adam, *What Is Postmodern Biblical Criticism?* (Minneapolis: Fortress, 1995), pp. 18-25; J. Severino Croatto, *Biblical Hermeneutics: Toward a Theory of Reading as the Production of Meaning* (New York: Orbis Books, 1984), p. 3. Croatto refers especially to the work of Ricoeur. See also Loretta Dornisch, "Symbolic Systems and the Interpretation of Scripture: An Introduction to the Work of Paul Ricoeur" *Semeia* 4 (1975): 1-19.

[28] John Dillenberger, *Protestant Theology and Natural Science,* pp. 15, 16; Holmes Rolston III, *Science and Religion* (Philadelphia: Temple University Press, 1987), pp. 306-322. On the tension between the theology of Barth and Tillich, see Paul Tillich, "Kritisches und positives Paradox. Eine Auseinandersetzung mit Karl Barth und Friedrich Gogarten," *Theologische Blätter* 2 (1923): 263ff.; Karl Barth, "Von der Paradoxie des positiven Paradoxes. Antworten und Fragen an Paul Tillich," *Theologische Blätter* 2 (1923): 278ff.; James M. Robinson, ed., *The Beginnings of Dialectic Theology* (Richmond, Va.: John Knox, 1968), vol. 1.

[29] Langdon Gilkey, *Religion and the Scientific Future,* pp. 18, 123; *Message and Existence,* pp. 7-65, 178, 179, 181; *Gilkey on Tillich* (New York: Crossroad, 1990); "A Retrospective Glance at My Work," in *The Whirlwind in Culture: Frontiers in Theology,* ed. Donald W. Musser and Joseph L. Price (Bloomington, Ind.: Meyer-Stone Books, 1988), pp. 14, 25-30; "An Appreciation of Karl Barth," *How Karl Barth Changed My Mind,* ed. Donald K. McKim (Grand Rapids: Eerdmans, 1986), pp. 150-155; *Maker of Heaven and Earth: A Study of the Christian Doctrine of Creation* (New York: Doubleday, 1959); "Empirical Science and Theological Knowing," in *Foundations of Theology: Papers From the International Lonergan Congress, 1970,* ed. Philip McShane (Notre Dame, Ind.: University of Notre Dame Press, 1972), pp. 76-101; "Religion and Science in an Advanced Scientific Culture," in *Knowing Religiously* (Notre Dame, Ind.: University of Notre Dame, 1985); *Nature, Reality and the Sacred: The Nexus of Science and Religion* (Minneapolis: Fortress, 1993).

[30] Thomas Torrance, *Space Time, and Resurrection* (Edinburgh: Handsel Press, 1976), p. 87; *Transformation and Convergence in the Frame of Knowledge: Explorations in the Interrelations of Scientific and Theological Enterprise* (Grand Rapids: Eerdmans, 1984), pp. 245-250; *Karl Barth, Biblical and Evangelical Theologian* (Edinburgh: T. & T. Clark, 1990); "My Interaction With Barth," *How Karl Barth Changed My Mind,* ed. Donald K. McKim (Grand Rapids: Eerdmans, 1986), pp. 52-64;

Christian Theology and Scientific Culture (New York: Oxford University Press, 1981); *Reality and Evangelical Theology* (Philadelphia: Westminster, 1982); *The Christian Frame of Mind: Reason, Order, and Openness in Theology and Natural Science* (Colorado Springs, Colo.: Helmers and Howard, 1989).

[31] On the cosmological approach to biblical interpretation, see some of the references in note 6. On the Christocentric approach to biblical interpretation, see Samuel Terrien, *The Elusive Presence: The Heart of Biblical Theology* (New York: Harper and Row, 1978); Pierre Benoit, Ronald Murphy, and Bastiaan Van Iersel, eds., *Scripture: The Presence of God* (New York: Paulist Press, 1969); Kenneth S. Kantzer, "The Christ-Revelation as Act and Interpretation," in *Jesus of Nazareth: Saviour and Lord,* ed. Carl F. H. Henry (Grand Rapids: Eerdmans, 1966), pp. 241-264; B. Engelbrecht, "Is Christ the Scopus of the Scriptures?" in *Calvinus Reformator: His Contribution to Theology, Church and Society* (Potchefstroom, South Africa: Potchefstroom University for Higher Education, 1982), pp. 192-200. According to the book *Seventh-day Adventists Believe* (p. 13): "All human wisdom must be subject to the authority of Scripture. The Bible truths are the norm by which all other ideas must be tested. Judging the Word of God by finite human standards is like trying to measure the stars with a yardstick. The Bible must not be subjected to human norms." Fernando Canale points out that "both biblical and systematic theologies need to interpret the same issues as philosophy interprets (God, human nature, reality, reason, etc.). Thus, the issues cannot be dismissed. However, theology does not need to follow any humanly conceived interpretation. On the contrary, if biblical thinking is taken seriously, theology should develop an understanding of these issues on the basis of—and in full harmony with—the interpretation they receive in Scripture" (Fernando Canale, "Revelation and Inspiration: Method for a New Approach," pp. 184, 185). Canale's proposal "has broad consequences for the way in which Scripture should be understood as source of theological data. Some of the most salient implications relate to the nature, scope, exegetical methodology, theological interpretation, and subordinate and limited role of extrabiblical sources of theological data" ("Revelation and Inspiration: The Historical-Cognitive Model," p. 33). According to Canale, "Philosophy, science and tradition are not to be conceived as data on which Christian theology should be built or its methodologies and presuppositional structure determined. Extrabiblical sources are to be approached critically. . . . In a secondary sense, however, there may be times and opportunities in which some facts resulting from the activities of philosophy, science, and tradition might become useful for the theological task" (*ibid.,* pp. 35, 36).

[32] In addition, both "the revelation recorded in Holy Writ and [the revelation] seen in the person and life of Jesus Christ is necessary in order to know the personal God of Scripture." "Science and Religion," in *Seventh-day Adventist Encyclopedia* (Washington, D.C.: Review and Herald, 1996), vol. 11, p. 562. (Bracketed words mine.)

[33] *Seventh-day Adventists Believe,* p. 13.

[34] *Ibid.,* p. 6. (Bracketed words mine.) See also Jacques-Marie Pohier, "The Hermeneutic of Sin in the Light of Science, Technology and Ethics," in *Moral Evil Under Challenge,* ed. Johannes B. Metz (New York: Herder and Herder, 1970), pp. 90-103; Donivan Bessinger, *Religion Confronting Science: And There Was Light* (Greenville, S.C.: Orchard Park Press, 1991).

[35] Gerhard Hasel, "Scripture and Theology," *Journal of the Seventh-day Adventist Theological Society* 4 (Autumn, 1993), p. 47; "The Crisis of the Authority of the Bible as the Word of God," *Journal of the Adventist Theological Society* 1, No. 1 (Spring 1990): 16-38.

[36] Fritz Guy, "Contemporary Adventism and the Crisis of Belief," *Spectrum* 4, No. 1 (Winter 1972): 21; J. E. Ballagas, *The Seventh-day Adventist Theology Crisis Confronted* (Mayagüez, P.R.: the author, 1988); A. Leroy Moore, "Theology in Crisis," (Ph.D. diss., New York University, 1979); *Adventism in Conflict: Resolving the Issues That Divide Us* (Hagerstown, Md.: Review and Herald, 1995); Anne Marie Freed, "Adventists in a Pluralist Society: The Relevance of Lesslie Newbigin's Hermeneutical Approach to the Adventist Identity Crisis," (M.A., thesis, Andrews University, 1992); Jack W. Provonsha, *A Remnant in Crisis* (Hagerstown, Md.: Review and Herald, 1993); Robert M. Price, "The Crisis of Biblical Authority: The Setting and Range of the Current Evangelical Crisis" (Ph.D. diss., Drew University, 1981); Andrew Dooman Chang, "Crisis in Biblical Authority: A Critical Examination of Biblical Authority in Contemporary Theology With Special Reference to Functionalism" (Th.D. diss., Dallas Theological Seminary, 1985).

[37] Raoul Dederen, "On Inspiration and Biblical Authority," in *Issues in Revelation and*

Inspiration, ed. Frank Holbrook and Leo Van Dolson (Berrien Springs, Mich.: Adventist Theological Society Publications, 1992), p. 91; "Revelation, Inspiration and Hermeneutics," in *A Symposium on Biblical Hermeneutics,* ed. Gordon M. Hyde (Washington, D.C.: General Conference of Seventh-day Adventists, 1974), pp. 1-15; "Toward a Seventh-day Adventist Theology of Revelation-Inspiration," in *North American Bible Conference 1974,* ed. Biblical Research Committee (Washington, D.C.: General Conference of Seventh-day Adventists, 1974); Richard M. Davidson, "The Authority of Scripture: A Personal Pilgrimage," *Journal of the Adventist Theological Society* 1, No. 1 (Spring 1990): 39-56; Robert K. Johnston, *Evangelicals at an Impasse* (Atlanta: John Knox, 1979), p. 2; Anthony C. Thiselton, "Authority and Hermeneutics: Some Proposals for a More Creative Agenda," in *A Pathway Into the Holy Scripture,* ed. P. E. Satterthwaite and D. F. Wright (Grand Rapids: Eerdmans, 1994), pp. 107-142; Yves Simon, *A General Theory of Authority* (Notre Dame, Ind.: University of Notre Dame Press, 1962); Robert Gnuse, *The Authority of the Bible: Theories of Inspiration, Revelation and the Canon of Scripture* (New York: Paulist Press, 1985); James D. G. Dunn, "The Authority of Scripture According to Scripture," *Churchman* 96 (1982): 104-122, 201-225; James M. Boice, ed., *The Foundation of Biblical Authority* (Grand Rapids: Zondervan, 1978); Robert Hyman Ayers, "A Study of the Problem of Biblical Authority in Selected Contemporary American Theologians" (Ph.D. diss., Vanderbilt University, 1958).

[38] Edward Lugenbeal, "The Conservative Restoration at Geoscience," *Spectrum* 15, No. 2 (1984): 23.

[39] Martin Hanna, "Contemporary Tensions Within Adventism Concerning the Relations of Science to the Doctrine of Creation" (unpublished research paper, Andrews University, 1992); Molleurus Couperus, "Tensons Between Religion and Science," *Spectrum* 10, No. 4 (1978): 74; Richard Rice, "Dominant Themes in Adventist Theology," *Spectrum* 10, No. 4 (1989): 59.

[40] John T. Baldwin, "Historicization and Christian Theological Method," *Journal of the Adventist Theological Society* 4, No. 2 (Autumn 1933): 168, 169. (Bracketed word mine.) See also Baldwin's "Inspiration, the Natural Sciences and a Window of Opportunity," *Journal of the Adventist Theological Society* 5, No. 1 (Spring 1994): 106-130. On the history of SDA theology, see P. Gerard Damsteegt, *Foundations of the Seventh-day Adventist Message and Mission* (Grand Rapids: Eerdmans, 1977); George R. Knight, *Anticipating the Advent: A Brief History of Seventh-day Adventists* (Boise, Idaho: Pacific Press, 1993); Edwin S. Gaustad, ed., *The Rise of Adventism: Religion and Society in Mid-Nineteenth-Century America* (New York: Harper and Row, 1974); John N. Loughborough, *The Great Second Advent Movement: Its Rise and Progress* (Nashville: Southern Pub., 1905); M. Ellsworth Olsen, *A History of the Origins and Progress of Seventh-day Adventists* (Washington, D.C.: Review and Herald, 1925); Arthur W. Spalding, *Origin and History of Seventh-day Adventists* (Washington, D.C.: Review and Herald, 1961-1962); Malcolm Bull and Keith Lockhart, *Seeking a Sanctuary: Seventh-day Adventism and the American Dream* (San Francisco: Harper and Row, 1989); LeRoy Edwin Froom, *Movement of Destiny* (Washington, D.C.: Review and Herald, 1971); Gary Land, *Adventism in America* (Grand Rapids: Eerdmans, 1986); C. Mervyn Maxwell, *Tell It to the World* (Mountain View, Calif.: Pacific Press, 1976).

[41] Fernando Canale, "Revelation and Inspiration: Method for a New Approach," p. 182. (Bracketed word mine.) Our approach is not an attempt to be compatible with every other model called postmodern. It is postmodern, in part, because we resist the modern "hyperactive pursuit of precise definitions" and the modern overemphasis on distinctions between disciplines such as science and theology. See A.K.M. Adam, *What Is Postmodern Biblical Criticism?* pp. xii, 1; J. Piaget, *Main Trends in Interdisciplinary Thought* (New York: Harper and Row, 1970); Oliver L. Reiser, *The Integration of Human Knowledge* (Boston: Porter Sargent, 1958).

[42] Gerhard Hasel, "Scripture and Theology," *Journal of the Adventist Theological Society* 4, No. 2 (Autumn 1992): 77, 78; *Biblical Interpretation Today* (Washington, D.C.: Biblical Research Institute, 1985); *Understanding the Living Word of God* (Mountain View, Calif.: Pacific Press, 1980).

[43] John Baldwin, "Historicization and Christian Theological Method," p. 170, n. 34; Norman R. Gulley, "The Influence of Philosophical and Scientific World Views on the Development of Theology," p. 137.

[44] *Seventh-day Adventists Believe* (Washington, D.C.: General Conference of Seventh-day Adventists, 1988), pp. 206-214; Paul A. Gordon, "Ellen G. White's Role in Ministering to God's

Remnant," *Journal of the Adventist Theological Society* 2, No. 2 (Autumn 1991): 210-218; Phyllis C. Bailey, *Fascinating Facts About the Spirit of Prophecy* (Hagerstown, Md.: Review and Herald, 1983); James H. Burry, "An Investigation to Determine Ellen White's Concepts of Revelation, Inspiration, 'the Spirit of Prophecy,' and Her Claims About the Origin, Production and Authority of Her Writings" (M.A. thesis, Andrews University, 1991); W. H. Littlejohn, "Seventh-day Adventists and the Testimony of Jesus Christ," *Review and Herald Extra,* Aug. 14, 1883, pp. 13-16; Dudley M. Canright, *Adventism Refuted in a Nutshell* (New York: Fleming H. Revell, 1889); William Henry Branson, *In Defense of the Faith: A Reply to Canright* (Washington, D.C.: Review and Herald, 1933); Lewis Harrison Christian, *The Fruitage of Spiritual Gifts* (Washington, D.C.: Review and Herald, 1947); D. A. Delafield, *Ellen White and the Seventh-day Adventist Church* (Mountain View, Calif.: Pacific Press, 1963); Robert L. Shull, "Ellen G. White in Adventist Theology," *Spectrum* 6, Nos. 3, 4 (1974): 78-85; Stephen T. Hand, "The Conditionality of Ellen White's Writings," *Spectrum* 6, Nos. 3, 4 (1974): 88-90; W. Paul Bradley, "Ellen G. White and Her Writings," *Spectrum* 3, No. 2 (Spring 1971): 43-65; Joseph J. Battistone, "Ellen White's Authority as Bible Commentator," *Spectrum* 8, No. 2 (January 1977): 37-40; Roy E. Graham, "Ellen G. White: An Examination of her Position and Role in the Seventh-day Adventist Church" (Ph.D. thesis, University of Birmingham, 1977).

[45] According to J. I. Packer: "The incarnation . . . was the climax of a long revelatory process in history and is the critical norm for future speech and thought about God for as long as this world will last. The Lord Jesus Christ, we may say, is divine revelation in paradigmatic form. "God uses language to communicate with us. God incarnate was a rabbi, a teacher, a talker, and a language user, and when he spoke, God was speaking. A priori doubts, rife since Kant, as to whether God could or would use language to tell us things, and whether therefore the Holy Scripture could possibly be his verbal word to the world, are thus resolved. God uses language" (see Packer, "Is Systematic Theology a Mirage?" in *Doing Theology in Today's World,* ed. John D. Woodbridge and Thomas Edward McComiskey [Grand Rapids: Zondervan, 1991], pp. 19-21).

[46] Brian S. Rosner, "'Written for Us': Paul's View of Scripture," in *A Pathway Into the Holy Scripture,* ed. P. E. Satterthwaite and D. F. Wright (Grand Rapids: Eerdmans, 1994), pp. 81-106; Langdon Gilkey, "The Spirit and the Discovery of the Truth Through Dialogue," in *Experience of the Spirit* (New York: Seabury Press, 1976), pp. 58-68.

[47] Judah Landa, *Torah and Science* (Hoboken, N.J.: KTAV Pub. House, 1991); Gerhard F. Hasel, "The Polemic Nature of the Genesis Cosmology," *Evangelical Quarterly* 46 (1974): 81-102.

[48] John Collins, "New Testament Cosmology," *Cosmology and Theology,* ed. David Tracy and Nicholas Lash (New York: Seabury Press, 1983), pp. 3-7.

[49] Bruce Norman, "Pauline Cosmology: Relic or Relevant?" *Journal of the Adventist Theological Society* 3, No. 2 (Autumn 1992): 127, 128; Frank M. Hasel, "Theology and the Role of Reason," in *Journal of the Adventist Theological Society* 4, No. 2 (1993): 172-189; Abraham J. Malherbe, *Paul and the Popular Philosophers* (Minneapolis: Fortress, 1989); Richard H. Akeroyd, *Reason and Revelation From Paul to Pascal* (Macon, Ga.: Mercer University Press, 1991), p. 8; John D. Moores, *Wrestling With Rationality in Paul: Romans 1-8 in a New Perspective* (Cambridge: Cambridge University Press, 1995).

[50] Dieter Werner Kemmler, *Faith and Human Reason: A Study of Paul's Method of Preaching as Illustrated by 1-2 Thessalonians and Acts 17:2-4* (Leiden: E. J. Brill, 1975).

[51] Philosophers identify three channels of knowledge: intuitive experience apprehends knowledge without demonstration; pragmatic experience confirms the usefulness of knowledge; reason extends knowledge beyond experience.

[52] "You grow faint in your mind *(psuche)*" (see Heb. 12:3). "Without your mind *(gnome)* I would do nothing" (see Philemon 14). "The minds *(noema)* of unbelievers are blinded" (see 2 Cor. 4:4). There is a contrast between the carnally minded and spiritually minded *(phronema)* (Rom. 8:6). God writes laws in the mind *(dianoia)* (Heb. 8:10; 10:16).

[53] Yandall Woodfin, *With All Your Mind: A Christian Philosophy* (Nashville: Abingdon, 1980), pp. 22-37; Frank Chamberlin Porter, *The Mind of Christ in Paul: Light From Paul on Present Problems of Christian Thinking* (New York: Charles Scribner's Sons, 1930); Harry Blamires, *The Christian Mind* (Ann Arbor, Mich.: Servant Books, 1978); Gene Edward Veith, *Loving God With All Your*

Mind (Westchester, Ill.: Crossway Books, 1987); Arthur F. Holmes, *Contours of a World View* (Grand Rapids: Eerdmans, 1983); *The Making of a Christian Mind: A Christian World View and the Academic Enterprise* (Downers Grove, Ill.: InterVarsity, 1985); W. Andrew Hoffecker, ed., *Building a Christian World View: God, Man and Knowledge* (Phillipsburg, N.J.: Presbyterian and Reformed Pub. Co., 1986), vol. 1; Ninian Smart, *World Views: Crosscultural Explorations of Human Beliefs* (New York: Charles Scribner's Sons, 1983).

[54] James A. Davis, *Wisdom and Spirit: An Investigation of 1 Corinthians 1:18-3:20 Against the Background of Jewish Sapiential Traditions in the Greco-Roman Period* (Lanham, Md.: University Press of America, 1984).

[55] Paul W. Gooch, *Partial Knowledge: Philosophical Studies in Paul* (Notre Dame, Ind.: University of Notre Dame Press, 1987), pp. 142-161.

[56] J. Collins, "New Testament Cosmology," pp. 3-7.

[57] E. W. Shideler, *Believing and Knowing*, pp. 27, 47.

[58] Rolf P. Knierim, "Science in the Bible," *Word and World* 13, No. 3 (Summer 1993): 242; Eugene H. Maly, "The Interplay of World and Worship in the Scriptures," *Liturgy in Transition*, ed. Herman Schmidt (New York: Herder and Herder, 1971).

[59] R. P. Knierim, "Science in the Bible," p. 243. He identifies Scripture references to the following sciences: rhetoric, library science, legal science, historiography, biology (anatomy, botany, zoology), psychology, medicine, management, logistics, administration, government, architecture, construction, metallurgy, philosophy, cosmology (pp. 242-255).

[60] Scott Hafemann, "The Righteousness of God," introduction to Stuhlmacher's *How to Do Biblical Theology* (Allison Park, Pa.: Pickwick Pub., 1995), pp. xv-xli.

[61] Abraham Kuyper, *Principles of Sacred Theology* (Grand Rapids: Eerdmans, 1954), pp. 150-175. Some would even argue that modern science would be impossible without the influence of the Bible. See Henry M. Morris, *The Biblical Basis for Modern Science* (Grand Rapids: Baker, 1984); Henning Graf Reventlow, *The Authority of the Bible and the Rise of the Modern World*, trans. John Bowden (Philadelphia: Fortress, 1984); R. Hooykaas, *Religion and the Rise of Modern Science* (Grand Rapids: Eerdmans, 1972); Eugene M. Klaaren, *The Religious Origins of Modern Science* (Grand Rapids: Eerdmans, 1977); M. B. Foster, "The Christian Doctrine of Creation and the Rise of Modern Science," *Mind* 43 (1934): 446-468; Edwin Burtt, *The Metaphysical Foundations of Modern Science* (Garden City, N.Y.: Doubleday, 1954); L. Gilkey, *Naming the Whirlwind*, p. 35; *Society and the Sacred* (New York: Crossroad, 1981), p. 103; J. P. Moreland, *Christianity and the Nature of Science* (Grand Rapids: Baker, 1989); Christopher B. Kaiser, *Creation and the History of Science* (Grand Rapids: Eerdmans, 1991).

[62] Bruce Norman, "Pauline Cosmology: Relic or Relevant?" pp. 131, 132; Thomas Luther Marberry, "The Place of the Natural World in the Theology of the Apostle Paul" (Ph.D. diss., Baylor University, 1982); Lewis O. Anderson, "A Study of the Pauline Theology of Creation and Its Relation to the Old Testament Creation Accounts" (M.A. thesis, Andrews University, 1970); Peter Stuhlmacher, *Paul's Letter to the Romans* (Louisville: John Knox, 1994); Werner G. Kümmel, *The Theology of the New Testament According to Its Major Witnesses: Jesus—Paul—John* (Nashville: Abingdon, 1973); F. F. Bruce, *Paul: Apostle of the Heart Set Free* (Grand Rapids: Eerdmans, 1977); Willem Van Gemeren, *The Progress of Redemption: The Story of Salvation From Creation to the New Jerusalem* (Grand Rapids: Zondervan, 1988).

[63] Everett N. Dick, *Founders of the Message* (Washington, D.C.: Review and Herald, 1938). On the metaphor of light, see Ellen G. White, "An Open Letter," *Review and Herald*, Jan. 20, 1903, in *Colporteur Ministry* (Mountain View, Calif.: Pacific Press, 1953), p. 125; Roger Coon, *A Gift of Light* (Hagerstown, Md.: Review and Herald, 1983); William Clyde Sands, "Nature as a Biblical Hermeneutic Device: The Role and Use of Light in the Experience and Writings of Ellen G. White" (M.A. thesis, Andrews University, 1989). On revelation, inspiration, and hermeneutics in Ellen White's writings, see Martin Hanna, "Reasonable Faith and the Knowledge of Revealed Truth: An Analysis of Ellen G. White's Theology of Revelation" (unpublished research paper, Andrews University, 1992); P. Gerard Damsteegt, "Ellen White on Theology, Its Methods, and the Use of Scripture," *Journal of the Adventist Theological Society* 4, No. 2 (Autumn 1993): 115-136; "The Inspiration of Scripture in the Writings of Ellen G. White," *Journal of the Adventist Theological*

Society 5, No. 1 (Spring 1994): 155-179; J. E. Ballagas, "Ellen G. White's Concept of the Hermeneutic Principle—The Bible Its Own Interpreter and Some of the Implications Related to the Use of Secondary Sources in Biblical Investigation" (M.A. project report, 1980); Maurice Barnett, *Ellen G. White and Inspiration* (Louisville: Gospel Anchor, 1983); Frederick E. J. Harder, "Revelation a Source of Knowledge as Conceived by Ellen G. White" (Ph.D. diss., New York University, 1991); Gil G. Fernandez, "Ellen G. White's Philosophy of History" (M.A. thesis, Andrews University, 1968); T. Housel Jemison, *A Prophet Among You* (Mountain View, Calif.: Pacific Press, 1955).

[64] Ellen G. White manuscript 86, 1898, in *E. G. White Manuscript Releases* (Silver Spring, Md.: Ellen G. White Estate, 1990), vol. 3, pp. 348, 349.

[65] *Ibid.*, p. 348. On nature as a source of light, see E. G. White, *The Desire of Ages* (Mountain View, Calif.: Pacific Press, 1898), p. 638; *Testimonies for the Church* (Mountain View, Calif.: Pacific Press, 1855-1909), vol. 2, p. 589; vol. 4, pp. 579, 580.

[66] ———, *The Desire of Ages*, pp. 207, 638; *The Ministry of Healing* (Mountain View, Calif.: Pacific Press, 1905), pp. 424, 425; *Testimonies*, vol. 2, pp. 589; vol. 4, pp. 579, 580; *Christ's Object Lessons* (Mountain View, Calif.: Pacific Press, 1900), pp. 81, 82.

[67] ———, *The Ministry of Healing*, p. 413; in *Review and Herald*, July 11, 1882; Feb. 23, 1892; *Youth's Instructor*, May 6, 1897; in *Principles of True Science* (Takoma Park: Washington College Press, 1929), pp. 381, 382; *Steps to Christ* (Washington, D.C.: Review and Herald, 1908, 1956), pp. 86, 87; *The Desire of Ages*, p. 308.

[68] ———, *Counsels to Parents and Teachers* (Mountain View, Calif.: Pacific Press, 1913), p. 186.

[69] ———, *Review and Herald*, Nov. 12, 1901.

[70] ———, *Education* (Mountain View, Calif.: Pacific Press, 1952), p. 209.

[71] ———, in *Review and Herald*, June 21, 1877.

[72] ———, *Selected Messages* (Washington, D.C.: Review and Herald, 1958), book 1, pp. 15-21; *Spiritual Gifts* (Battle Creek, Mich.: Review and Herald, 1858), vol. 1, p. 117; in *Bible Echo*, Aug. 26, 1895; *The Seventh-day Adventist Bible Commentary*, Ellen G. White Comments, ed. Francis D. Nichol (Washington, D.C.: Review and Herald, 1952-1957), vol. 6, p. 1065.

[73] ———, *Selected Messages*, book 1, p. 22.

[74] "The Bible is written by inspired men, but it is not God's mode of thought and expression. It is that of humanity. God, as a writer, is not represented. Men will often say such an expression is not like God. But God has not put Himself in words, in logic, in rhetoric, on trial in the Bible. The writers of the Bible were God's penmen, not His pen. Look at the different writers. It is not the words of the Bible that are inspired, but the men that were inspired. Inspiration acts not on the man's words or his expressions but on the man himself, who, under the influence of the Holy Ghost, is imbued with thoughts. But the words receive the impress of the individual mind. The divine mind is diffused. The divine mind and will is combined with the human mind and will; thus the utterances of the man are the word of God" (White, *Selected Messages*, book 1, p. 21 (manuscript 24, 1886).

[75] E. G. White, *Patriarchs and Prophets* (Mountain View, Calif.: Pacific Press, 1890, 1958), p. 504.

[76] ———, in *Signs of the Times*, Apr. 17, 1879.

[77] ———, *The Great Controversy* (Mountain View, Calif.: Pacific Press, 1911), pp. v-vii; *Selected Messages*, book 1, p. 15; *Spiritual Gifts*, vol. 1, p. 117; *Lift Him Up* (Hagerstown, Md.: Review and Herald, 1988), p. 118; *Patriarchs and Prophets*, p. 504 (see also Martin Hanna, "Ellen White's Concept of the Bible History in *Patriarchs and Prophets*" [unpublished research paper, Andrews University, 1991]); *Ellen G. White Manuscript Releases*, vol. 11, p. 155; *Counsels to Parents and Teachers*, p. 447.

[78] ———, in *Review and Herald*, Aug. 30, 1906.

[79] E. G. White letter 280, 1904, in *The Seventh-day Adventist Bible Commentary*, Ellen G. White Comments, vol. 5, p. 1113; White, in *Review and Herald*, Feb. 18, 1890.

[80] ———, in *Review and Herald*, Jan. 11, 1881; see also Dec. 31, 1872; Oct. 27, Dec. 1, 1885; June 11, 1889; Feb. 4, 18, June 10, 1890; Dec. 20, 1892; Apr. 3, 1894; Feb. 5, Apr. 23, July 9, 1895; Sept. 22, 1896; Jan. 25, 1898; July 18, Oct. 17, Nov. 21, 1899; Jan.13, Sept. 3, 1903; Aug. 30, 1906; Apr. 6, 1911; Feb. 15, 1912; July 16, 1914; *The Desire of Ages*, pp. 326, 507; E. G. White

manuscript 76, 1903, quoted in *The Seventh-day Adventist Bible Commentary*, Ellen G. White Comments, vol. 6, p. 1074.

[81] ———, *The Desire of Ages*, pp. 48, 49.

[82] *Ibid.* (My emphasis.)

[83] *Ibid.*, p. 129.

[84] ———, *Education*, p. 130.

[85] ———, in *Signs of the Times*, Mar. 20, 1884. (My emphasis.)

[86] ———, in *Signs of the Times*, Mar. 13, 1884. (My emphasis.)

[87] ———, *Education*, p. 128. (My emphasis.)

[88] ———, *The Desire of Ages*, p. 220.

[89] ———, *That I May Know Him* (Washington, D.C.: Review and Herald, 1964), p. 97. (Italics supplied.) "He who came to save the world could not be endured by those He came to rescue, and they killed the Lord of life and glory, thinking to extinguish His divine light from the world. But it was impossible for the grave to hold Him. He burst the fetters of the tomb, and proclaimed in triumph over the rent sepulcher, 'I am the resurrection and the life.' Thus Christ became a present Saviour, a divine presence, *in every place*. All who believe may obtain clear views of Christ's true glory. When they behold Him, all these minor things sink into insignificance, just as the lesser lights vanish when the sun appears. He who catches a glimpse of the matchless love of Christ, counts all other things as loss, and looks upon Him as the chiefest among ten thousand, and as the one altogether lovely" (White, in *Review and Herald*, Feb. 25, 1896; my emphasis). For more on lesser and greater lights, see E. G. White, *Spirit of Prophecy* [Battle Creek, Mich.: Review and Herald, 1884], vol. 2, p. 83; in *Review and Herald*, Apr. 8, 1873).

[90] ———, in *The Seventh-day Adventist Bible Commentary*, Ellen G. White Comments, vol. 7, p. 907. (My emphasis.) Cf. p. 921; *Education*, p. 132.

[91] ———, *Education*, p. 134.

[92] ———, in *Signs of the Times*, Mar. 20, 1884.

[93] ———, *Testimonies*, vol. 4, p. 427.

[94] ———, *This Day With God* (Washington, D.C.: Review and Herald, 1947), p. 246. The quotation continues: "Those who despise the blessings and glory of the Jewish age are not prepared to be benefited by the preaching of the gospel. The brightness of the Father's glory, and the excellence and perfection of His sacred law, are only understood through the atonement made upon Calvary by His dear Son; but even the atonement loses its significance when the law of God is rejected."

[95] ———, *Christ's Object Lessons*, p. 107.

[96] ———, *Counsels to Parents and Teachers*, p. 510.

[97] ———, *Christ's Object Lessons*, p. 107.

[98] ———, *Fundamentals of Christian Education* (Nashville: Southern Pub. Assn., 1923), p. 285.

[99] ———, *Education*, p. 134.

[100] ———, *Patriarchs and Prophets*, p. 113.

[101] ———, in *Signs of the Times*, Mar. 13, 1884.

[102] ———, *The Ministry of Healing*, p. 462; *Christ's Object Lessons*, p. 107.

[103] ———, *Testimonies*, vol. 4, p. 274.

[104] ———, *Patriarchs and Prophets*, p. 599.

[105] ———, *Education*, p. 120.

[106] ———, *The Ministry of Healing*, p. 462.

[107] ———, *Medical Ministry* (Mountain View, Calif.: Pacific Press, 1932), p. 97.

[108] ———, in *Signs of the Times*, Mar. 27, 1884.

[109] ———, *Spiritual Gifts* (Battle Creek, Mich.: Seventh-day Adventist Pub. Assn., 1864), vol. 3, pp. 90-96; in *Signs of the Times*, Mar. 20, 1879; *Selected Messages*, book 2, p. 351; in *Signs of the Times*, Mar. 13, 1884; in *The Seventh-day Adventist Bible Commentary*, Ellen G. White Comments, vol. 2, p. 1011.

[110] ———, in *Signs of the Times*, Mar. 27, 1884.

[111] *Ibid.*

[112] *E. G. White Manuscript Releases*, vol. 3, p. 353.

[113] ———, in *Review and Herald*, Mar. 8, 1887.

[114] ————, *Mind, Character, and Personality* (Nashville: Southern Pub., 1977), vol. 1, p. 7; vol. 2, p. 743; in *Review and Herald*, Jan. 19, 1886; E. G. White manuscript 4, 1882; in *Signs of the Times*, May 12, 1909; *The Great Controversy*, pp. 522, 600, 601; *The Ministry of Healing*, p. 427.

[115] ————, in *Review and Herald*, Jan. 24, 1899; *Testimonies*, vol. 5, pp. 703, 704; *Mind, Character, and Personality*, vol. 1, p. 91.

[116] E. G. White letter 4, 1889, in *Mind, Character, and Personality*, vol. 2, pp. 535, 536. See also E. G. White, *Maranatha* (Washington, D.C.: Review and Herald, 1976), p. 252; *E. G. White Manuscript Releases*, vol. 18, p. 127; in *Review and Herald*, Mar. 8, 1887; *Spirit of Prophecy*, vol. 4, p. 349; in *Signs of the Times*, Mar. 20, 1879. White assesses the quality of faith by the ability to give a reason for faith. "Many . . . will be found wanting. They have neglected the weightier matters. Their conversion is superficial, not deep, earnest, and thorough. They do not know why they believe the truth. . . . They can give no intelligent reason why they believe" (*Christian Service* [Washington, D.C.: Review and Herald, 1947], p. 45).

[117] Frederick J. Harder, "Revelation a Source of Knowledge as Conceived by Ellen G. White," pp. 486, 487. A similar perspective to that of Ellen G. White appears in Arthur F. Holmes, *All Truth Is God's Truth* (Leicester, Eng.: InterVarsity, 1977).

[118] G. G. Fernandez, *Ellen G. White's Philosophy of History* (M.A. thesis, Philippine Union College, 1968), p. 134.

[119] Raymond F. Cottrell, "Ellen White's Evaluation and Use of the Bible," in *A Symposium on Biblical Hermeneutics*, ed. Gordon M. Hyde (Washington, D.C.: General Conference of Seventh-day Adventists, 1974), pp. 149-161.

[120] Martin Hanna, "Low Views of Scripture as Sign of the Times in the Writings of Ellen White" (unpublished research paper, Andrews University, 1992).

[121] Seventh-day Adventists accept the Bible as their only creed and hold certain fundamental beliefs to be the teaching of the Holy Scriptures. These beliefs . . . constitute the church's understanding and expression of the teaching of Scripture. Revision of these statements may be expected at a General Conference session when the church is led by the Holy Spirit to a fuller understanding of Bible truth or finds better language in which to express the teachings of God's Holy Word" (*Seventh-day Adventist Yearbook* [1998], p. 5). These words appear in the introduction to the fundamental beliefs accepted by the vote of the 1980 General Conference session. See also Winfried Corduan, *Handmaid to Theology* (Grand Rapids: Baker, 1981), pp. 9-22.

[122] Clyde L. Webster, *The Earth: Origins and Early History* (Silver Spring, Md.: General Conference of Seventh-day Adventists, 1989), p. 16.

[123] V. Philips Long, *The Art of Biblical History* (Grand Rapids: Zondervan, 1994), pp. 186-195.

[124] C. Raschke, *Theological Thinking*, p. 22; John B. Cobb., Jr., *A Christian Natural Theology: Based on the Thought of Alfred North Whitehead* (Philadelphia: Westminster, 1965; Philip Hefner, "Can a Theology of Nature Be Coherent With Scientific Cosmology?" in *Evolution and Creation: A European Perspective*, ed. Svend Andersen and Arthur Peacocke (Aarhus: Aarhus University Press, 1987), pp. 141-151.

[125] F. M. Hasel, "Theology and the Role of Reason," pp. 172-198.

[126] E. G. White *Fundamentals of Christian Education*, p. 186.

[127] E. G. White letter 197, 1904, in *Ellen G. White Manuscript Releases*, vol. 21, p. 426.

[128] Philip Hefner, "Theology in the Context of Science, Liberation, and Christian Tradition," in *Worldviews and Warrants: Plurality and Authority in Theology* (Lanham, Md.: University Press, 1987), pp. 33-49.

[129] Malachi Martin, *The Keys of His Blood: The Struggle for World Dominion Between Pope John Paul II, Mikhail Gorbachev, and the Capitalist West* (New York: Simon and Schuster, 1990), pp. 280-292.

[130] George W. Reid, "The Theologian as Conscience for the Church," in *Journal of the Adventist Theological Society* 4, No. 2 (Autumn 1993): 12, 13, 18, 19.

INDEX OF SUBJECTS AND AUTHORS

A

accommodationist position, 32
Adam, 86, 159,162
    and Eve, 46
Adam's transgression, 73
Adriatic coast, 98
Adventism, postmodern, 178
Adventist
    faith, 166
    Theological Society, 8
    theology, 160, 180, 186, 193
    historic, 180
aeon, 54, 62
Ager, Darek, 116
agnosticism, 124
allegorical sense, 63
allegorical method, 42
    Alexandrian, 42
    of interpretation, 41
allegory, 42, 50
allusion, 19
    cryptic, 24
altruism, 157
anagogical sense, 63
analogy, 49, 66
    principle of, 51
anatomy, 124
Andrews University, 14
animal kingdom, 141
Aquinas, Thomas, 126, 175
Archer, Gleason L., 88
archetype, 61
Aristotle, 127
ark, 82, 87
ascension, bodily, 177
Athens, 108
atonement, 108, 109, 115, 119, 125
    substitutionary, 11, 114
Augustine of Hippo, 41, 126, 151, 175
Austin, William, 173
autonomy, 164
Ayer, A. J., 133

B

Babel, Tower of, 81, 86
Bailey, Lloyd R., 47
Baldwin, John Templeton, 7, 108, 180
Barr, James, 54
Barth, Karl, 12, 16, 50, 125, 177, 178

Bavinck, Herman, 173
beginning, new, 86, 89
beyôm, 57
biblical, 44
    authority, 44, 160, 179
    concept of creation, 160
    cosmology, 85
    creationism, 129
    fundamentalism, 149
    interpretation, 42, 160
    scholars, 7
    terminology, 80
    worldview, 26, 150
bibliolatry, 191
biological kingdom, 7, 111
biology
    molecular, 127, 132, 141, 148, 149
Bird, W. R., 128, 141
Blenkinsopp, Joseph, 85
Blyth, Edward, 144
botanical world, 72
bouleversement, 84, 91
boundary
    Cretaceous, 110
    Permian, 110
    Tertiary, 110
    Triassic, 110
Bowler, Peter J., 127, 128
Bräumer, Hansjörg, 45
breccia's deposition, 117
Briscoe, D. Stuart, 45
Brueggermann, Walter, 50
Buckland, William, 120
Bultmann, Rudolph, 65, 159, 160

C

Calvary, 10, 108, 113, 115, 119, 121
Cambrian, 110, 117
    strata, 147
Canale, Fernando Luis, 180
cannibalism, 125
Carnap, Rudolf, 133
Cassuto, Umberto, 9, 72, 73, 84
catastrophe, 116, 117
    aquatic, 100, 120, 121
    cosmic, 84
    global, 5
catastrophism, 151
    diluvial, 80

Catechism, 63, 126
category translation, 12, 30
Catholicism, Roman, 42
Cenozoic, 103, 118
Chadwick, Arthur, 103, 118
chaos, 84, 85
Christ-centeredness, 189
Christian theism, 151
Christianity, 162
Christians, Bible-believing, 71
Christendom, 42
church councils, 161
Civitas Dei, 151
cladistics, 148
Clayton, Philip, 7, 28
Clines, David, 84, 85, 89
Clouser, Roy, 173
Coconino Sandstone, 95, 100, 101, 103
Collingwood, R. G., 52
Colorado River, 93-95, 104, 107
colossal scale, 26
column, geological, 25, 89, 100-102, 108-
    114, 118-121, 147, 148, 151
commandment, fourth, 19, 23
Communism, 125
concordism, 48
concordist, Christian, 43
    broad, 43-49, 54
    neoevangelical broad, 50
conservative theology, 176
contextual criteria, 46
conventional geologists, 109
cosmic
    catastrophe, 84
    destiny, 8
    reversal of creation, 89
cosmogonic myths, 53
cosmogony, 20
cosmology, 66
cosmos, 85
councils, church, 161
covenant, 86
    remnant, 90
creation, 8, 85, 96, 113
    continuing, 126
    cosmic reversal of, 89
    divine, 43, 132
    eschatological, 185
    progressive, 11, 126

scientists, 109
sin-free, 76
six-day, 96, 106, 160, 166
Sumerian account of, 74
undoing of, 84
week, 8
creation science, 40, 62
creationism, 40, 126, 128
creationists, progressive, 109
Creator-God, 11
Cretaceous boundary, 110
Crick, Francis, 127, 132, 134
criteria
    linguistic, 46
    phraseological, 46
criticism
    form, 53
    reader-response, 66
Cush, 88

D

Daniel, 181
Darwin, Charles, 41, 109, 124-127, 130-
    132, 138, 139, 142-145, 148, 153
Darwinism, 127, 129
Davidson, Richard, 9, 79, 115
Davis, Percival, 128
Dawkins, Richard, 132, 135, 137-141
day-age theory, 43, 47, 62, 64
day-night, 60
day, divine, 45
days
    of creation as revelation days, 48
    of restoration, 43
    of revelation, 43, 47, 48
    seven consecutive 24-hour, 40
    six historical, 29
    six literal 24-hour, 48, 89, 159
de Vries, Hugo, 146
de Cameron, Nigel M., 108, 109
Decalogue, the, 20, 165
deconstructionalism, 66
Deity, 70
Democritus, 127
demythologization, 65
Denton, Michael, 128, 134-141, 149
Descartes, René, 175
deshe, 72
dichotomy, 183

Dillard, R. B., 71
Dillenberger, John, 177
divine
    creation, 43, 132
    day, 45
    Exemplar, 61
    investigative judgment, 85
    judgment, 27, 86
    mercy, 86
    promulgations, 62
    revelation, 24, 44
    Substitute, 108
    wisdom, 27
divine-human
    communication, 178
    communion, 187
    encounter, 176
    revelations, 186
    union, 187
DNA, 127, 132, 135, 136, 141, 152
Dodd, C. H., 20
Dooyeweerd, Herman, 151
Dose, Klaus, 133
Doukhan, Jacques, 89
Dutton, Clarence E., 100, 105

E

E (for "Elohist"), 70
economic imperialism, 125
economy of words, 24
Eden, Garden of, 75, 88, 166
Eiseley, Loren, 127
el-Dreijat (Jordan), 14
Eldredge, Niles, 127, 128, 146
electrophysiological studies, 139
Elohim, 70
embryologists, 127
empiricism, 130
Enlightenment humanism, 151
Enumah Elish, 126
Epicurus, 127
epistemological holism, 32
epistemology, 31
Erickson, Millard J., 133
Eridu Genesis, 74
eschatological creation, 185
eschatology, 89
eschaton, 27
Euphrates, 88

evangelical
    Christians, 80
    Theological Society, 8
    theology, 12, 125
evening and morning, 46, 54, 55, 60, 63, 69
Everest, Mount, 87
evolution, 40, 96
    abrupt, 146, 147
    explosive, 147
    humanistic concept of, 159
    macro-, 11, 25
    micro-, 7, 11, 128, 143
    naturalistic, 40, 48
    organic, 28
    parallel, 147
    process of, 163-165
    secular concept of, 159
    spiritual, 161
    theistic, 114, 126, 154, 159-166
evolutionary
    era, 24
    gradualism, 146
    model of origins, 54
    theory, 8, 43, 45, 124-131, 136-138, 143-148, 152, 153
existentialist, 176

F

face of the ground, 81
Fairbridge, Rhodes, 116
fall, 85
false worship, 22
Feigel, Herbert, 133
feminist, 177
Fertile Crescent, 85, 86
Feyerabend, Paul K., 130
first
    angel's message, 21-35, 152
    Cause, 130
    principles, 8
fittest, the, 144
    arrival of, 144
    survival of, 153, 163
Fitzmyer, Joseph A., 112, 113
flood
    account, 80
    diminishing, 10
    geology, 8, 11

global, 8, 25, 87, 90, 104, 106, 115, 119, 120,151
local, 87, 90
Noahic, 84
typology, 79, 89
universal, 84
worldwide, 82, 88, 89, 98, 106
forgiveness of sins, 8
form criticism, 53
form-critical genre, 51
40 days, 88
fossil coral reefs, 15
fountains of water, 26
Fretheim, Terence, 61
fruit trees, 72
Frymer-Kensky, Tikva, 84
futurist, 23

G

galactic universe, 7
Garden of Eden, 75, 88, 166
genealogical frame, 79
genetic
 heredity, 155
 random mutation, 129, 152, 155
 random variation, 139
geneticists, 127
genetics, Mendellian, 127
genocide, 125
genre
 form-critical, 51
 literary, 66
geologic,
 column, 25, 89, 100-102, 108-114, 118-121, 147, 148, 151
 time scale, 102
 uniformitarianism, 116
geological theory, 8
 conventional, 116, 117
German Pietism, 173
Gibson, John C. L., 45
Gihon, 88
Gilgamesh Epic, 91
Gilkey, Langdon, 29, 177, 178
God, 11
 image of, 166
 nature of, 163
 power of, 162
 signs of, 7

Word of, 8, 161, 162, 179
God's
 promise, 87
 revelation, 161, 181, 186
 self-revelation, 178, 179
 supreme revelation, 185
Gould, Stephen Jay, 109, 127, 140, 146-149
gradualism, 127, 129
grammatical-syntactical view, 46
Grand Canyon, 93-106, 110, 117-120
Gray, Asa, 138
Greco-Roman philosophy, 183, 184
Greene, John C., 127
Gulf of Mexico, 104
Gulley, Norman R., 11, 16
Gunkel, Hermann, 49, 52, 54
Gustafsson, Bengt, 172

H

Hallam, A., 144
Halstead, L. Beverly, 127, 128, 146
Hamilton, Victor P., 48, 49, 54
Hanna, Martin, 11, 17
Hasel, Gerhard F., 9, 40, 80, 83, 106, 115, 179, 180
Havasupai, 105
Havilah, 88
Hefner, Philip, 193
Hellenistic Judaism, 184
Hennig, Willi, 127, 148
heredity, genetic, 155
hermeneutical principles, 23
Hermit Shale, 100, 101
Hick, John, 111
historical
 future, 68
 narrative-prose, 52, 79
historical-critical
 approaches, 77
 principle, 23
 method, 49, 63
 scholarship, 69
historical-cultural approach, 49
historical-grammatical method, 42
historicist
 perspective, 23
 principles of interpretation, 22
historicization, 39

historiography, 51
history, 44, 160, 161
    inaugural, 53
Hitchcock, Edward, 111, 120
Ho, Mae-Wan, 134
Hodge, Charles, 9, 32
holism, epistemological, 32
Holocaust, 124
homo sapiens, 46
homology, 131
Hooke, S. H., 50
Hopper, Jerrey, 176
horticulture, 78
Hoyle, Frederick, 132
Hualapai, 105
humanity, 11
Hummel, Charles E., 49
Huse, Scott M., 128, 136
Hutton, James, 43, 109
Huxley, Julian, 131, 151
hymn, 50

I

immanence, 176
imminent return, 7
immortality of the soul, 162
immunologists, 127
incarnation, 165, 180
    divine-human, 191
    pre-, 23
inclusio, 59
inclusive model, 12, 178, 191
infanticide, 125
inspiration, 44, 186
    of Scripture, 175, 178
instant speciation, 147
intellectualism, 184
intellectual suicide, 192
intelligent
    cause theory, 138
    design theory, 8
interpretation
    biblical, 42, 160
    figurative, 44
    grammatical, 42
    historicist principles of, 22
    literal, 42
investigation
    linguistic, 41

    semantic, 41
irrationalism, 176, 178
Israel, 14

J

J (for "Yahwist"), 70
Jellema, Harry, 151
Jenni, Ernst, 55
Jerusalem, 108
Jesuit, 126
Jewett, Paul K., 125
Johnson, Phillip E., 128, 140, 142, 147, 149, 150
Jordan, 14
Josephus, 71
Judaism, Hellenistic, 184
judgment, 76, 120
    agent of God's, 76
    divine, 27, 86
    divine investigative, 85
    universal, 85
justification through righteousness, 185

K

Kaibab-Coconino Uplift, 93
Kaiser, Walter, 79
karst surfaces, 98-100
Kant, Immanuel, 175
Kenyon, Dean H., 128
King, Robert, 172
kingdom
    animal, 141
    biological, 7, 111
    plant, 72
Knierim, Rolf P., 185
Kouznetsov, Dimitri, 149
Krebs cycle, 137, 138
Kuhn, Thomas, 150
Küng, Hans, 112
Kuyper, Abraham, 151, 186

L

Lamarkism, 137
Lane, David H., 114
legend, 49
Leith, Brian, 128, 137, 144
Lenior, Timothy, 134
Leupold, H. C., 83
Lexicography, 54

liberalism, Protestant, 176
liberal scholars, 50
liberal-critical commentators, 80
liberation, 177
life-and-death cycle, 111
life-forms, 87, 96, 110, 147
limited theory, 79
Lindbeck, George, 32
Lings, Martin, 124
linguistic
    criteria, 46
    investigation, 41
Linnaeus, Carolus, 144
Lipson, H. S., 150
literary
    critical methodology, 51
    form, 66
    genre, 53
liturgy, cultic, 50, 52
living souls, 162
logical positivism, 133
Logos, 23
Lohflink, Norbert F., 112, 113
Long ages, 44, 96, 100
Longman, T., 71
Lord, resurrected, 7
Lot, 87
Lugenbeal, Edward, 179
Luther, Martin, 8, 42
LXX, 27

M

mabbûl, 10, 83
Macquarrie, John, 12, 126
macroevolutionary
    change, 128
    theory, 138
Madaba Plains Project, 14
Manakacha formation, 102
marriage, 125, 165
Mayr, Ernst, 124
McKee, E. D., 106
medieval Catholic theologians, 42
mega universe, 137
Mendellian genetics, 127
Mesopotamia, 83, 85, 86
Mesopotamian, 79
    primeval histories, 74, 75
Mesozoic, 103, 118

Messianic seed, 85
metaphor, 45
metaphysics, 129, 173
methodological naturalism, 129, 177
Meyer, Stephen C., 131, 134, 137
micro universe, 137
microevolutionary
    changes, 127
militarism, 125
millennium, 42
Miller, Stanley, 131
Miller, Hugh, 47
Miller-Urey model, 132
Mishnah, 71
model, inclusive, 12, 178, 191
molecular biology, 127, 132, 141, 148, 149
Monad, Jacques, 142
monogenous, 180
Montagu, 128
Monterey Canyon, 105
Moody, Dale, 174
moral values, 159
Moreland, J. P., 128-130
morphogenesis, 136
morphology, 135
Morris, Henry M., 125, 130
Mosaic authorship, 71
Moses, 81
Mount Everest, 87
Murphy, Nancey, 32
mutations, 143
myths, 50
    cosmogonic, 53
myth-and-ritual school, 50

N

NASA, 139
natural
    data, 44
    knowledge, 183
    laws of cause and effect, 126
    science, 125, 129
    selection, 7, 124-131, 134, 136, 139, 142-144, 149, 152-157
    theology, 175, 192
naturalism, 126, 129, 130, 150-152
    methodological, 129, 130, 177
    perennial, 151

naturalistic
    evolutionary worldview, 49
    model, 44
    view, 173
nature, 8
    of God, 163
Navajo, 105
Nazism, 125
Near Eastern, ancient
    accounts, 80
    literature, 70
    society, 161
Nelson, Paul, 194, n. 6
neo-
    Darwinian, 23, 124, 127
    evangelical, 177
    evangelical broad concordist, 50
    orthodox, 50, 176
new beginning, 86, 89
New Age philosophy, 152
nihilism, 176, 178
Nilsson, Dan E., 140
Nilsson, Susanne, 140
nineteenth century, 42, 47
Nintur, 75
Noah, 29, 82, 86-88
Noahic flood, 84
Nobel Prize, 132, 140
Noll, Mark, 32
norma normans, 174
normae normatae, 174
Norman, Bruce, 186
nous, 183

O

obscurantism, 192
ocean tidal movement, 88
oceanic energy impulse model, 88
Oller, John W., 135
Omdahl, John L., 135
omniscience, 82
Origen, 41
origin science, 40
Origin of Species, 41, 109, 124, 127, 130, 131, 138, 142, 145, 151
origins, 8
Overton, William, 129
oxymoron, 129
O'Connor, M., 59

P

P (for "priestly"), 69
pagan philosophical modes of thinking, 42
paleocurrent patterns, 118
Paleontologists, 127, 129, 145
paleontology, 124
Paleozoic
    Era, 103
    Karst, 107
    paleocurrents, 103
    portion, 117
parable, 50, 52
parallels
    structural, 19, 35
    thematic, 19, 35
    verbal, 19
pars pro toto, 60
Patterson, Colin, 127, 129
Paulien, Jon, 19
Pearl, Henry F., 37
pēgē, 27
Pentateuch, 81
Permian boundary, 110
Phanerozoic, 97, 101
Pharisees, 71
Philo, 71
philosophy
    Greco-Roman, 183, 184
    rational, 184
philosophical modes of thinking
    pagan, 42
photosynthesis, 138
phraseological criteria, 46
phraseology, 88
Pietism, German, 173
Pishon, 88
plan of
    redemption, 85
    salvation, 163-165
plant
    kingdom, 72
    of the field, 69, 72, 73
Plantinga, Alvin, 128, 139, 143, 147, 149, 150
plants
    obnoxious, 73
    seed-bearing, 72
Plato, 175
pluralism

theological, 172, 173
Polanyi, Michael, 128, 135
pope, 42, 161
Popper, Karl, 129
positivism, logical, 133
post-
    Darwinianism, 115, 127, 155
    Enlightenment, 30
    flood, 86
    modern, 8, 23, 30
    modern Adventism, 178
Precambrian, 97, 103, 118
preflood, 86
"present truth," 23
preservation, 126
preterist, 23
primitive cell, 142
process
    of gradualism, 129
    subcellular, 138
progressive creationists, 109
prooftexts, 20
prose genealogy, 52
Protestant
    liberalism, 176
    Reformation, 175
Protognosticism, 184
protology, 89
prototokon, 180
providence, 126
psychology, 124
punctuated equilibrium, 127, 146, 147,
    155

Q
Quine, 32

R
racism, 125
rain, 76
rainbow, 7, 8, 86, 119, 120
Ramm, Bernard, 49
random genetic
    mutation, 129, 152, 155
    variation, 139
ransom, 108, 112
Raschke, Carl, 173, 192
rational philosophy, 184
Ratzsch, Del, 9

Raup, David M., 110
re-creation, 89, 90
    of the earth, 164–166
reader-response criticism, 66
    theories, 35
reason, 161, 174, 190
reconciliation, 108, 112, 166
redemption, 108, 112, 114
    Christ's work of, 11
    plan of, 85
Red Sea, 164
Redwall Limestone, 98–100
Reformation, 42
    Protestant, 175
Reid, George, 193
Rensch, Bernhard, 147
restoration, days of, 43
resurrected Lord, 7
resurrection, 162, 165, 177, 178
    of Christ, 159, 164
return, imminent, 7
revelation
    days of, 47, 48
    divine, 24, 44, 173, 182, 185, 188, 191
    of God, 175, 178–180, 181, 185, 186
    general, 178, 181, 185, 189, 191
    hierarchy of, 188
    special, 178, 181, 185, 188, 190, 191
    supreme, 191
Rice, Richard, 28
RNA, 132
Rocky Mountains, 99
Rolston III, Holmes, 28
Roman Catholicism, 42
Roosevelt, Theodore, 93
Roth, Ariel A., 10, 15, 93, 115
Rudwick, Martin J., 146
Ruse, Michael, 128, 130

S
Sabbath, 165
Saeboe, Magne, 55
saga, 50
Sahara, 116
salvation, 187
    science of, 189
sanctuary, 36
    heavenly, 166
    ministry, 165

Sarna, Nahum, 84
Satan, 28, 152, 165
Saunders, Peter T., 134
Schleiermacher, Friedrich D. E., 32, 176
Schlick, Moritz, 133
Schmitz-Moormann, Karl, 112
science, 44
    highest, 187
    origin, 40
    theistic, 40, 129
science-theology,
    conflict, 176
    relations, 172-175, 178, 179, 181, 183,
       191
scientific creationism, 129
    existentialist theology, 177
    hypothesis, 42, 44
    worldview, 125
scriptura
    prima, 178
    sola, 178, 180, 191
    tota, 178
Scripture
    authority of, 159
    totality of, 44
Second Coming, 159, 164-166
Second Vatican Council, 126
seed-bearing plants, 72
selection, natural, 7, 124-131, 134, 136,
       139, 142-144, 149, 152-157
semantic investigation, 41
semantic-syntactical usages of the Hebrew
       language, 56, 57, 59, 62
Semler, Johann, 31
serpent, 85
seventh day, 69, 159
Seventh-day Adventist
    church, 161
    eschatology, 166
    global mission, 193
    theology, 159, 160, 164, 172, 174,
       178
Seventh-day Adventists, 9, 151, 153
Shideler, Emerson, 185
shorthand method of endorsing, 24
shrub of the field, 69, 72
sign, 119, 120
signs of God, 7
Silurian shale beds, 116

Simpson, G. G., 127, 134
sin-free
    creation, 76
    human being, 77
sinful person, 74
sins, forgiveness of, 8
six-day creation, 96, 106, 160, 166
six-plus-one schema, 60
sixteenth century, 42
skepticism, 132
Skinner, John, 83, 84
Smith, Huston, 141
sociology, 44, 159
Sodom, 87
solar system, 43
Sölle, Dorothee, 174
soul, immortality of, 162
souls, living, 162
sovereignty, 82
speciation, instant, 147
species, transmutation of, 127
Sperry, Roger, 140
spiritual gifts, 180
Stek, John H., 50, 53, 54
Stent, Gunther S., 129
Stiling, Rodney, 10, 111
Stob, Henry, 151
structural parallel, 19, 35
substructure, 20
sui generis, 53
suicide, intellectual, 192
Sumerian account of creation, 74
supernaturalism, 126, 152
symbolic
    reading, 48
    representations, 40
systematic theologians, 7

T

Talmud, 71
Tapeats Sandstone, 117, 118
tautological relationship, 145
taxonomy, 127, 148
tēḇēl, 81
Teilhard de Chardin, Pierre, 126, 152
Tell Jalul, 14
Tell Gezer (Israel), 14
Tell el' Umeiri, 14
ten-commandment law, 20, 165

terminology, 42, 84, 85
Terreros, Marco, 114, 115
Tertiary boundary, 110
tertium quid, 108
Thaxton, Charles B., 130
theistic
    evolution, 6, 90, 109, 114, 126, 154,
       159-166
    science, 40, 129
thematic parallel, 19, 35
theodicy, 38
theologians
    medieval Catholic, 42
    systematic, 7
theology
    conservative, 176
    evangelical, 12, 125
    fundamentalist, 176
    scientific existentialist, 177
    Seventh-day Adventist, 159, 160, 164,
       172, 174, 178
    trans-scientific, 177
    Western, 175
theory
    conventional geological, 116, 117
    day-age, 43, 47, 62, 64
    days of revelation, 48
    evolutionary, 8, 43, 45, 124-131, 136-
       138, 143-148, 152, 153
    expressivist, 32
    geological, 8
    intelligent cause, 138
    intelligent design, 8
    limited, 79
    local flood, 79
    macroevolutionary, 138
    of gravitation, 149
    referential, 32
    supernatural, 131
    traditional flood, 79
    vision, 48
thorns and thistles, 73
Tigris, 88
Tillich, Paul, 12, 177, 178
time
    astronomical unit of, 55
    calendrical unit of, 55
time scale, geologic, 102
timeless, 41

topography,
    prediluvian, 87, 88
    postdiluvian, 87, 88
Torrance, Thomas F., 12, 16, 177, 178
Tower of Babel, 81, 86
traditional flood theory, 79
transcendence, 176
transmutation of species, 127
trees, fruit, 72
Triassic boundary, 110
Troeltsch, Ernst, 51
tropological sense, 63
tropology, 42
typologists, 148
24-hour days, literal, 40, 41, 51, 54, 58

U

uncreation, 89, 90
undoing of creation, 84
uniformitarian principle of analogy, 51
uniformitarianism, 43, 80, 151
    geologic, 116
uniformity, 51
universe
    galactic, 7
    mega, 137
    micro, 137
University of Arizona, 14
Ury, Thane, 28

V

values, moral, 159
Vanderbilt University, 14
Vatican Council, second, 126
Vegetation, 72
verbal parallel, 19
von Rad, Gerhard, 50, 54, 85, 90

W

Wallace, Alfred R., 124
Waltke, Bruce K., 59
Warfield, Benjamin B., 33, 176
water, fountains of, 26
Watson, James, 127, 134
Webster, Clyde, 192
Weeks, Noel, 50
Wenham, Gordon, 50, 54, 74
weqos we-dardar, 73
Wescogame formation, 102

Westermann, Claus, 84
White, Ellen G., 71, 166, 180, 186, 190–192
Whitehead, Alfred, 126
Wise, Kurt P., 137
Wiseman, P. J., 47, 48
Wittgenstein, Ludwig, 133
Wolf, Abraham, 130
Wordsworth, William, 7
work the ground, 75, 76
work-and-rest, 49
worldview, 26, 150
    biblical, 26, 150
    Copernican, 43
    naturalistic evolutionary, 49
    Ptolemaic, 43
    secular, 5
    scientific, 125
    six-contiguous-creative-day creation, 31
    theoretical, 172

worldwide
    deluge, 86
    destruction, 82
    flood, 82, 88, 89, 98 , 106
worship, false, 22
Wright, Robert, 125

X

xerophyte, 72, 73

Y

Yahweh (Lord), 70
Yahweh-elohim (Lord God), 70
yôm, 45, 53, 55, 56, 58, 59, 62
Young, Davis A., 10
Younker, Randall W., 9, 69, 106, 115

Z

Zinke, E. Edward, 11, 16, 159
Zohary, M., 73